LIFE IN SOUTH AFRICA.

By LADY BARKER,

AUTHOR OF

"STATION LIFE IN NEW ZEALAND," "STORIES ABOUT," Etc., Etc.

NEGRO UNIVERSITIES PRESS
NEW YORK

Originally published in 1877
by J. B. Lippincott & Co., Philadelphia

Reprinted 1969 by
Negro Universities Press
A DIVISION OF GREENWOOD PUBLISHING CORP.
NEW YORK

SBN 8371-2441-7

LIFE IN SOUTH AFRICA.

PART I.

CAPE TOWN, October 16, 1875.

SAFE, safe at last, after twenty-four days of nothing but sea and sky, of white-crested waves—which made no secret of their intention of coming on board whenever they could or of tossing the good ship Edinburgh Castle hither and thither like a child's plaything—and of more deceitful sluggish rolling billows, looking tolerably calm to the unseafaring eye, but containing a vast amount of heaving power beneath their slow, undulating water-hills and valleys. Sometimes sky and sea have been steeped in dazzling haze of golden glare, sometimes brightened to blue of a sapphire depth. Again, a sudden change of wind has driven up serried clouds from the south and east, and all has been gray and cold and restful to eyes wearied with radiance and glitter of sun and sparkling water.

Never has there been such exceptional weather, although the weather of my acquaintance invariably *is* exceptional. No sooner had the outlines of Madeira melted and blended into the soft darkness of a summer night than we appeared to sail straight into tropic heat and a sluggish vapor, brooding on the water like steam from a giant geyser. This simmering, oily, exhausting temperature carried us close to the line. "What is before us," we asked each other languidly, "if it be hotter than this? How can mortal man, woman, still less child, endure existence?" Vain alarms! Yet another shift of the light wind, another degree passed, and we are all shivering in winter wraps. The line was crossed in greatcoats and shawls, and the only people whose complexion did not resemble a purple plum were those lucky ones who had strength of mind and steadiness of body to lurch up and down the deck all day enjoying a strange method of movement which they called walking.

The exceptional weather pursued us right into the very dock. Table Mountain ought to be seen—and very often is seen—seventy miles away. I am told it looks a fine bold bluff at that distance. Yesterday we had blown off our last pound of steam and were safe under its lee before we could tell there was a mountain there at all, still less an almost perpendicular cliff more than three thousand feet high. Robben Island looked like a dun-colored hillock as we shot past it within a short distance, and a more forlorn and discouraging islet I don't think I have ever beheld. When I expressed something of this impression to a cheery fellow-voyager, he could only urge in its defence that there were a great many rabbits on it. If he had thrown the lighthouse into the bargain, I think he would have summed up all its attractive features. Unless Langalibalele is of a singularly unimpressionable nature, he must have found his sojourn on it somewhat monotonous, but he always says he was very comfortable there.

3

And now for the land. We are close alongside of a wharf, and still a capital and faithful copy of a Scotch mist wraps houses, trees and sloping uplands in a fibry fantastic veil, and the cold drizzle seems to curdle the spirits and energies of the few listless Malays and half-caste boys and men who are lounging about. Here come hansom cabs rattling up one after the other, all with black drivers in gay and fantastic head and shoulder gear; but their hearts seem precisely as the hearts of their London brethren, and they single out new-comers at a glance, and shout offers to drive them a hundred yards or so for exorbitant sums, or yell laudatory recommendations of sundry hotels. You must bear in mind that in a colony every pothouse is a hotel, and generally rejoices in a name much too imposing to fit across its frontage. These hansoms are all painted white with the name of some ship in bright letters on the side, and are a great deal cleaner, roomier and more comfortable than their London "forbears." The horses are small and shabby, but rattle along at a good pace; and soon each cab has its load of happy home-comers and swings rapidly away to make room for fresh arrivals hurrying up for fares. Hospitable suggestions come pouring in, and it is as though it were altogether a new experience when one steps cautiously on the land, half expecting it to dip away playfully from under one's feet. A little boy puts my thoughts into words when he exclaims, "How steady the ground is !" and becomes a still more faithful interpreter of a wave-worn voyager's sensations when, a couple of hours later, he demands permission to get *out* of his delicious little white bed that he may have the pleasure of getting *into* it again. The evening is cold and raw and the new picture is all blurred and soft and indistinct, and nothing seems plain except the kindly grace of our welcome and the never-before-sufficiently-appreciated delights of space and silence.

OCTOBER 17.

How pleasant is the process familiarly known as "looking about one," particu-larly when performed under exceptionally favorable circumstances ! A long and happy day commenced with a stroll through the botanic gardens, parallel with which runs, on one side, a splendid oak avenue just now in all the vivid freshness of its young spring leaves. The gardens are beautifully kept, and are valuable as affording a sort of experimental nursery in which new plants and trees can be brought up on trial and their adaptability to the soil and climate ascertained. For instance, the first thing that caught my eye was the gigantic trunk of an Australian blue-gum tree, which had attained to a girth and height not often seen in its own land. The flora of the Cape Colony is exceptionally varied and beautiful, but one peculiarity incidentally alluded to by my charming guide struck me as very noticeable. It is that in this dry climate and porous soil all the efforts of uncultivated nature are devoted to the *stems* of the vegetation : on their sap-retaining power depends the life of the plant, so blossom and leaf, though exquisitely indicated, are fragile and incomplete compared to the solidity and bulbous appearance of the stalk. Everything is sacrificed to the practical principle of keeping life together, and it is not until these stout-stemmed plants are cultivated and duly sheltered and watered, and can grow, as it were, with confidence, that they are able to do justice to the inherent beauty of penciled petal and veined leaf. Then the stem contracts to ordinary dimensions, and leaf and blossom expand into things which may well be a joy to the botanist's eye. A thousand times during that shady saunter did I envy my companions their scientific acquaintance with the beautiful green things of earth, and that intimate knowledge of a subject which enhances one's appreciation of its charms as much as bringing a lamp into a darkened picture-gallery. There are the treasures of form and color, but from ignorant eyes more than half their charms and wonders are held back.

A few steps beyond the garden stand the library and natural history museum. The former is truly a credit to the Colony.

Spacious, handsome, rich in literary treasures, it would bear comparison with similar institutions in far older and wealthier places. But I have often noticed in colonies how much importance is attached to the possession of a good public library, and how fond, as a rule, colonists are of books. In a new settlement other shops may be ill supplied, but there is always a good bookseller's, and all books are to be bought there at pretty nearly the same prices as in England. Here each volume costs precisely the same as it would in London, and it would puzzle ever so greedy a reader to name a book which would not be instantly handed to him.

The museum is well worth a visit of many more hours than we could afford minutes, and, as might be expected, contains numerous specimens of the *Bok* family, whose tapering horns and slender legs are to be seen at every turn of one's head. Models are there also of the largest diamonds, and especially well copied is the famous "Star of South Africa," a magnificent brilliant of purest water, sold here originally for something like twelve thousand pounds, and resold for double that sum three or four years back. In these few hours I perceive, or think I perceive, a certain soreness, if one may use the word, on the part of the Cape Colonists about the unappreciativeness of the English public toward their produce and possessions. For instance, an enormous quantity of wine is annually exported, which reaches London by a devious route and fetches a high price, as it is fairly entitled to do from its excellence. If that same wine were sent direct to a London merchant and boldly sold as Cape wine, it is said that the profit on it would be a very different affair. The same prejudice exists against Cape diamonds. Of course, as in other things, a large proportion of inferior stones are forced into the market and serve to give the diamonds that bad name which we all know is so fatal to a dog. But it is only necessary to pretend that a really fine Cape diamond has come from Brazil to ensure its fetching a handsome price, and in that way even jewelers themselves have been known

to buy and give a good round sum, too, for stones they would otherwise have looked upon with suspicion. Already I have seen a straw-colored diamond from "Du Zoit's pan" in the diamond-fields cut in Amsterdam and set in London, which could hold its own for purity, radiance and color against any other stone of the same rare tint, without fear or favor; but of course such gems are not common, and fairly good diamonds cost as much here as in any other part of the world.

The light morning mists from that dampness of yesterday have rolled gradually away as the beautiful sunshine dried the atmosphere, and by mid-day the table-cloth, as the colonists affectionately call the white, fleece-like vapor which so often rests on their pet mountain, has been folded up and laid aside in Cloudland for future use. I don't know what picture other people may have made to their own minds of the shape and size of Table Mountain, but it was quite a surprise and the least little bit in the world of a disappointment to me to find that it cuts the sky (and what a beautiful sky it is!) with a perfectly straight and level line. A gentle, undulating foreground broken into ravines, where patches of green *velts* or fields, clumps of trees and early settlers' houses nestle cosily down, guides the eye halfway up the mountain. There the rounder forms abruptly cease, and great granite cliffs rise, bare and straight, up to the level line stretching ever so far along. "It is so characteristic," and "You grow to be so fond of that mountain," are observations I have heard made in reply to the carping criticisms of travelers, and already I begin to understand the meaning of the phrases. But you need to see the mountain from various points of view and under different influences of sun and cloud before you can take in its striking and peculiar charms.

On each side of the straight line which is emphatically Table Mountain, but actually forming part of it, is a bold headland of the shape one is usually accustomed to in mountains. The "Devil's Peak" is uncompromising enough for any one's taste, whilst the "Lion's Head" charms the eye by its bluff form and deep purple fissures. These grand promontories are not, however, half so beloved by Cape Colonists as their own Table Mountain, and it is curious and amusing to notice how the influence of this odd straight ridge, ever before their eyes, has unconsciously guided and influenced their architectural tastes. All the roofs of the houses are straight—straight as the mountain; a gable is almost unknown, and even the few steeples are dwarfed to an imperceptible departure from the prevailing straight line. The very trees which shade the Parade - ground and border the road in places have their tops blown absolutely straight and flat, as though giant shears had trimmed them; but I must confess, in spite of a natural anxiety to carry out my theory, that the violent "sou'-easters" are the "straighteners" in their case.

Cape Town is so straggling that it is difficult to form any idea of its real size, but the low houses are neat and the streets are well kept and look quaint and lively enough to my new eyes this morning. There are plenty of people moving about with a sociable, business-like air; lots of different shades of black and brown Malays, with pointed hats on the men's heads: the women encircle their dusky, smiling faces with a gay cotton handkerchief and throw another of a still brighter hue over their shoulders. When you add to this that they wear a full, flowing, stiffly-starched cotton gown of a third bright color, you can perhaps form some idea of how they enliven the streets. Swarms of children everywhere, romping and laughing and showing their white teeth in broadest of grins. The white children strike me at once as looking marvelously well—such chubby cheeks, such sturdy fat legs—and all, black or white, with that amazing air of independence peculiar to baby-colonists. Nobody seems to mind them and nothing seems to harm them. Here are half a dozen tiny boys shouting and laughing at one side of the road, and half a dozen baby-girls at the other (they all seem to play separately): they are all

driving each other, for "horses" is the one game here. By the side of a pond sit two toddles of about three years old, in one garment apiece and pointed hats: they are very busy with string and a pin; but who is taking care of them and why don't they tumble in? They are as fat as ortolans and grin at us in the most friendly fashion.

We must remember that this chances to be the very best moment of the whole year in which to see the Cape and the dwellers thereat. The cold weather has left its bright roses on the children's cheeks, and the winter rains exceptionally having this year made every blade of grass and leaf of tree to laugh and sing in freshest green. After the dry, windy summer I am assured there is hardly a leaf and never a blade of grass to be seen in Cape Town, and only a little straggling verdure under the shelter of the mountain. The great want of this place is water. No river, scarcely a brook, refreshes one's eye for many and many a league inward. The necessary water for the use of the town is brought down by pipes from the numerous springs which trickle out of the granite cliffs of Table Mountain, but there is never a sufficiency to spare for watering roads or grassplots. This scarcity is a double loss to residents and visitors, for one misses it both for use and beauty.

Everybody who comes here rides or drives round the "Kloof." That may be; but what I maintain is that very few do it so delightfully as I did this sunny afternoon with a companion who knew and loved every turn of the romantic road, who could tell me the name of every bush or flower, of every distant stretch of hills, and helped me to make a map in my head of the stretching landscape and curving bay. Ah! how delicious it was, the winding, climbing road, at whose every angle a fresh fair landscape fell away from beneath our feet or a shining stretch of sea, whose transparent green and purple shadows broke in a fringe of feathery spray at the foot of bold, rocky cliffs, or crept up to a smooth expanse of silver sand in a soft curling line of foam! "Kloof" means simply cleft, and is the pass between the Table Mountain and the Lion's Head. The road first rises, rises, rises, until one seems halfway up the great mountain, and the little straight-roofed white houses, the green velts or fields and the parallel lines of the vineyards have sunk below one's feet far, far away. The mountain gains in grandeur as one approaches it, for the undulating spurs which run from it down to the sea-shore take away from the height looking upward. But when these are left beneath, the perpendicular walls of granite, rising sheer and straight up to the bold sky-line, and the rugged, massive strength of the buttress-like cliffs, begin to gain something of their true value to the stranger's eye. The most beautiful part of the road, however, to my taste, is the descent, when the shining expanse of Camp's Bay lies shimmering in the warm afternoon haze with a thousand lights and shadows from cloud and cliff touching and passing over the crisp water-surface. By many a steep zigzag we round the Lion's Head, and drop once more on a level road running parallel to the sea-shore, and so home in the balmy and yet bracing twilight. The midday sun is hot and scorching even at this time of year, but it is always cool in the shade, and no sooner do the afternoon shadows grow to any length than the air freshens into sharpness, and by sundown one is glad of a good warm shawl.

October 18.

Another bright, ideal day, and the morning passed in a delicious flower-filled room looking over old books and records and listening to odd, quaint little scraps from the old Dutch records. But directly after luncheon (and how hungry we all are, and how delicious everything tastes on shore!) the open break with four capital horses comes to the door, and we start for a long, lovely drive. Half a mile or so takes us out on a flat red road with Table Mountain rising straight up before it, but on the left stretches away a most enchanting panorama. It is all so soft in coloring and tone, distinct and yet not hard, and exquisitely beautiful!

The Blue-Berg range of mountains stretch beyond the great bay, which, unless a "sou'-easter" is tearing over it, lies glowing in tranquil richness. This afternoon it is colored like an Italian lake. Here are lines of chrysoprase, green-fringed, white with little waves, and beyond lie dark, translucent, purple depths, which change with every passing cloud. Beyond these amethystic shoals again stretches the deep blue water, and again beyond, and bluer still, rise the five ranges of "Hottentots' Holland," which encircle and complete the landscape, bringing the eye round again to the nearer cliffs of the Devil's Peak. When the Dutch came here some two hundred years ago, they seized upon this part of the coast and called it Holland, driving the Hottentots beyond the neighboring range and telling them that was to be their Holland—a name it keeps to this day. Their consciences must have troubled them after this arbitrary division of the soil, for up the highest accessible spurs of their own mountain they took the trouble to build several queer little square houses called "block-houses," from which they could keep a sharp look-out for foes coming over the hills from Hottentots' Holland. The foes never came, however, and the roofs and walls of the block-houses have gradually tumbled in, and the gun-carriages—for they managed to drag heavy ordnance up the steep hillside—have rotted away, whilst the old-fashioned cannon lie, grim and rusty, amid a tangled profusion of wild geranium, heath and lilies. I scrambled up to one of the nearest block-houses, and found the date on the dismounted gun to be more than a hundred years old. The view was beautiful and the air fresh and fragrant with scent of flowers.

But to return to our drive. I could gaze and gaze for ever at this lovely panorama, but am told this is the ugliest part of the road. The road itself is certainly not pretty just here, and is cloudy with a fine red dust, but this view of sea and distant hills is enchanting. Soon we get under the lee of the great mountain, and then its sheltering arms show their protective power; for splendid oak avenues begin to border the road all the way, and miniature forests of straight-stemmed pines and shimmering belts of the ghostly silver tree run up all the mountain-clefts. Stem and leaf of the silver tree are all of purest white; and when one gets a gleam of sunlight on a distant patch of these trees, the effect is quite indescribable, contrasting, as they do, with green of field and vineyard. The vines all about here and towards Constantia, thirteen miles off, are dwarf-plants, and only grow to the height of gooseberry-bushes. It is a particular species, which is found to answer best as requiring less labor to train and cultivate, and is less likely to be blown out of the ground by the violent "sou'-easters" which come sweeping over the mountain. These gales are evidently the greatest annoyance which Cape Colonists have to endure; and although everybody kindly suggests that I *ought* to see one, just to understand what it is like, I am profoundly thankful that I only know it from their description and my own distinct recollection of the New Zealand "nor'-westers." Those were hot winds, scorching and curling up everything, whereas this is rather a cold breeze, although it blows chiefly in summer. It whirls along clouds of dust from the red clay roads and fields which penetrates and clings to everything in the most extraordinary manner. All along the road the stems and lower branches of the trees are dyed a deep brick-dust color, and I hear moving and pathetic stories of how it ruins clothes, not only utterly spoiling black silk dresses, but staining white petticoats and children's frocks and pinafores with a border of color exactly like the ruddle with which sheep are branded. Especially is it the terror of sailors, rendering the navigation along the coast dangerous and difficult; for it blends land and water into one indistinct whirl of vaporous cloud, confusing and blurring everything until one cannot distinguish shore from sea.

The vineyards of Constantia originally took their pretty name from the fair daughter of one of the early Dutch governors, but now it has grown into a generic word, and you see "Cloete's Constantia," "Von Reybeck Constantia," written upon great stone gateways leading by long avenues into the various vine-growing plantations. It was to the former of these constantias, which was also the farthest off, that we were bound that pleasant summer afternoon, and from the time we got out of the carriage until the moment we re-entered it—all too soon, but it is a long drive back in the short cold twilight—I felt as though I had stepped through a magic portal into the scene of one of Washington Irving's stories. It was all so simple and homely, so quaint and so inexpressibly picturesque. The house had stood there for a couple of hundred years, and looks as though it might last for ever, with its air of cool, leisurely repose and comfort and strength.

In the flagged hall stands a huge stalactite some ten feet high, brought a hundred years ago from caves far away in the distant ranges. It is shaped something like a Malay's hat, only the peak tapers to a point about eight feet high. The drawing-room—though it seems a profanation to call that venerable stately room by so flippant and modern a name—is large, ceiled with great beams of cedar, and lighted by lofty windows, which must contain many scores of small panes of glass. There were treasures of rarest old china and delfware, and curious old carved stands for fragile dishes. A wealth of swinging-baskets of flowers and ferns and bright girl-faces lighted up the solemn, shady old room, in which we must not linger, for there is much to see outside. First to the cellar, as it is called, though it is far from being under ground, and is, in fact, a spacious stone building with an elaborately-carved pediment. Here are rows and rows of giant casks, stretching on either hand into avenues in the black distance, but these are mere children in the nursery, compared to those we are going to see. First we must pause in a middle room full of quaintest odds and ends — crossbows, long whips of hippopotamus hide, strange rusty old swords and firearms—to look at a map of South Africa drawn somewhere about 1640. It hangs on the wall and is hardly to be touched, for the paint and varnish crack and peel off at a breath. It is a marvel of accurate geographical knowledge, and is far better filled in than the maps of yesterday. All poor Livingstone's great geographical discoveries are marked on it as being —perhaps only from description—known or guessed at all that long time ago. It was found impossible to photograph it on account of the dark shade which age has laid over the original yellow varnish, but a careful tracing has been made and, I believe, sent home to the Geographical Society. It is in the long corridor beyond this that the "stuck-vats" live—puncheons which hold easily some thousand gallons or so, and are of a solemn rotundity calculated to strike awe into the beholder's heart. Here is white constantia, red constantia, young constantia, middle-aged constantia, and constantia so old as to be a liqueur almost beyond price. When it has been kept all these years, the sweetness by which it is distinguished becomes so absorbed and blended as to be hardly perceptible.

Presently one of the party throws a door suddenly open, and, behold, we are standing right over a wild wooded glen with a streamlet running through it, and black washerwomen beating heaps of white clothes on the strips of shingle. Turtledoves are cooing, and one might almost fancy one was back again on the wild Scotch west coast, until some one else says calmly, "Look at the ostriches!" Here they come, with a sort of dancing step, twisting their long necks and snakelike heads from side to side in search of a tempting pebble or trifle of hardware. Their wings are slightly raised, and the long fringe of white feathers rustles softly as they trot easily and gracefully past us. They are young male birds, and in a few months more their plumage, which now resembles that of a turkey-cock, will be jet black, except the wing-feathers. A few drops of rain are falling, so we hurry back to where the carriage is standing under some splendid oak trees, swallow a sort of stirrup-cup of delicious hot tea, and so home again as fast as we can go.

OCTOBER 19.

It is decided that I must take a drive in a Cape cart; so directly after breakfast a smart workman-like-looking vehicle, drawn by a pair of well-bred iron-gray cobs, dashes up under the portico. There are capital horses here, but they fetch a good price, and such a pair as these would easily find purchasers at one hundred and fifty pounds. The cart itself is very trim and smart, with a framework sort of head, which falls back at pleasure, and it holds four people easily. It is a capital vehicle, light and strong and uncommonly comfortable, but I am warned not to imagine that all Cape carts are as easy as this one. Away we go at a fine pace through the delicious sparkling morning sunshine and crisp air, soon turning off the red high-road into a sandy, marshy flat with a sort of brackish back-water standing in pools here and there. We are going to call on Langalibalele, and his son, Malambuli, who are located at Uitvlugt on the Cape downs, about four miles from the town. It is a sort of farm-residence; and considering that the chief has hitherto lived in a reed hut, he is not badly off, for he has plenty of room out of doors as well as a good house over his head. We bump over some strange and rough bits of sandy road and climb up and down steep banks in a manner seldom done on wheels. There is a wealth of lovely flowers blooming around, but I can't help fixing my eyes on the pole of the cart, which is sometimes sticking straight up in the air, its silver hook shining merrily in the sun, or else it has disappeared altogether, and I can only see the horses' haunches. That is when we are going *down* hill, and I think it is a more terrible sensation than when we are playfully scrambling up some sandy hillock as a cat might.

Here is the location at last, thank Heaven! and there is Langalibalele sitting in the verandah stoep (pronounced "stoup") on his haunches on a brick. He looks as comfortable as if he were in an arm-chair, but it must be a difficult thing to do if you think seriously of it. The etiquette seems to be to take no notice of him as we pass into the parlor, where we present our pass and the people in authority satisfy themselves that we are quite in rule. Then the old chief walks quietly in, takes off his soft felt hat and sits himself down in a Windsor arm-chair with grave deliberation. He is uncommonly ugly ; but when one remembers that he is nearly seventy years of age, it is astonishing to see how young he looks. Langalibalele is not a true Kafir at all : he is a Fingor, a half-caste tribe contemptuously christened by the Kafirs "dogs." His wool grows in distinct and separate clumps like hassocks of grass all over his head. He is a large and powerful man and looks the picture of sleek contentment, as well he may. Only one of his sons, a good-natured, fine young man, black as ebony, is with him, and the chief's one expressed grievance is that none of his wives will come to him. In vain he sends commands and entreaties to these dusky ladies to come and share his solitude. They return for answer that "they are working for somebody else ;" for, alas ! the only reason their presence is desired is that they may cultivate some of the large extent of ground placed at the old chief's disposal. Neither he nor his stalwart son would dream for a moment of touching spade or hoe ; but if the ladies of the family could only be made to see their duty, an honest penny might easily be turned by oats or rye. I gave him a large packet of sugar-plums, which he seized with childish delight and hid away exactly like the big monkeys at the Zoo.

By way of a joke, Malambuli pretended to want to take them away, and the chattering and laughing which followed was almost deafening. But by and by a gentleman of the party presented a big parcel of the best tobacco, and the chuckling old chief made over at once all my sweetmeats "jintly" to his son, and proceeded to hide away his new treasure. He was

dressed exactly like a dissenting minister, and declared through the interpreter he was perfectly comfortable. The impression here seems to be that he is a restless, intriguing and mischief-making old man, who may consider himself as having come out of the hornets' nest he tried to stir up uncommonly well.

We don't want to bump up and down the sandy plain again, so a lively conversation goes on in Dutch about the road between one of my gentlemen and somebody who looks like a "stuck-vat" upon short legs. The dialogue is fluent and lively, beginning with "Ja, ja !" and ending with "All right !" but it leads to our hitting off the right track exactly, and coming out at a lovely little cottage-villa under the mountain, where we rest and lunch and then stroll about up the hill spurs, through myrtle hedges and shady oak avenues. Then, before the afternoon shadows grow too long, we drive off to "Groote Schuur," the ancient granary of the first settlers, which is now turned into a roomy, comfortable country-house, perfect as a summer residence, and securely sheltered from the "sou'-easters." We approach it through a double avenue of tall Italian pines, and after a little while go out once more for a ramble up some quaint old brick steps, and so through a beautiful glen all fringed and feathered with fresh young fronds of maiden-hair ferns, and masses of hydrangea bushes, which must be beautiful as a poet's dream when they are covered with their great bunches of pale blue blossom. That will not be until Christmas-tide, and, alas ! I shall not be here to see, for already my three halcyon days of grace are ended and over, and this very evening we must steam away from a great deal yet unvisited of what is interesting and picturesque, and from friends who three days ago were strangers, but who have made every moment since we landed stand out as a bright and pleasant landmark on life's highway.

PART II.

TWO days ago we steamed out of Table Bay on just such a gray, drizzling afternoon as that on which we entered it. But the weather cleared directly we got out to sea, and since then it has carried us along as though we had been on a pleasant summer cruise. All yesterday we were coasting along the low downs which edge the dangerous sea-board for miles upon miles. From the deck of the Edinburgh Castle the effect is monotonous enough, although just now everything is brightly green; and, with their long ribbon fringe of white breaker-foam glinting in the spring sunshine, the stretches of undulating hillocks looked their best. This part of the coast is well lighted, and it was always a matter of felicitation at night when, every eighty miles or so, the guiding rays of a lighthouse shone out in the soft gloom of the starlight night. One of these lonely towers stands more than eight hundred feet above the sea-level, and warns ships off the terrible Agulhas Bank.

We have dropped our anchor this fresh bright morning a mile or so from the shore on which Port Elizabeth stands. Algoa Bay is not much of a shelter, and it is always a chance whether a sudden south-easter may not come tearing down upon the shipping, necessitating a sudden tripping of anchors and running out to sea to avoid the fate which is staring us warningly in the face in the shape of the gaunt ribs or rusty cylinders of sundry cast-away vessels. To-day the weather is on its good behavior; the south-easter rests on its

    aëry nest
  As still as a brooding dove;

and sun and sea are doing their best to show off the queer little straggling town creeping up the low sandy hills that lie before us. I am assured that Port Elizabeth is a flourishing mercantile place.

From the deck of our ship I can't at all perceive that it is flourishing, or doing anything except basking in the pleasant sunshine. But when I go on shore an hour or two later I am shown a store which takes away my breath, and before whose miscellaneous contents the stoutest-hearted female shopper must needs *baisser son pavillon*. Everything in this vast emporium looked as neat and orderly as possible, and, though the building was twice as big as the largest co-operative store in London, there was no hurry or confusion. Thimbles and ploughs, eau-de-cologne and mangles, American stoves, cotton dresses of astounding patterns to suit the taste of Dutch ladies, harmoniums and flat-irons, —all stood peaceably side by side together. But these were all "unconsidered trifles" next the more serious business of the establishment, which was wool—wool in every shape and stage and bale. In this department, however, although for the sake of the dear old New Zealand days my heart warms at the sight of the huge packages, I was not supposed to take any interest; so we pass quickly out into the street again, get into a large open carriage driven by a black coachman, and make the best of our way up to a villa on the slope of the sandy hill. Once I am away from the majestic influence of that store the original feeling of Port Elizabeth being rather a dreary place comes back upon me; but we drive all about—to the Park, which may be said to be in its swaddling-clothes *as* a park, and to the Botanic Gardens, where the culture of foreign and colonial flowers and shrubs is carried on under the chronic difficulties of too much sun and wind and too little water. Everywhere there is building going on — very modest building, it is true, with rough-and-ready masonry or timber, and roofs of zinc painted in strips of light colors, but everywhere there are signs of progress and growth. People look bored, but healthy, and it does not surprise me in the least to hear that though there are a good many inhabitants, there is not much society. A pretty little luncheon and a pleasant hour's chat in a cool, shady drawing-room, with plenty of new books and music and flowers, gave me an agreeable impression to carry back on board the ship; which, by the way, seemed strangely silent and deserted when we returned, for most of our fellow-passengers had disembarked here on their way to different parts of the interior.

As I saunter up and down the clean, smart-looking deck of what has been our pleasant floating home during these past four weeks, I suddenly perceive a short, squat pyramid on the shore, standing out oddly enough among the low-roofed houses. If it had only been red instead of gray, it might have passed for the model of the label on Bass's beer-bottles; but, even as it is, I feel convinced that there is a story connected with it: and so it proves, for this ugly, most unsentimental-looking bit of masonry was built long ago by a former governor as a record of the virtues and perfections of his dead wife, whom, among other lavish epithets of praise, he declares to have been "the most perfect of women." Anyhow, there it stands, on what was once a lonely strip of sand and sea, a memorial—if one can only believe the stone story, now nearly a hundred years old—of a great love and a great sorrow; and one can envy the one and pity the other just as much when looking at this queer, unsightly monument as when one stands on the pure marble threshold of the exquisite Taj Mahal at Agra, and reads that it too, in all its grace and beauty, was reared "in memory of an undying love."

Although the day has been warm and balmy, the evening air strikes chill and raw, and our last evening on board the dear old ship has to be spent under shelter, for it is too cold to sit on deck. With the first hours of daylight next morning we have to be up and packing, for by ten o'clock we must be on board the Florence, a small, yacht-like coasting-steamer which can go much closer into the sand-blocked harbors scooped by the action of the rivers all along the coast. It is with a very heavy heart that I, for one, say good-bye to the Edinburgh Castle, where I have passed so many happy hours and made some pleasant acquaintances. A ship is a very forcing-house of friendship, and no one who has not taken a voyage can realize how rapidly an acquaintance grows and ripens into a friend under the lonely influences of sea and sky. We have all been so happy together, everything has been so comfortable, everybody so kind, that one would indeed be cold-hearted if, when the last moment of our halcyon voyage arrived, it could bring with it anything short of a regret.

With the same chivalrous goodness and courtesy which has taken thought for the comfort of our every movement since we left Dartmouth, our captain insists on seeing us safely on board the Florence (what a toy-boat she looks after our stately ship!) and satisfying himself that we can be comfortably settled once more in our doll's house of a new cabin. Then there comes a reluctant "Good-bye" to him and all our kind care-takers of the Edinburgh Castle; and the last glimpse we catch of her— for the Florence darts out of the bay like a swallow in a hurry—is her dipping her ensign in courteous farewell to us.

In less than twenty-four hours we had reached another little port, some hundred and fifty miles or so up the coast, called East London. Here the harbor is again only an open roadstead, and hardly any vessel drawing more than three or four feet of water can get in at all near the shore, for between us and it is a bar of shifting sand, washed down, day by day, by the strong current of the river Buffalo. All the cargo has to be transferred to lighters, and a little tug steamer bustles backward and forward with messages of entreaty to those said lighters to come out and take away their loads. We had dropped our anchor by daylight, yet at ten o'clock scarcely a boat had made its appearance alongside, and every one was fuming and fretting at the delay and consequent waste of fine weather and daylight. That is to say, it was a fine bright day overhead, with sunshine and sparkle all round, but the heavy roll of the sea never ceased for a moment. From one side to the other, until her ports touched the water, backward and forward, with slow, monotonous heaving, our little vessel swayed with the swaying rollers until everybody on board felt sick and sorry. "This is comparatively a calm day," I was told: "you can't possible imagine from this what rolling really is." But I *can* imagine quite easily, and do not at all desire a closer acquaintance with this restless Indian Ocean. Breakfast is a moment of penance: little G—— is absolutely fainting from agonies of sea-sickness, though he has borne all our South-Atlantic tossings with perfect equanimity; and it is with real joy that I hear the lifeboat is alongside, and that the kind-hearted captain of the Florence (*how* kind sailors are!) offers to take babies, nurse and me on shore, so as to escape a long day of this agonizing rolling. In happy unconsciousness of what landing at East London, even in a lifeboat, meant when a bar had to be crossed, we were all tumbled and bundled, more or less unceremoniously, into the great, roomy boat, and were immediately taken in hand by the busy little tug. For half a mile or more we made good progress in her wake, being in a position to set at naught the threatening water-mountains which came tumbling in furious haste from seaward. It was not until we seemed close to the shore and all our troubles over that the tug was obliged to cast us off, owing to the rapidly shoaling water, and we prepared to make the best of our own way in. Bad was that best, indeed, though the peril came and went so quickly that it is but a confused impression I retain of what seemed to me a really terrible moment. One instant I hear felicitations exchanged between our captain—who sits protectingly close to me and poor, fainting little G——, who lies like death in my arms—and the captain of the lifeboat. The next moment, in spite of sudden panic and presence of danger, I could laugh to hear the latter sing out in sharpest tones of terror and dismay, "Ah, you would, would you?" coupled with rapid orders to the stout rowers and shouts to us of "Look out!" and I *do* look out, to see on one side sand which the retreating wave has sucked dry, and in which the boat seems trying to bury herself as though she were a mole: on the other hand there towers above us a huge green wave, white-crested and curled, which is rushing at us like a devouring monster. I glance, as I think, for the last time, at the pale nurse, on whose lap lies the baby placidly sucking his bottle. I see a couple of sailors lay hold of her and the child with one hand each, whilst with the other they cling desperately to the thwarts. A stout seafaring man flings the whole weight of his ponderous pilot-coated body upon G—— and me: I hear a roar of water, and, lo! we are washed right up alongside of the rude landing-place, still *in* the boat indeed, but wet and frightened to the last degree. Looking back on it all, I can distinctly remember that it was not the sight of the overhanging wave which cost me my deadliest pang of sickening fright, but the glimpse I caught of the shining, cruel-looking sand, sucking us in so silently and greedily. We were all trembling so much that it seemed as impossible to stand upright on the earth as on the tossing waters, and it was with reeling, drunken-looking steps that we rolled and staggered through the heavy sand-street until we reached the shelter of an exceedingly dirty hotel. Everything in it required courage to touch, and it was with many qualms that I deposited limp little G—— on a filthy sofa. However, the mistress of the house looked clean, and so did the cups and saucers she quickly produced; and by the time we had finished a capital breakfast we were all quite in good spirits again, and so sharpened up as to be able to "mock ourselves" of our past perils and present discomforts. Outside there were strange, beautiful shrubs in flower, tame pigeons came cooing and bowing in at the door, and above all there was an enchanting freshness and balminess in the sunny air.

In about an hour "Capting Florence" (as G—— styles our new commander) calls for us and takes us out sight-seeing. First and foremost, across the river to the rapidly-growing railway lines, where a brand-new locomotive was hissing away with full steam up. Here we were met and welcomed by the energetic superintendent of this iron road, and, to my intense delight, after explaining to me what a long distance into the interior the line had to go and how fast it was getting on, considering the difficulties in the way of doing anything in South Africa, from washing a pocket-handkerchief up to laying down a railway, he proposed that we should get *on* the engine and go as far as the line was open for anything like safe traveling. Never were such delightful five minutes as those spent in whizzing along through the park-like country and cutting fast through the heavenly air. In vain did I smell that my serge skirts were getting dreadfully singed, in vain did I see most uncertain bits of rail before me : it was all too perfectly enchanting to care for danger or disgrace, and I could have found it in my heart to echo G——'s plaintive cry for "More !" when we came to the end and had to get off. But it consoled us a little to watch the stone-breaking machine crunching up small rocks as though they had been lumps of sugar, and after looking at that we set off for the unfinished station, and could take in, even in its present skeleton state, how commodious and handsome it will all be some day. You are all so accustomed to be whisked about the civilized world when and where you choose that it is difficult to make you understand the enormous boon the first line of railway is to a new country — not only for the convenience of travelers, but for the transport of goods, the setting free of hundreds of cattle and horses and drivers—all sorely needed for other purposes — and the fast-following effects of opening up the resources of the back districts. In these regions labor is the great difficulty, and one needs to hold both patience and temper fast with both

one's hands when watching either Kafir or Coolie at work. The white man cannot or will not do much with his hands out here, so the navvies are slim-looking blacks, who jabber and grunt and sigh a good deal more than they work.

It is a fortunate circumstance that the delicious air keeps us all in a chronic state of hunger, for it appears in South Africa that one is expected to eat every half hour or so. And, shamed am I to confess, we *do* eat—and eat with a good appetite too — a delicious luncheon at the superintendent's, albeit it followed closely on the heels of our enormous breakfast at the dirty hotel. Such a pretty little bachelor's box as it was !—so cool and quiet and neat ! — built somewhat after the fashion of the Pompeian houses, with a small square garden full of orange trees in the centre, and the house running round this opening in four corridors. After lunch a couple of nice, light Cape carts came to the door, and we set off to see a beautiful garden whose owner had all a true Dutchman's passion for flowers. Here was fruit as well as flowers. Pineapples and jasmine, strawberries and honeysuckle, grew side by side with bordering orange trees, feathery bamboos and sheltering gum trees. In the midst of the garden stood a sort of double platform, up whose steep border we all climbed : from this we got a good idea of the slightly undulating land all about, waving down like solidified billows to where the deep blue waters sparkled and rolled restlessly beyond the white line of waves ever breaking on the bar. I miss animal life sadly in these parts : the dogs I see about the streets are few in number, and miserably currish specimens of their kind. "Good dogs don't answer out here," I am told : that is to say, they get a peculiar sort of distemper, or ticks bite them, or they got weak from loss of blood, or become degenerate in some way. The horses and cattle are small and poor-looking, and hard-worked, very dear to buy and very difficult to keep and to feed. I don't even see many cats, and a pet bird is a rarity. However, as we stood on the breezy platform I saw a most beautiful wild bird fly over the rose-hedge just below us. It was about as big as a crow, but with a strange iridescent plumage. When it flitted into the sunshine its back and wings shone like a rainbow, and the next moment it looked perfectly black and velvety in the shade. Now a turquoise-blue tint comes out on its spreading wings, and a slant in the sunshine turns the blue into a chrysoprase green. Nobody could tell me its name: our Dutch host spoke exactly like Hans Breitmann, and declared it was a "bid of a crow," and so we had to leave it and the platform and come down to more roses and tea. There was so much yet to be seen and to be done that we could not stay long, and, laden with magnificent bouquets of *gloire de Dijon* roses and honeysuckle, and divers strange and lovely flowers, we drove off again in our Cape carts. I observed that instead of saying "Whoa!" or checking the horses in any way by the reins, the driver always whistles to them— a long, low whistle—and they stand quite still directly. We bumped up and down, over extraordinarily rough places, and finally slid down a steep cutting to the brink of the river Buffalo, over which we were ferried, all standing, on a big punt, or rather pontoon. A hundred yards or so of rapid driving then took us to a sort of wharf which projected into the river, where the important-looking little tug awaited us; and no sooner were we all safely on board—rather a large party by this time, for we had gone on picking up stragglers ever since we started, only three in number, from the hotel—than she sputtered and fizzed herself off upstream. By this time it was the afternoon, and I almost despair of making you see the woodland beauty of that broad mere, fringed down to the water's edge on one side with shrubs and tangle of roses and woodbine, with ferns and every lovely green creeping thing. That was on the bank which was sheltered from the high winds: the other hillside showed the contrast, for there, though green indeed, only a few feathery tufts of pliant shrubs had survived the force of some of these south-eastern gales. We paddled steadily along in mid-stream,

and from the bridge (where little G—— and I had begged "Capting Florence" to let us stand) one could see the double of each leaf and tendril and passing cloud mirrored sharp and clear in the crystalline water. The lengthening shadows from rock and fallen crag were in some places flung quite across our little boat, and so through the soft, lovely air, flooded with brightest sunshine, we made our way, up past Picnic Creek, where another stream joins the Buffalo, and makes miniature green islands and harbors at its mouth, up as far as the river was navigable for even so small a steamer as ours. Every one was sorry when it became time to turn, but there was no choice: the sun-burned, good-looking captain of the tug held up a warning hand, and round we went with a wide sweep, under the shadows, out into the sunlight, down the middle of the stream, all too soon to please us.

Before we left East London, however, there was one more great work to be glanced at, and accordingly we paid a hasty visit to the office of the superintendent of the new harbor-works, and saw plans and drawings of what will indeed be a magnificent achievement when carried out. Yard by yard, with patient under-sea sweeping, all that waste of sand brought down by the Buffalo is being cleared away; yard by yard, two massive arms of solidest masonry are stretching themselves out beyond those cruel breakers: the river is being forced into so narrow a channel that the rush of the water must needs carry the sand far out to sea in future, and scatter it in soundings where it cannot accumulate into such a barrier as that which now exists. Lighthouses will guard this safe entrance into a tranquil anchorage, and so, at some not too far distant day, there is good hope that East London may be one of the most valuable harbors on this vast coast; and when her railway has reached even the point to which it is at present projected, nearly two hundred miles away, it will indeed be a thriving place. Even now, there is a greater air of movement and life and progress about the little seaport, what with the railway and the harbor-works, than at any other place I have yet seen; and each great undertaking is in the hands of men of first-rate ability and experience, who are as persevering as they are energetic. After looking well over these most interesting plans there was nothing left for us to do except to make a sudden raid on the hotel, pick up our shawls and bags, pay a most moderate bill of seven shillings and sixpence for breakfast for three people and luncheon for two, and the use of a room all day, piteously entreat the mistress of the inn to sell us half a bottle of milk for G—— 's breakfast to-morrow—as he will not drink the preserved milk—and so back again on board the tug. The difficulty about milk and butter is the first trouble which besets a family traveling in these parts. Everywhere milk is scarce and poor, and the butter such as no charwoman would touch in England. In vain does one behold from the sea thousands of acres of what looks like undulating green pasturage, and inland the same waving green hillocks stretch as far as the eye can reach: there is never a sheep or cow to be seen, and one hears that there is no water, or that the grass is sour, or that there is a great deal of sickness about among the animals in that locality. Whatever the cause, the result is the same—namely, that one has to go down on one's knees for a cupful of milk, which is but poor, thin stuff at its best, and that Irish salt butter out of a tub is a costly delicacy.

Having secured this precious quarter of a bottle of milk, for which I was really as grateful as though it had been the Koh-i-noor, we hastened back to the wharf and got on board the little tug again. "Now for the bridge!" cry G—— and I, for has not Captain Florence promised us a splendid but safe tossing across the bar? And faithfully he and the bar and the boat keep their word, for we are in no danger, it seems, and yet we appear to leap like a race-horse across the strip of sand, receiving a staggering buffet first on one paddle-wheel and then on the other from the angry guardian breakers, which seem sworn foes of boats and passengers. Again and again are we knocked aside by huge billows, as though the poor little tug were a walnut-shell; again and again do we recover ourselves, and blunder bravely on, sometimes with but one paddle in the water, sometimes burying our bowsprit in a big green wave too high to climb, and dashing right through it as fast as if we shut our eyes and went at everything. The spray flies high over our heads, G—— and I are drenched over and over again, but we shake the sparkling water off our coats, for all the world like Newfoundland dogs, and are all right again in a moment. "Is that the very last?" asks G—— reluctantly as we take our last breaker like a five-barred gate, flying, and find ourselves safe and sound, but quivering a good deal, in what seems comparatively smooth water. Is it smooth, though? Look at the Florence and all the other vessels. Still at it, seesaw, backward and forward, roll, roll, roll! How thankful we all are to have escaped a long day of sickening, monotonous motion! But there is the getting on board to be accomplished, for the brave little tug dare not come too near to her big sister steamboat or she would roll over on her. So we signal for a boat, and quickly the largest which the Florence possesses is launched and manned—no easy task in such a sea, but accomplished in the smartest and most seamanlike fashion. The sides of the tug are low, so it is not very difficult to scramble and tumble into the boat, which is laden to the water's edge by new passengers from East London and their luggage. When, however, we have reached the rolling Florence it is no easy matter to get out of the said boat and on board. There is a ladder let down, indeed, from the Florence's side, but how are we to use it when one moment half a dozen rungs are buried deep in the sea, and the next instant ship and ladder and all have rolled right away from us? It has to be done, however, and what a tower of strength and encouragement does "Capting Florence" prove himself at this juncture! We are all to sit perfectly still: no one is to move until his name is called, and then he is to come unhesitatingly and do exactly what he is told.

"Pass up the baby!" is the first order which I hear given, and that astonishing baby is "passed up" accordingly. I use the word "astonishing" advisedly, for never was an infant so bundled about uncomplainingly. He is just as often upside down as not; he is generally handed from one quartermaster to the other by the gathers of his little blue flannel frock; seas break over his cradle on deck, but nothing disturbs him. He grins and sleeps and pulls at his bottle through everything, and grows fatter and browner and more impudent every day. On this occasion, when—after rivaling Léotard's most daring feats on the trapeze in my scramble up the side of a vessel which was lurching away from me—I at last reached the deck, I found the ship's carpenter nursing the baby, who had seized the poor man's beard firmly with one hand, and with the finger and thumb of the other was attempting to pick out one of his merry blue eyes. "Avast there!" cried the long-suffering sailor, and gladly relinquished the mischievous bundle to me.

Up with the anchor, and off we go once more into the gathering darkness of what turns out to be a wet and windy night. Next day the weather had recovered its temper, and I was called upon deck directly after breakfast to see the "Gates of St. John," a really fine pass on the coast where the river Umzimvubu rushes through great granite cliffs into the sea. If the exact truth is to be told, I must confess I am a little disappointed with this coast-scenery. I have heard so much of its beauty, and as yet, though I have seen it under exceptionally favorable conditions of calm weather, which has allowed us to stand in very close to shore, I have not seen anything really fine until these "Gates" came in view. It has all been monotonous, undulating downs, here and there dotted with trees, and in some places the ravines were filled with what we used to call in New Zealand *bush*—i. e., miscellaneous greenery. Here and there a bold cliff or tumbled pile of red rock makes a landmark for the passing ships, but otherwise the uniformity is great indeed. The ordinary weather along this coast is something frightful, and the great reputation of our little Florence is built on the method in which she rides dry and safe as a duck among these stormy waters. Now that we are close to "fair Natal," the country opens out and improves in beauty. There are still the same sloping, rolling downs, but higher downs rise behind them, and again beyond are blue and purpling hills. Here and there, too, are clusters of fat, dumpy haystacks, which in reality are no haystacks at all, but Kafir kraals. Just before we pass the cliff and river which marks where No-Man's Land ends and Natal begins these little locations are more frequently to be observed, though what their inhabitants subsist on is a marvel to me, for we are only a mile or so from shore, and all the seeing power of all the field-glasses on board fails to discern a solitary animal. We can see lots of babies crawling about the hole which serves as door to a Kafir hut, and they are all as fat as little pigs; but what do they live on? Buttermilk, I am told—that is to say, sour milk, for the true Kafir palate does not appreciate fresh, sweet milk—and a sort of porridge made of *mealies*. I used to think "mealies" was a coined word for potatoes, but it really signifies maize or Indian corn, which is rudely crushed and ground, and forms the staple food of man and beast.

In the mean time, we are speeding gayly over the bright waters, never very calm along this shore. Presently we come to a spot clearly marked by some odd-colored, tumbled-down cliffs and the remains of a great iron butt, where, more than a hundred years ago, the Grosvenor, a splendid clipper ship, was wrecked. The men nearly all perished or were made away with, but a few women were got on shore and carried off as prizes to the kraals of the Kafir "inkosis" or chieftains. What sort of husbands these stalwart warriors made to their reluctant brides tradition does not say, but it is a fact that almost all the children were born mad, and their descendants are, many of them, lunatics or idiots up to the present time. As the afternoon draws on a chill mist creeps over the hills and provokingly blots out the coast, which gets more beautiful every league we go. I wanted to remain up and see the light on the bluff just outside Port d'Urban, but a heavy shower drove me down to my wee cabin before ten o'clock. Soon after midnight the rolling of the anchor-chains and the sudden change of motion from pitching and jumping to the old monotonous roll told us that we were once more outside a bar, with a heavy sea on, and that there we must remain until the tug came to fetch us. But, alas! the tug had to make short work of it next morning, on account of the unaccommodating state of the tide, and all our hopes of breakfasting on shore were dashed by a hasty announcement at 5 A. M. that the tug was alongside, the mails were rapidly being put on board of her, and that she could not wait for passengers or anything else, because ten minutes later there would not be water enough to float her over the bar.

"When shall *we* be able to get over the bar?" I asked dolefully.

"Not until the afternoon," was the prompt and uncompromising reply, delivered through my keyhole by the authority in charge of us. And he proved to be quite right; but I am bound to say the time passed more quickly than we had dared to hope or expect, for an hour later a bold little fishing-boat made her way through the breakers and across the bar in the teeth of wind and rain, bringing F—— on board. He has been out here these eight months, and looks a walking advertisement of the climate and temperature of our new home, so absolutely healthy is his appearance. He is very cheery about liking the place, and particularly insists on the blooming faces and sturdy limbs I shall see belonging to the young Natalians. Altogether, he appears thoroughly happy and contented, liking his work, his position, everything and everybody; which is all extremely satisfactory to hear. There is so much to tell and so much to behold that, as G—— declares, "it is afternoon

directly," and, the signal-flag being up, we trip our anchor once more and rush at the bar, two quartermasters and an officer at the wheel, the pilot and captain on the bridge, all hands on deck and on the alert, for always, under the most favorable circumstances, the next five minutes hold a peril in every second. "Stand by for spray!" sings out somebody, and we do stand by, luckily for ourselves, for "spray" means the top of two or three waves. The dear little Florence is as plucky as she is pretty, and appears to shut her eyes and lower her head and go *at* the bar. Scrape, scrape, scrape! "We've stuck! No, we haven't! Helm hard down! Over!" and so we are. Among the breakers, it is true, buffeted hither and thither, knocked first to one side and then to the other; but we keep right on, and a few more turns of the screw take us into calm water under the green hills of the bluff. The breakers are behind us, we have twenty fathoms of water under our keel, the voyage is ended and over, the captain takes off his straw hat to mop his curly head, everybody's face loses the expression of anxiety and rigidity it has worn these past ten minutes, and boats swarm like locusts round the ship. The baby is passed over the ship's side for the last time, having been well kissed and petted and praised by every one as he was handed from one to the other, and we row swiftly away to the low sandy shore of the "Point."

Only a few warehouses, or rather sheds of warehouses, are to be seen, and a rude sort of railway-station, which appears to afford indiscriminate shelter to boats as well as to engines. There are leisurely trains which saunter into the town of D'Urban, a mile and a half away, every half hour or so, but one of these "crawlers" had just started. The sun was very hot, and we voyagers were all sadly weary and headachy. But the best of the colonies is the prompt, self-sacrificing kindness of old-comers to new-comers. A gentleman had driven down in his own nice, comfortable pony-carriage, and without a moment's hesitation he insisted on our all getting into it and making the best of our way to our hotel. It is too good an offer to be refused, for the sun is hot and the babies are tired to death; so we start, slowly enough, to plough our way through heavy sand up to the axles. If the tide had been out we could have driven quickly along the hard, dry sand; but we comfort ourselves by remembering that there had been water enough on the bar, and make the best of our way through clouds of impalpable dust to a better road, of which a couple of hundred yards land us at our hotel. It looks bare and unfurnished enough, in all conscience, but it is a new place, and must be furnished by degrees. At all events, it is tolerably clean and quiet, and we can wash our sunburned faces and hands, and, as nurse says, "turn ourselves round."

Coolies swarm in every direction, picturesque fish- and fruit-sellers throng the verandah of the kitchen a little way off, and everything looks bright and green and fresh, having been well washed by the recent rains. There are still, however, several feet of dust in the streets, for they are *made* of dust; and my own private impression is, that all the water in the harbor would not suffice to lay the dust of D'Urban for more than half an hour. With the restlessness of people who have been cooped up on board ship for a month, we insist, the moment it is cool enough, on being taken out for a walk. Fortunately, the public gardens are close at hand, and we amuse ourselves very well in them for an hour or two, but we are all thoroughly tired and worn out, and glad to get to bed, even in gaunt, narrow rooms on hard pallets.

The two following days were spent in looking after and collecting our cumbrous array of boxes and baskets. Tin baths, wicker chairs and baskets, all had to be counted and recounted, until one got weary of the word "luggage;" but that is the penalty of drafting babies about the world. In the intervals of the serious business of tracing No. 5 or running No. 10 to earth in the corner of a warehouse, I made many pleasant acquaintances and received kindest words and notes of welcome from unknown friends. All this warm-hearted, unconventional kindness goes far to make the stranger forget his "own people and his father's house," and feel at once at home amid strange and unfamiliar scenes. After all, "home" is portable, luckily, and a welcoming smile and hand-clasp act as a spell to create it in any place. We also managed, after business-hours, when it was of no use making expeditions to wharf or custom-house after recusant carpet-bags, to drive to the Botanic Gardens. They are extensive and well kept, but seem principally devoted to shrubs. I was assured that this is the worst time of year for flowers, as the plants have not yet recovered from the winter drought. A dry winter and wet summer is the correct atmospheric fashion here: in winter everything is brown and dusty and dried up, in summer green and fragrant and well watered. The gardens are in good order, and I rather regretted not being able to examine them more thoroughly. Another afternoon we drove to the Berea, a sort of suburban Richmond, where the rich semi-tropical vegetation is cleared away in patches, and villas with pretty pleasure-grounds are springing up in every direction. The road winds up the luxuriantly-clothed slopes, with every here and there lovely sea-views of the harbor, with the purpling lights of the Indian Ocean stretching away beyond. Every villa must have an enchanting prospect from its front door, and one can quite understand how alluring to the merchants and business-men of D'Urban must be the idea of getting away after office-hours, and sleeping on such high ground in so fresh and healthy an atmosphere. And here I must say that we Maritzburgians (I am only one in prospective) wage a constant and deadly warfare with the D'Urbanites on the score of the health and convenience of our respective cities. *We* are two thousand feet above the sea and fifty-two miles inland, so we talk in a pitying tone of the poor D'Urbanites as dwellers in a very hot and unhealthy place. "Relaxing" is the word we apply to their climate when we want to be particularly nasty, and they retaliate by reminding us that they are ever so much older than we are (which is an advantage in a colony), and that they are on the coast, and can grow all manner of nice things which we cannot compass, to say nothing of their climate being more equable than ours, and their thunderstorms, though longer in duration, mere flashes in the pan compared to what we in our amphitheatre of hills have to undergo at the hands of the electric current. We never can find answer to that taunt, and if the D'Urbanites only follow up their victory by allusions to their abounding bananas and other fruits, their vicinity to the shipping, and consequent facility of getting almost anything quite easily, we are completely silenced, and it is a wonder if we retain presence of mind enough to murmur "Flies." On the score of dust we are about equal, but I must in fairness confess that D'Urban is a more lively and a better-looking town than Maritzburg when you are in it, though the effect from a distance is not so good. It is very odd how unevenly the necessaries of existence are distributed in this country. Here at D'Urban anything hard in the way of stone is a treasure: everything is soft and friable: sand and finest shingle, so fine as to be mere dust, are all the available material for road-making. I am told that later on I shall find that a cartload of sand in Maritzburg is indeed a rare and costly thing: there we are all rock, a sort of flaky, slaty rock underlying every place.

Our last day, or rather half day, in D'Urban was very full of sightseeing and work. F—— was extremely anxious for me to see the sun rise from the signal-station on the bluff, and accordingly he, G—— and I started with the earliest dawn. We drove through the sand again in a hired and springless Cape cart down to the Point, got into the port-captain's boat and rowed across a little strip of sand at the foot of a winding path cut out of the dense vegetation which makes the bluff such a refreshingly green headland to eyes of wave-worn voyagers. A stalwart Kafir carried our picnic basket, with tea and milk, bread and butter and eggs, up the hill, and it was delightful to follow the windings of

the path through beautiful bushes bearing strange and lovely flowers, and knit together in patches in a green tangle by the tendrils of a convolvulus or clematis, or sort of wild passion-flower, whose blossoms were opening to the fresh morning air. It was a cool but misty morning, and though we got to our destination in ample time, there was never any sunrise at all to be seen. In fact, the sun steadily declined to get up the whole day, so far as I knew, for the sea looked gray and solemn and sleepy, and the land kept its drowsy mantle of haze over its flat shore; which haze thickened and deepened into a Scotch mist as the morning wore on. We returned by the leisurely railway—a railway so calm and stately in its method of progression that it is not at all unusual to see a passenger step calmly out of the train when it is at its fullest speed of crawl, and wave his hand to his companions as he disappears down the by-path leading to his little home. The passengers are conveyed at a uniform rate of sixpence a head, which sixpence is collected promiscuously by a small boy at odd moments during the journey. There are no nice distinctions of class, either, for we all travel amicably together in compartments which are a judicious mixture of a third-class carriage and a cattle-truck. Of course, wood is the only fuel used, and that but sparingly, for it is exceedingly costly.

There was still much to be done by the afternoon—many visitors to receive, notes to write and packages to arrange, for our traveling of these fifty-two miles spreads itself over a good many hours, as you will see. About three o'clock the government mule-wagon came to the door. It may truly and literally be described as "stopping the way," for not only is the wagon itself a huge and cumbrous machine, but it is drawn by eight mules in pairs, and driven by a couple of black drivers. I say "driven by a couple of drivers," because the driving was evidently an affair of copartnership: one held the reins—such elaborate reins as they were! a confused tangle of leather — and the other had the care of two or three whips of differing lengths. The drivers were both jet black—not Kafirs, but Cape blacks—descendants of the old slaves taken by the Dutch. They appeared to be great friends, these two, and took earnest counsel together at every rut and drain and steep pinch of the road, which stretched away, over hill and dale, before us, a broad red track, with high green hedges on either hand. Although the rain had not yet fallen long or heavily, the ditches were all running freely with red, muddy water, and the dust had already begun to cake itself into a sticky, pasty red clay. The wagon was shut in by curtains at the back and sides, and could hold eight passengers easily. Luckily for the poor mules, however, we were only five grown-up people, including the drivers. The road was extremely pretty, and the town looked very picturesque as we gradually rose above it and looked down on it and the harbor together. Of a fine, clear afternoon it would have been still nicer, though I was much congratulated on the falling rain on account of the absence of its alternative —dust. Still, it was possible to have too much of a good thing, and by the time we reached Pine Town, only fourteen miles away, the heavy roads were beginning to tell on the poor mules, and the chill damp of the closing evening made us all only too thankful to get under the shelter of a roadside inn (or hotel, as they are called here), which was snug and bright and comfortable enough to be a credit to any colony. It seemed the most natural thing in the world to be told that this inn was not only a favorite place for people to come out to from D'Urban to spend their holiday time in fine weather (there is a pretty little church in the village hard by), but also that it was quite *de rigueur* for all honeymoons to be spent amid its pretty scenery.

A steady downpour of rain all through the night made our early start next day an affair of doubt and discouragement and dismal prophecy; but we persevered, and accomplished another, long stage through a cold persistent drizzle before reaching an inn, where we enjoyed simply the best breakfast I ever tasted, or at all events the best I have tasted in Natal. The mules were also unharnessed, and after taking, each, a good roll on the damp grass, turned out in the drizzling rain for a rest and a nibble until their more substantial repast was ready. The rain cleared up from time to time, but an occasional heavy shower warned us that the weather was still sulky. It was in much better heart and spirits, however, that we made a second start about eleven o'clock, and struggled on through heavy roads up and down weary hills, slipping here, sliding there, and threatening to stick everywhere. Our next stage was to a place where the only available shelter was a filthy inn, at which we lingered as short a time as practicable—only long enough, in fact, to feed the mules—and then, with every prospect of a finer afternoon, set out once more on the last and longest stage of our journey. All the way the road has been very beautiful, in spite of the shrouding mist, especially at the Inchanga Pass, where round the shoulder of the hill as fair a prospect of curved green hills, dotted with clusters of timber exactly like an English park, of distant ranges rising in softly-rounded outlines, with deep violet shadows in the clefts and pale green lights on the slopes, stretches before you as the heart of painter could desire. Nestling out of sight amid this rich pastureland are the kraals of a large Kafir location, and no one can say that these, the children of the soil, have not secured one of the most favored spots. To me it all looked like a fair mirage. I am already sick of beholding all this lovely country lying around, and yet of being told that food and fuel are almost at famine-prices. People say, "Oh, but you should see it in winter. *Now* it is green, and there is plenty of feed on it, but three months ago no grass-eating creature could have picked up a living on all the country-side. It is all as brown and bare as parchment for half the year. *This* is the spring." Can you not imagine how provoking it is to hear such statements made by old settlers, who know the place only too well, and to find out that all the radiant beauty which greets the traveler's eye is illusive, for in many places there are miles and miles without a drop of water for the flock and herds; consequently, there are no means of transport for all this fuel until the days of railways? Besides which, through Natal lies the great highway to the Diamond Fields, the Transvaal and the Free States, and all the opening-up country beyond; so it is more profitable to drive a wagon than to till a farm. Every beast with four legs is wanted to drag building materials or provisions. The supply of beef becomes daily more precarious and costly, for the oxen are all "treking," and one hears of nothing but diseases among animals —"horse sickness," pleuro-pneumonia, fowl sickness (I feel it an impertinence for the poultry to presume to be ill), and even dogs set up a peculiar and fatal sort of distemper among themselves.

But to return to the last hours of our journey. The mules struggle bravely along, though their ears are beginning to flap about any way, instead of being held straight and sharply pricked forward, and the encouraging cries of "Pull up, Capting! now then, Blue-bok, hi!"

become more and more frequent: the driver in charge of the whips is less nice in his choice of a scourge with which to urge on the patient animals, and whacks them soundly with whichever comes first. The children have long ago wearied of the confinement and darkness of the back seats of the hooded vehicle; we are all black and blue from jolting in and out of deep holes hidden by mud which occur at every yard; but still our flagging spirits keep pretty good, for *our* little Table Mountain has been left behind, whilst before us, leaning up in one corner of an amphitheatre of hills, are the trees which mark where Maritzburg nestles. The mules see it too, and, sniffing their stables afar off, jog along faster. Only one more rise to pull up: we turn a little off the high-road, and there, amid a young plantation of trees, with roses, honeysuckle and passion-flowers climbing up the posts of the wide verandah, a fair and enchanting prospect lying at our feet, stands our new home, with its broad red tiled roof stretching out a friendly welcome to the tired, belated travelers.

PART III.

THE weather at the beginning of this month was lovely and the climate perfection, but now (I am writing on its last day) it is getting very hot and trying. If ever people might stand excused for talking about the weather when they meet, it is we Natalians, for, especially at this time of year, it varies from hour to hour. All along the coast one hears of terrible buffeting and knocking about among the shipping in the open roadsteads which have to do duty for harbors in these parts; and it was only a few days ago that the lifeboat, with the English mail on board, capsized in crossing the bar at D'Urban. The telegram was —as telegrams always are—terrifying in its vagueness, and spoke of the mail-bags as "floating about." When one remembers the vast size of the breakers on which this floating would take place, it sounded hopeless for our letters. They turned up, however, a few days later—in a pulpy state, it is true, but quite readable, though the envelopes were curiously blended and engrafted upon the letters inside—so much so that they required to be taken together, for it was impossible to separate them. I had recourse to the expedient of spreading my letters on a dry towel and draining them before attempting to dissever the leaves. Still, we were all only too thankful to get our correspondence in any shape or form, for precious beyond the power of words to express are home-letters to us, so far away from home.

But to return to our weather. At first it was simply perfect. Bright hot days—not too hot, for a light breeze tempered even the midday heat—and crisp, bracing nights succeeded each other during the first fortnight. The country looked exquisitely green in its luxuriant spring tints over hill and dale, and the rich red clay soil made a splendid contrast on road and track with the brilliant green on either hand. Still, people looked anxiously for more rain, declaring that not half enough had fallen to fill tanks or "shuits" (as the ditches are called), and it took four days of continuous downpour to satisfy these thirsty souls even for the moment. Toward the middle of the month the atmosphere became more oppressive and clouds began to come up in thick masses all round the horizon, and gradually spread themselves over the whole sky. The day before the heaviest rain, though not particularly oppressive, was remarkable for the way in which all manner of animals tried to get under shelter at nightfall. The verandah was full of big frogs: if a door remained open for a moment they hopped in, and then cried like trapped birds when they found themselves in a corner. As for the winged creatures, it was something wonderful the numbers in which they flew in at the windows wherever a light attracted them. I was busy writing English letters that evening: I declare the cockroaches fairly drove me away from the table by the mad way in which they flung themselves into my ink-bottle, whilst the smell of singed moths at the other lamp was quite overpowering. Well, after this came rain indeed—not rain according to English ideas, but a tropical deluge, as many inches falling in a few hours as would fill your rain-gauges for months. I believe my conduct was very absurd that first rainy night. The little house had just been newly papered, and as the ceiling was not one to inspire confidence, consisting as it did merely of boards roughly joined together and painted white, through which and through the tiles beyond the sky could be seen quite plainly, I suffered the gravest doubts about the water getting in and spoiling my pretty new paper. Accordingly, whenever any burst of rain came heavier than its immediate predecessor, I jumped out of bed in a perfect agony of mind,

23

and roamed, candle in hand, all over the house to see if I could not detect a leak anywhere. But the unpromising-looking roof and ceiling stood the test bravely, and not a drop of all that descending downpour found its way to my new walls.

By the way, I must describe the house to you, remarking, first of all, that architecture, so far as my observation extends, is at its lowest ebb in South Africa. I have not seen a single pretty building of any sort or kind since I arrived, although in these small houses it would be so easy to break by gable and porch the severe simplicity of the unvarying straight line in which they are built. Whitewashed outer walls with a zinc roof are not uncommon, and they make a bald and hideous combination until kindly, luxuriant Nature has had time to step in and cover up man's ugly handiwork with her festoons of roses and passion-flowers. Most of the houses have, fortunately, red-tiled roofs, which are not so ugly, and mine is among the number. It is so squat and square, however, that, as our landlord happens to be the chief baker of Maritzburg, it has been proposed to christen it "Cottage Loaf," but this idea requires consideration on account of the baker's feelings. In the mean time, it is known briefly as "Smith's," that being the landlord's name. It has, as all the houses here have, a broad projecting roof extending over a wide verandah. Within are four small rooms, two on either side of a narrow passage which runs from one end to the other. By a happy afterthought, a kitchen has been added beyond this extremely simple ground-plan, and on the opposite side a corresponding projection which closely resembles a packing-case, and which has been painted a bright blue inside and out. This is the dining-room, and evidently requires to be severely handled before its present crude and glaring tints can be at all toned down. At a little distance stands the stable, saddle-room, etc., and a good bedroom for English servants, and beyond that, again, among large clumps of rose-bushes, a native hut. It came up here half built—that is, the frame was partly put together elsewhere —and it resembled a huge crinoline more than anything else in its original state. Since that, however, it has been made more secure by extra pales of bamboo, each tied in its place with infinite trouble and patience by a knot every inch or two. The final stage consisted of careful thatching with thick bundles of grass laid on the framework, and secured by long ropes of grass binding the whole together. The door is the very smallest opening imaginable, and inside it is of course pitch dark. All this labor was performed by stalwart Kafir women, one of whom, a fearfully repulsive female, informed my cook that she had just been bought back by her original husband. Stress of circumstances had obliged him to sell her, and she had been bought by three other husband-masters since then, but was now resold, a bargain, to her first owner, whom, she declared, she preferred to any of the others. But few as are these rooms, they yet are watertight —which is a great point out here—and the house, being built of large, awkward blocks of stone, is cool and shady. When I have arranged things a little, it will be quite comfortable and pretty ; and I defy any one to wish for a more exquisite view than can be seen from any corner of the verandah. We are on the brow of a hill which slopes gently down to the hollow wherein nestles the picturesque little town, or rather village, of Maritzburg. The intervening distance of a mile or so conceals the real ugliness and monotony of its straight streets, and hides all architectural shortcomings. The clock-tower, for instance, is quite a feature in the landscape, and from here one cannot perceive that the clock does not go. Nothing can be prettier than the effect of the red-tiled roofs and white walls peeping out from among thick clumps of trees, whilst beyond the ground rises again to low hills with deep purple fissures and clefts in their green sides. It is only a couple of years since this little house was built and the garden laid out, and yet the shrubs and trees are as big as if half a dozen years had passed over their leafy heads. As for the roses, I never saw anything like the way they flourish at their own sweet will. Scarcely a leaf is to be seen on the ugly straggling tree—nothing but masses of roses of every tint and kind and old-fashioned variety. The utmost I can do in the way of gathering daily basketsful appears only in the light of judicious pruning, and next day a dozen blossoms have burst forth to supply the place of each theft of mine. And there is such a variety of trees! Oaks and bamboos, blue gums and deodars, seem to flourish equally well within a yard or two of each other, and the more distant flower-beds are filled with an odd mixture of dahlias and daturas, white fleur-de-lis and bushy geraniums, scarlet euphorbias and verbenas. But the weeds! They are a chronic eyesore and grief to every gardener. On path and grass-plat, flower-bed and border, they flaunt and flourish. "Jack," the Zulu refugee, wages a feeble and totally inadequate warfare against them with a crooked hoe, but he is only a quarter in earnest, and stops to groan and take snuff so often that the result is that our garden is precisely in the condition of the garden of the sluggard, gate and all. This hingeless condition of the gate, however, is, I must in fairness state, neither Jack's nor our fault. It is a new gate, but no one will come out from the town to hang it. That is my standing grievance. Because we live about a mile from the town it is next to impossible to get anything done. The town itself is one of the shabbiest assemblages of dwellings I have ever seen in a colony. It is not to be named on the same day with Christchurch, the capital of Canterbury, New Zealand, which ten years ago was decently paved and well lighted by gas. Poor sleepy Maritzburg consists now, at more than forty years of age (Christchurch is not twenty-five yet), of a few straight, wide, grass-grown streets, which are only picturesque at a little distance on account of their having trees on each side. On particularly dark nights a dozen oil-lamps standing at long intervals apart are lighted, but when it is even moderately starlight these aids to finding one's way about are prudently dispensed with. There is not a

single handsome and hardly a decent building in the whole place. The streets, as I saw them after rain, are veritable sloughs of despond, but they are capable of being changed by dry weather into deserts of dust. It is true, I have only been as yet twice down to the town, but on both visits it reminded me more of the sleepy villages in Washington Irving's stories than of a smart, modern, go-ahead colonial "city." There are some fairly good shops, but they make no show outside, and within the prices of most of the articles sold are nearly double the same things would bring either at Melbourne or at Christchurch. As D'Urban is barely a month away from London in point of communication, and New Zealand (when I knew it) nearly treble the distance and time, this is a great puzzle to me.

A certain air of quaint interest and life is given to the otherwise desolate streets by the groups of Kafirs and the teams of wagons which bring fuel and forage into the town every day. Twenty bullocks drag these ponderous contrivances —bullocks so lean that one wonders how they have strength to carry their wide-spreading horns aloft; bullocks of a stupidity and obstinacy unparalleled in the natural history of horned beasts. At their head walks a Kafir lad called a "forelooper," who tugs at a rope fastened to the horns of the leading oxen, and in moments of general confusion invariably seems to pull the wrong string and get the whole team into an inextricable tangle of horns and yokes. Sometimes of a quiet Sunday morning these teams and wagons I see "out-spanned" on the green slopes around Maritzburg, making a picturesque addition to the sylvan scenery. Near each wagon a light wreath of smoke steals up into the summer air, marking where some preparation of "mealies" is on foot, and the groups of grazing oxen—"spans," as each team is called—give the animation of animal life which I miss so sadly at every turn in this part of the world.

In Maritzburg itself I only noticed two buildings which made the least effect. One is the government house, standing in a nice garden and boasting of a rather pretty porch, but otherwise reminding one — except for the sentinel on duty — of a quiet country rectory : the other is a small block comprising the public offices. The original idea of this square building must have come from a model dairy. But the crowning absurdity of the place is the office of the colonial secretary, which stands nearly opposite. I am told that inside it is tolerably comfortable, being the remains of an old Dutch building : outside, it can only be compared to a dilapidated barn on a bankrupt farm, and when it was first pointed out to me I had great difficulty, remembering similar buildings in other colonies, in believing it was a public office.

The native police look very smart and shiny in their white suits, and must be objects of envy to their black brethren on account of their "knobkerries," the knobbed sticks which they alone are permitted to carry officially in their hands. The native loves a stick, and as he is forbidden to carry either an assegai — which is a very formidable weapon indeed — or even a knobkerry, only one degree less dangerous, he consoles himself with a wand or switch in case of coming across a snake. You never see a Kafir without something of the sort in his hand : if he is not twirling a light stick, then he has a sort of rude reed pipe from which he extracts sharp and tuneless sounds. As a race, the Kafirs make the effect of possessing a fine *physique :* they walk with an erect bearing and a light step, but in true leisurely savage fashion. I have seen the black race in four different quarters of the globe, and I never saw one single individual move quickly of his own free will. We must bear in mind, however, that it is a new and altogether revolutionary idea to a Kafir that he should do any work at all. Work is for women — war or idleness for men ; consequently, their fixed idea is to do as little as they can ; and no Kafir will work after he has earned money enough to buy a sufficient number of wives who will work for him. "Charlie," our groom — who is, by the way, a very fine gentleman and speaks

"Ingeliss" after a strange fashion of his own — only condescends to work until he can purchase a wife. Unfortunately, the damsel whom he prefers is a costly article, and her parents demand a cow, a kettle and a native hut as the price of her hand — or hands, rather — so Charlie grunts and groans through about as much daily work as an English boy of twelve years old could manage easily. He is a very amusing character, being exceedingly proud, and will only obey his own master, whom he calls his great inkosi or chief. He is always lamenting the advent of the inkosi-casa, or chieftainess, and the piccaninnies and their following, especially the "vaiter," whom he detests. In his way, Charlie is a wag, and it is as good as a play to see his pretence of stupidity when the "vaiter" or French butler desires him to go and eat "sa paniche." Charlie understands perfectly that he is told to go and get his breakfast of mealy porridge, but he won't admit that it is to be called "paniche," preferring his own word "scoff ;" so he shakes his head violently and says, "Nay, nay, paniche." Then, with many nods, "Scoff, ja ;" and so in this strange gibberish of three languages he and the Frenchman carry on quite a pretty quarrel. Charlie also "mocks himself" of the other servants, I am informed, and asserts that he is the "indema" or headman. He freely boxes the ears of Jack, the Zulu refugee — poor Jack, who fled from his own country, next door, the other day, and arrived here clad in only a short flap made of three bucks' tails. That is only a month ago, and "Jack" is already quite a *petit maître* about his clothes. He ordinarily wears a suit of knickerbockers and a shirt of blue check bound with red, and a string of beads round his neck, but he cries like a baby if he tears his clothes, or still worse if the color of the red braid washes out. At first he hated civilized garments, even when they were only two in number, and begged to be allowed to assume a sack with holes for the arms, which is the Kafir compromise when near a town between clothes and flaps made of the tails of wild beasts or strips of hide. But he soon came to delight in them, and is now always begging for "something to wear."

I confess I am sorry for Jack. He is the kitchen-boy, and is learning with much pains and difficulty the *wrong language*. My cook is also French, and, naturally, all that Jack learns is French, and not English. Imagine poor Jack's dismay when, after his three years' apprenticeship to us is ended, he seeks perhaps to better himself, and finds that no one except madame can understand him! Most of their dialogues are carried on by pantomime and the incessant use, in differing tones of voice, of the word "Ja." Jack is a big, loutish young man, but very ugly and feeble, and apparently under the impression that he is perpetually "wanted" to answer for the little indiscretion, whatever it was, on account of which he was forced to flee over the border. He is timid and scared to the last degree, and abjectly anxious to please if it does not entail too much exertion. He is, as it were, apprenticed to us for three years. We are bound to feed and clothe and doctor him, and he is to work for us, in his own lazy fashion, for small wages. The first time Jack broke a plate his terror and despair were quite edifying to behold. Madame called him a "maladroit" on the spot. Jack learned this word, and after his work was over seated himself gravely on the ground with the fragments of the plate, which he tried to join together, but gave up the attempt at last, announcing in his own tongue that it was "dead." After a little consideration he said slowly, several times, "Maldraw, ja," and hit himself a good thump at each "ja." *Now*, I grieve to say, Jack breaks plates, dishes and cups with a perfectly easy and unembarrassed conscience, and is already far too civilized to care in the least for his misfortunes in that line. Whenever a fowl is killed—and I came upon Jack slowly putting one to death the other day with a pair of nail-scissors—he possesses himself of a small store of feathers, which he wears tastefully placed over his left ear. A gay ribbon, worn like a bandeau across the forehead, is what he really loves. Jack is very proud of a tawdry ribbon of many colors with a golden ground which I found for him the other day, only he never can make up his mind where to wear it; and I often come upon him sitting in the shade with the ribbon in his hands, gravely considering the question.

The Pickle and plague of the establishment, however, is the boy Tom, a grinning young savage fresh from his kraal, up to any amount of mischief, who in an evil hour has been engaged as the baby's body-servant. I cannot trust him with the child out of my sight for a moment, for he "snuffs" enormously, and smokes coarse tobacco out of a cow's horn, and is anxious to teach the baby both these accomplishments. Tom wears his snuff-box—which is a brass cylinder a couple of inches long—in either ear impartially, there being huge slits in the cartilage for the purpose, and the baby never rests till he gets possession of it and sneezes himself nearly into fits. Tom likes nursing Baby immensely, and croons to him in a strange buzzing way which lulls him to sleep invariably. He is very anxious, however, to acquire some words of English, and I was much startled the other day to hear in the verandah my own voice saying, "What is it, dear?" over and over again. This phrase proceeded from Tom, who kept on repeating it, parrot-fashion—an exact imitation, but with no idea of its meaning. I had heard the baby whimpering a little time before, and Tom had remarked that these four words produced the happiest effect in restoring good-humor; so he learned them, accent and all, on the spot, and used them as a spell or charm on the next opportunity. I think even the poor baby was puzzled. But one cannot feel sure of what Tom will do next. A few evenings ago I trusted him to wheel the perambulator about the garden-paths but, becoming anxious in a very few minutes to know what he was about, I went to look for him. I found him grinning in high glee, watching the baby's efforts at cutting his teeth on a live young bird. Master Tom had spied a nest, climbed the tree, and brought down the poor little bird, which he presented to the child, who instantly put it into his mouth. When I arrived on the scene Baby's mouth was full of feathers, over which he was making a very disgusted face, and the unhappy bird was nearly dead of fright and squeezing, whilst Tom was in such convulsions of laughter that I nearly boxed his ears. He showed me by signs how Baby insisted on sucking the bird's head, and conveyed his intense amusement at the idea. I made Master Tom climb the tree instantly and put the poor little half-dead creature back into its nest, and sent for Charlie to explain to him he should have no sugar—the only punishment Tom cares about—for two days. I often think, however, that I must try and find another penalty, for when Tom's allowance of sugar is stopped he "requisitions" that of every one else, and so gets rather more than usual. He is immensely proud of the brass chin-strap of an old artillery bushy which has been given to him. He used to wear it across his forehead in the favorite Kafir fashion, but as the baby always made it his first business to pull this shining strap down over Tom's eyes, and eventually over Tom's mouth, it has been transferred to his neck.

These Kafir-lads make excellent nurse-boys generally, and English children are very fond of them. Nurse-girls are rare, as the Kafir women begin their lives of toil so early that they are never very handy or gentle in a house, and boys are easier to train as servants. I heard to-day, however, of an excellent Kafir nursemaid who was the daughter of a chief, and whose only drawback was the size of her family. She was actually and truly one of *eighty* brothers and sisters, her father being a rich man with twenty-five wives. That simply means that he had twenty - five devoted slaves, who worked morning, noon and night for him in field and mealy-patch without wages. Jack the Zulu wanted to be nurse-boy dreadfully, and used to follow Nurse about with a towel rolled up into a bundle, and another towel arranged as drapery, dandling an imaginary baby on his arm, saying plaintively, "Piccaninny, piccaninny!" This Nurse translated to mean that he was an experienced nurse-boy, and had taken care of a baby in his own country, but as I had no confidence in maladroit Jack, who chanced to be very deaf besides, he was ruthlessly relegated to his pots and pans.

It is very curious to see the cast-off clothes of all the armies of Europe finding their way hither. The natives of South Africa prefer an old uniform coat or tunic to any other covering, and the effect of a short scarlet garment when worn with bare legs is irresistibly droll. The apparently inexhaustible supply of old-fashioned English coatees with their worsted epaulettes is just coming to an end, and being succeeded by ragged red tunics, franc-tireurs' brownish-green jackets and much-worn Prussian gray coats. Kafir-Land may be looked upon as the old-clothes shop of all the fighting world, for sooner or later every cast-off scrap of soldier's clothing drifts toward it. Charlie prides himself much upon the possession of an old gray great-coat, so patched and faded that it may well have been one of those which toiled up the slopes of Inkerman that rainy Sunday morning twenty years ago ; whilst scampish Tom got well chaffed the other day for suddenly making his appearance clad in a stained red tunic with buff collar and cuffs, and the number of the old "dirty Half-hundred" in tarnished metal on the shoulder-scales. "Sir Garnet," cried Charlie the witty, whilst Jack affected to prostrate himself before the grinning imp, exclaiming, "O great inkosi !"

Charlie is angry with me just now, and looks most reproachfully my way on all occasions. The cause is that he was sweeping away sundry huge spiders' webs from the roof of the verandah (the work of a single night) when I heard him coughing frightfully. I gave him some lozenges, saying, "Do your cough good, Charlie." Charlie received them in both hands held like a cup, the highest form of Kafir gratitude, and gulped them all down on the spot. Next day I heard the same dreadful cough, and told F—— to give him some more lozenges. But Charlie would have none of them, alleging he "eats plenty to-morrow's yesterday, and dey no good at all;" and he evidently despises me and my remedies.

If only there were no hot winds! But the constant changes are so trying and so sudden. Sometimes we have a hot, scorching gale all day, drying and parching one's very skin up, and shriveling one's lovely roses like the blast from a furnace: then in the afternoon a dark cloud sails suddenly up from behind the hills to the west. It is over the house before one knows it is coming: a loud clap of thunder shakes the very ground beneath one's feet, others follow rapidly, and a thunderstorm bewilders one for some ten minutes or so. A few drops of cold rain fall to the sound of the distant thunder, now rolling away eastward, which yet "struggles and howls at fits." It is not always distant, but we have not yet seen a real thunderstorm; only a few of these short, sudden electrical disturbances, which come and go more like explosions than anything else. A few days ago there was a duststorm which had a very curious effect as we looked down upon it from this hill. All along the roads one could watch the dust being caught up, as it were, and whirled along in dense clouds, whilst the poor little town itself was absolutely blotted out by the blinding masses of fine powder. For half an hour or so we could afford to watch and smile at our neighbors' plight, but soon we had to flee for shelter ourselves within the house, for a furious hot gale drove heavily up behind the dust and nearly blew us away altogether. Still, there was no thunderstorm, though we quite wished for one to cool the air and refresh the parched and burnt-up grass and flowers. Such afternoons are generally pretty sure to be succeeded by a cold night, and perhaps a cold, damp morning; and one can already understand that these alternations during the summer months are apt to produce dysentery among young children. I hear just now of a good many such cases among babies.

I have been so exceedingly busy this month packing, arranging and settling that there has been but little time for going about and seeing the rather pretty environs of Maritzburg; besides which, the weather is dead against excursions, changing as it does to rain or threatening thunderstorms nearly every afternoon. One evening we ventured out for a walk in spite of growlings and spittings up above among the crass-looking clouds. Natal is not a nice country, for women at all events, to walk in. You have to keep religiously to the road or track, for woe betide the rash person who ventures on the grass, though from repeated burnings all about these hills it is quite short. There is a risk of your treading on a snake, and a certainty of your treading on a frog. You will soon find your legs covered with small and pertinacious ticks, who have apparently taken a "header" into your flesh and made up their minds to die sooner than let go. They must be the bull-dogs of the insect tribe, these ticks, for a sharp needle will scarcely dislodge them. At the last extremity of extraction they only burrow their heads deeper into the skin, and will lose this important part of their tiny bodies sooner than yield to the gentlest leverage. Then there are myriads of burs which cling to you in green and brown scales of roughness, and fringe your petticoats with their sticky little lumps. As for the poor petticoats themselves, however short you may kilt them, you bring them back from a walk deeply flounced with the red clay of the roads; and as the people who wash do not seem to consider this a disadvantage, and take but little pains to remove the earth-stains, one's garments gradually acquire, even when clean, a uniform bordering of dingy red. All the water at this time of year is red too, as the rivers are stirred up by the heavy summer rains, and resemble angry muddy ditches more than fresh-water streams. I miss at every turn the abundance of clear, clean, sparkling water in the creeks and rivers of my dear New Zealand, and it is only after heavy rain, when every bath and large vessel has been turned into a receptacle during the downpour, that one can compass the luxury of an inviting-looking bath or glass of drinking-water. Of course this turbid water renders it pretty difficult to get one's clothes properly washed, and the substitute for a mangle is an active Kafir, who makes the roughly-dried clothes up into a neat parcel, places them on a stone and dances up and down upon them for as long or short a time as he pleases. Fuel is so enormously dear that the cost of having clothes ironed is something astounding, and altogether washing is one of the many costly items of Natalian housekeeping. When I remember the frantic state of indignation and alarm we were all in in England three years ago when coals rose to £2 10s. a ton, and think how cheap I should consider that price for fuel here, I can't help a melancholy smile. Nine solid sovereigns purchase you a tolerable-sized load of wood, about equal for cooking purposes to a ton of coal; but whereas the coal is at all events some comfort and convenience to use, the wood is only a source of additional trouble and expense. It has to be cut up and dried, and finally coaxed and cajoled by incessant use of the bellows into burning. Besides the price of fuel, provisions of all sorts seem to me to be dear and bad. Milk is sold by the quart bottle: it is now fourpence per bottle, but rises to sixpence during the winter. Meat is eightpence a pound, but it is so thin and bony, and of such indifferent quality, that there is very little saving in that respect. I have not tasted any really good butter since we arrived, and we pay two shillings a pound for cheesy, rancid stuff. I hear that "mealies," the crushed maize, are also very dear, and so is forage for the horses. Instead of the horses being left out on the run night and day, summer and winter, as they used to be in New Zealand, with an occasional feed of oats for a treat, they need to be carefully housed at night and well fed with oaten straw and mealies to give them a chance against the mysterious and fatal "horse-sickness," which kills them in a few hours. Altogether, so far as my very limited experience—of only a few weeks, remember—goes, I should say that Natal was an expensive place to live in, owing to the scarcity and dearness of the necessaries of life. I am told that far up in the country food and

fuel are cheap and good, and that it is the dearness and difficulty of transport which forces Maritzburg to depend for its supplies entirely on what is grown in its own immediate vicinity, where there is not very much land under cultivation; so we must look to the coming railway to remedy all that.

If only one could eat flowers, or if wheat and other cereals grew as freely and luxuriously as flowers grow, how nice it would be! On the open grassy downs about here the blossoms are lovely — beautiful lilies in scarlet and white clusters, several sorts of periwinkles, heaths, cinnerarias, both purple and white, and golden bushes of citisus or Cape broom, load the air with fragrance. By the side of every "spruit" or brook one sees clumps of tall arum lilies filling every little water-washed hollow in the brook, and the ferns which make each ditch and watercourse green and plumy have a separate shady beauty of their own. This is all in Nature's own free, open garden, and when the least cultivation or care is added to her bounteous luxuriance a magnificent garden for fruit, vegetables and flowers is the result; always supposing you are fortunate enough to be able to induce these lazy Kafirs to dig the ground for you.

About a fortnight ago I braved the dirt and disagreeables of a cross-country walk in showery weather—for we have not been able to meet with a horse to suit us yet— and went to see a beautiful garden a couple of miles away. It was approached by a long double avenue of blue gum trees, planted only nine years ago, but tall and stately as though a century had passed over their lofty, pointed heads, and with a broad red clay road running between the parallel lines of trees. The ordinary practice of clearing away the grass as much as possible round a house strikes an English eye as bare and odd, but when one hears that it is done to avoid snakes, it becomes a necessary and harmonious adjunct to the rest of the scene. In this instance I found these broad smooth walks, with their deep rich red color, a very beautiful contrast to the glow of brilliant blossoms in the enormous flower-beds. For this garden was not at all like an ordinary garden, still less like a prim English parterre. The beds were as large as small fields, slightly raised and bordered by a thick line of violets. Large shrubs of beautiful semi-tropical plants made tangled heaps of purple, scarlet and white blossoms on every side ; the large creamy bells of the datura drooped toward the reddish earth ; thorny shrubs of that odd bluish-green peculiar to Australian foliage grew side by side with the sombre-leaved myrtle. Every plant grew in the most liberal fashion ; green things which we are accustomed to see in England in small pots shoot up here to the height of laurel bushes; a screen of scarlet euphorbia made a brilliant line against a background formed by a hedge of shell-like cluster-roses, and each pillar of the verandah of the little house had its own magnificent creeper. Up one standard an ipomea twined closely; another pillar was hidden by the luxuriance of a trumpet-honeysuckle; whilst a third was thickly covered by an immense passion-flower. In shady, damp places grew many varieties of ferns and blue hydrangeas, whilst other beds were filled by gay patches of verbenas of every hue and shade. The sweet-scented verbena is one of the commonest and most successful shrubs in a Natal garden, and just now the large bushes of it which one sees in every direction are covered by tapering spikes of its tiny white blossoms. But the feature of this garden was roses —roses on each side whichever way you turned, and I should think of at least a hundred different sorts. Not the stiff standard rose tree of an English garden, with its few precious blossoms, to be looked at from a distance and admired with respectful gravity. No: in this garden the roses grow as they might have grown in Eden—untrained, unpruned, in enormous bushes covered entirely by magnificent blossoms, each bloom of which would have won a prize at a rose-show. There was one cloth-of-gold rose bush that I shall never forget — its size, its fragrance, its wealth of creamy-yellowish blossoms. A few yards off stood a still bigger and more luxuriant pyramid, some ten feet high, covered with the large, delicate and regular pink bloom of the souvenir de Malmaison. When I talk of *a* bush I only mean one especial bush which caught my eye. I suppose there were fifty cloth-of-gold and fifty souvenir rose bushes in that garden. Red roses, white roses, tea roses, blush-roses, moss roses, and, last not least, the dear old-fashioned, homely cabbage rose, sweetest and most sturdy of all. You could wander for acres and acres among fruit trees and plantations of oaks and willows and other trees, but you never got away from the roses. There they were, beautiful, delicious things at every turn—hedges of them, screens of them and giant bushes of them on either hand. As I have said before, though kept free from weeds by some half dozen scantily-clad but stalwart Kafirs with their awkward hoes, it was not a bit like a trim English garden. It was like a garden in which Lalla Rookh might have wandered by moonlight talking sentimental philosophy with her minstrel prince under old Fadladeen's chaperonage, or a garden that Boccaccio might have peopled with his Arcadian fine ladies and gentlemen. It was emphatically a poet's or a painter's garden, not a gardener's garden. Then, as though nothing should be wanting to make the scene lovely, one could hear through the fragrant silence the tinkling of the little "spruit" or brook at the bottom of the garden, and the sweet song of the Cape canary, the same sort of greenish finch which is the parent stock of all our canaries, and whose acquaintance I first made in Madeira. A very sweet warbler it is, and the clear, flute-like notes sounded prettily among the roses. From blossom to blossom lovely butterflies flitted, perching quite fearlessly on the red clay walk just before me, folding and unfolding their big painted wings. Every day I see a new kind of butterfly, and the moths which one comes upon hidden away under the leaves of the creepers during the bright noisy day are lovely beyond the power of words. One little fellow is a great pet of mine. He wears pure white wings, with vermilion stripes drawn in regular horizontal lines across his back, and between the lines are shorter, broken streaks of black, which is at once neat and uncommon; but he is always in the last stage of sleepiness when I see him. I am so glad little G—— is not old enough to want to catch them all and impale them upon corks in a glass case; so the pretty creatures live out their brief and happy life in the sunshine, without let or hinderance from him.

The subject of which my mind is most full just now is the purchase of a horse. F—— has a fairly good chestnut cob of his own; G—— has become possessed, to his intense delight, of an aged and long-suffering Basuto pony, whom he fidgets to death during the day by driving him all over the place, declaring he is "only showing him where the nicest grass grows;" and I want a steed to draw my pony-carriage and to carry me. F—— and I are at dagger's drawn on this question. He wants to buy me a young, handsome, showy horse of whom his admirers predict that "he will steady down presently," whilst my affections are firmly fixed on an aged screw who would not turn his head if an Armstrong gun were fired behind him. His owner says Scotsman is "rising eleven:" F,—— declares Scotsman will never see his twentieth birthday again. F—— points out to me that Scotsman has had rough times of it, apparently, in his distant youth, and that he is strangely battered about the head, and has a large notch out of one ear. I retaliate by reminding him how sagely the old horse picked his way, with a precision of judgment which only years can give, through the morass which lies at the foot of the hill, and which must be crossed every time I go into town (and there is nowhere else to go). That morass is a bog in summer and a honeycomb of deep ruts and holes in winter, which, you must bear in mind, is the dry season here. Besides his tact in the matter of the morass, did I not drive Scotsman the other day to the park, and did he not comport himself in the most delightfully sedate fashion? You require experience to be on the lookout for the

perils of Maritzburg streets, it seems, for all their sleepy, deserted, tumble-down air. First of all, there are the transport-wagons, with their long span of oxen straggling all across the road, and a nervous bullock precipitating himself under your horse's nose. The driver, too, invariably takes the opportunity of a lady passing him to crack his whip violently, enough to startle any horse except Scotsman. Then when you have passed the place where the wagons most do congregate, and think you are tolerably safe and need only look out for ruts and holes in the street, lo! a furious galloping behind you, and some half dozen of the "gilded youth" of Maritzburg dash past you, stop, wheel round and gallop past again, until you are almost blinded with dust or smothered with mud, according to the season. This peril occurred several times during my drive to and from the park, and I can only remark that dear old Scotsman kept his temper better than I did: perhaps he was more accustomed to Maritzburg manners.

When the park was reached at last, across a frail and uncertain wooden bridge shaded by large weeping willows, I found it the most creditable thing I had yet seen. It is admirably laid out, the natural undulations of the ground being made the most of, and exceedingly well kept. This in itself is a difficult matter where all vegetation runs up like Jack's famous beanstalk, and where the old proverb about the steed starving whilst his grass is growing falls completely to the ground. There are numerous drives, made level by a coating of smooth black shale, and bordered by a double line of syringas and oaks, with hedges of myrtle or pomegranate. In some places the roads run alongside the little river—a very muddy torrent when I saw it—and then the oaks give way to great drooping willows, beneath whose trailing branches the river swirled angrily. On fine Saturday afternoons the band of the regiment stationed here plays on a clear space under some shady trees—for you can never sit or stand on the grass in Natal, and even croquet is played on bare leveled earth —and everybody rides or walks or drives about. When I saw the park there was not a living creature in it, for it was, as most of our summer afternoons are, wet and cold and drizzling; but, considering that there was no thunderstorm likely to break over our heads that day, I felt that I could afford to despise a silent Scotch mist. We varied our afternoon weather last week by a hailstorm, of which the stones were as big as large marbles. I was scoffed at for remarking this, and assured it was "nothing, absolutely nothing," to *the* great hailstorm of two years ago, which broke nearly every tile and pane of glass in Maritzburg, and left the town looking precisely as though it had been bombarded. I have seen photographs of some of the ruined houses, and it is certainly difficult to believe that hail could have done so much mischief. Then, again, stories reach me of a certain thunderstorm one Sunday evening just before I arrived in which the lightning struck a room in which a family was assembled at evening prayers, killing the poor old father with the Bible in his hand, and knocking over every member of the little congregation. My informant said, "I assure you it seemed as though the lightning were poured out of heaven in a jug. There were no distinct flashes: the heavens appeared to split open and pour down a flood of blazing violet light." I have seen noth-

ing like this yet, but can quite realize what such a storm must be like, for I have observed already how different the color of the lightning is. The flashes I have seen were exactly of the lilac color he described, and they followed each other with a rapidity of succession unknown in less electric regions. And yet my last English letters were full of complaints of the wet weather in London, and much self-pity for the long imprisonment in-doors. Why, those very people don't know what weather inconveniences are. If London streets are muddy, at all events there are no dangerous morasses in them. No matter how much it rains, people get their comfortable meals three times a day. *Here*, rain means a risk of starvation (if the little wooden bridge between us and the town were to be swept away) and a certainty of short commons. A wet morning means damp bread for breakfast and a thousand other disagreeables. No, I have no patience with the pampered Londoners, who want perpetual sunshine in addition to their other blessings, for saying one word about discomfort. They are all much too civilized and luxurious, and their lives are made altogether too smooth for them. Let them come out here and try to keep house on the top of a hill with servants whose language they don't understand, a couple of noisy children and a small income, and then, as dear Mark Twain says, "they'll know something about woe."

PART IV.

I MUST certainly begin this letter by setting aside every other topic for the moment and telling you of our grand event, our national celebration, our historical New Year's Day. We have "turned the first sod" of our first inland railway, and, if I am correctly informed, at least a dozen sods more, but you must remember, if you please, that our navvies are Kafirs, and that they do *not* understand what Mr. Carlyle calls the beauty and dignity of labor in the least. It is all very well for you conceited dwellers in the Old and New Worlds to laugh at us for making such a fuss about a projected hundred miles of railway — you whose countries are made into dissected maps by the magic iron lines — but for poor us, who have to drag every pound of sugar and reel of sewing-cotton over some sixty miles of vile road between this and Maritzburg, such a line, if it be ever finished, will be a boon and a blessing indeed.

I think I can better make you understand *how* great a blessing if I describe my journeys up and down — journeys made, too, under exceptionally favorable circumstances. The first thing which had to be done, some three weeks before the day of our departure, was to pack and send down by wagon a couple of portmanteaus with our smart clothes. I may as well mention here that the cost of the transit came to fourteen shillings each way for three or four small, light packages, and that on each occasion we were separated from our possessions for a fortnight or more. The next step to be taken was to secure places in the daily post-cart, and it required as much mingled firmness and persuasion to do this as though it had reference to a political crisis. But then there were some hundreds of us Maritzburgians all wanting to be taken down to D'Urban within the space of a few days, and there was nothing to take us except the open post-cart, which occupied six hours on the journey, and an omnibus, which took ten hours, but afforded more shelter from possible rain and probable sun. Within the two vehicles some twenty people might, at a pinch, find places, and at least a hundred wanted to go every day of that last week of the old year. I don't know how the others managed: they must have got down somehow, for there they were in great force when the eventful day had arrived.

This first journey was prosperous, deceitfully prosperous, as though it would fain try to persuade us that after all there was a great deal to be said in favor of a mode of traveling which reminded one of the legends of the glories of the old coaching days. No dust—for there had been heavy rain a few days before—a perfect summer's day, hot enough in the sun, but not disagreeably hot as we bowled along, fast as four horses could go, in the face of a soft, balmy summer breeze. We were packed as tightly as we could fit — two of us on the coach-box, with the mail-bags under our feet and the driver's elbows in our ribs. The ordinary light dog-cart which daily runs between Maritzburg and D'Urban was exchanged for a sort of open break, strong indeed, but very heavy, one would fancy, for the poor horses, who had to scamper along up and down veldt and berg, over bog and spruit, with this lumbering conveyance at their heels. Not for long, though: every seven miles, or even less, we pulled up—sometimes at a tidy inn, where a long table would be set in the open verandah laden with eatables (for driving fast through the air sharpens even the sturdy colonial appetite), sometimes at a lonely shanty by the roadside, from whence a couple of Kafir lads emerged tugging at the bridles of the fresh horses. But I am bound to say that although each of these teams did

34

a stage twice a day, although they were ill-favored and ill-groomed, their harness shabby beyond description, and their general appearance most forlorn, they were one and all in good condition and did their work in first-rate style. The wheelers were generally large, gaunt and most hideous animals, but the leaders often were ponies who, one could imagine, under happier circumstances might be handsome little horses enough, staunch and willing to the last degree. They knew their driver's cheery voice as well as possible, and answered to every cry and shout of encouragement he gave them as we scampered along. Of course, each horse had its name, and equally of course "Sir Garnet" was there in a team with "Lord Gifford" and "Lord Carnarvon" for leaders. Did we come to a steep hillside, up which any respectable English horse would certainly expect to walk in a leisurely, sober fashion, then our driver shook out his reins, blew a ringing blast on his bugle, and cried, "Walk along, Lord Gifford! think as you've another Victorian Cross to get top o' this hill! Walk along, Lord Carnarvon! you ain't sitting in a cab'net council *here*, you know. Don't leave Sir Garnet do all the work, you know. Forward, my lucky lads! creep up it!" and by the time he had shrieked out this and a lot more patter, behold! we were at the top of the hill, and a fresh, lovely landscape was lying smiling in the sunshine below us. It was a beautiful country we passed through, but, except for a scattered homestead here and there by the roadside, not a sign of a human dwelling on all its green and fertile slopes. How the railway is to drag itself up and round all those thousand and one spurs running into each other, with no distinct valley or flat between, is best known to the engineers and surveyors, who have declared it practicable. To the non-professional eye it seems not only difficult, but impossible. But oh how it is wanted! All along the road shrill bugle-blasts warned the slow trailing ox-wagons, with their naked "forelooper" at their head, to creep aside out of our way. I counted one hundred and twen-

ty wagons that day on fifty miles of road. Now, if one considers that each of these wagons is drawn by a span of some thirty or forty oxen, one has some faint idea of how such a method of transport must waste and use up the material of the country. Something like ten thousand oxen toil over this one road summer and winter, and what wonder is it not only that merchandise costs more to fetch up from D'Urban to Maritzburg than it does to bring it out from England, but that beef is dear and bad! As transport pays better than farming, we hear on all sides of farms thrown out of cultivation, and as a necessary consequence milk, butter, and so forth are scarce and poor, and in the neighborhood of Maritzburg, at least, it is esteemed a favor to let you have either at exorbitant prices and of most inferior quality. When one looks round at these countless acres of splendid grazing-land, making a sort of natural park on either hand, it seems like a bad dream to know that we have constantly to use preserved milk and potted meat as being cheaper and easier to procure than fresh.

No one was in any mood, however, to discuss political economy that beautiful day, and we laughed and chatted, and ate a great many luncheons, chiefly of tea and peaches, all the way along. Our driver enlivened the route by pointing out various spots where frightful accidents had occurred to the post-cart on former occasions: "You see that big stone? Well, it war jest there that Langabilile and Colenso, they takes the bits in their teeth, those 'osses do, and they sets off their own pace and their own way. Jim Stanway, he puts his brake down hard and his foot upon the reins, but, Lord love you! them beasts would ha' pulled his arms and legs both off afore they'd give in. So they runs poor Jim's near wheel right up agin that bank and upsets the whole concern, as neat as needs be, over agin that bit o' bog. Anybody hurt? Well, yes: they was all what you might call shook. Mr. Bell, he had his arm broke, and a foreign chap from the diamond-fields, he gets killed outright, and Jim himself had his head cut open.

It was a bad business, you bet, and rough upon Jim. Ja!"

All the driver's conversation is interlarded with "*Ja*," but he never says a worse word than that, and he drinks nothing but tea. As for a pipe, or a cigar even, when it is offered to him he screws up his queer face into a droll grimace and says, "No—thanks. I want all my nerves, I do, on this bit of road. —Walk along, Lady Barker : I'm ashamed of you, I am, hanging your head like that at a bit of a hill!" It was rather startling to hear this apostrophe all of a sudden, but as my namesake was a very hard-working little brown mare, I could only laugh and declare myself much flattered.

Here we are at last, amid the tropical vegetation which makes a green and tangled girdle around D'Urban for a dozen miles inland : yonder is the white and foaming line of breakers which marks where the strong current, sweeping down the east coast, brings along with it all the sand and silt it can collect, especially from the mouth of the Umgeni River close by, and so forms the dreaded bar which divides the outer from the inner harbor. Beyond this crisp and sparkling line of heaving, tossing snow stretches the deep indigo-blue of the Indian Ocean, whilst over all wonderful sunset tints of opal and flamecolor are hovering and changing with the changing, wind-driven clouds. Beneath our wheels are many inches of thick white sand, but the streets are gay and busy, with picturesque coolies in their bright cotton draperies and swiftly-passing Cape carts and vehicles of all sorts. We are in D'Urban indeed—D'Urban in unwonted holiday dress and on the tippest tiptoe of expectation and excitement. A Cape cart, with a Chinese coolie driver, and four horses apparently put in harness together for the first time, was waiting for us and our luggage at the post-office. We got into it, and straightway began to plunge through the sandy streets once more, turning off the highroad and beginning almost immediately to climb with pain and difficulty the red sandy slopes of the Berea, a beautiful wooded upland dotted with villas. The road is terrible for man and beast, and we had to stop every few yards to breathe the horses. At last our destination is reached, through fields of sugar-cane and plantations of coffee, past luxuriant fruit trees, rustling, broad-leafed bananas and encroaching greenery of all sorts, to a clearing where a really handsome house stands, with hospitable, wide-open doors, awaiting us. Yes, a good big bath first, then a cup of tea, and now we are ready for a saunter in the twilight on the wide level terrace (called by the ugly Dutch name "stoop") which runs round three sides of the house. How green and fragrant and still it all is! Straightway the glare of the long sunny day, the rattle and jolting of the post-cart, the toil through the sand, all slip away from mind and memory, and the tranquil delicious present, "with its odors of rest and of love," slips in to soothe and calm our jaded senses. Certainly, it is hotter here than in Maritzburg—that assertion we are prepared to die in defence of— but we acknowledge that the heat at this hour is *not* oppressive, and the tropical luxuriance of leaf and flower all around is worth a few extra degrees of temperature. Of course, our talk is of to-morrow, and we look anxiously at the purpling clouds to the west.

"A fine day," says our host; and so it ought to be with five thousand people come from far and wide to see the sight. Why, that is more than a quarter of the entire white population of Natal! Bed and sleep become very attractive suggestions, though made indecently soon after dinner, and it is somewhere about ten o'clock when they are carried out, and, like Lord Houghton's famous "fair little girl," we

Know nothing more till again it is day.

A fine day, too, is this same New Year's Day of 1876—a glorious day—sunny of course, but with a delicious breeze stealing among the flowers and shrubs in capricious puffs, and snatching a differing scent from each heavy cluster of blossom it visits. By mid-day F—— has got himself into his gold-laced coat and has lined the inside of his cocked hat with plaintain-leaves. He has also groaned much at the idea of substituting this futile head-gear for his hideous but convenient pith helmet. I too have donned my best gown, and am horrified to find how much a smart bonnet (the first time I have needed to wear one since I left England) sets off and brings out the shades of tan in a sun-browned face; and for a moment I too entertain the idea of retreating once more to the protecting depths of my old shady hat. But a strong conviction of the duty one owes to a "first sod," and the consoling reflection that, after all, everybody will be equally brown (a fallacy, by the way: the D'Urban beauties looked very blanched by this summer weather), supported me, and I followed F—— and his cocked hat into the waiting carriage.

No need to ask, "Where are we to go?" All roads lead to the first sod to-day. We are just a moment late: F—— has to get out of the carriage and plunge into the sand, madly rushing off to find and fall into his place in the procession, and we turn off to secure our seats in the grand stand. But before we take them I must go and look at the wheelbarrow and spade, and above all at the "first sod." For some weeks past it has been a favorite chaff with us Maritzburgians to offer to bring a nice fresh, lively sod down with us, but we were assured D'Urban could furnish one. Here it is exactly under the triumphal arch, looking very faded and depressed, with a little sunburned grass growing feebly on it, but still a genuine sod and no mistake. The wheelbarrow was really beautiful, made of native woods with their astounding names. All three specimens of the hardest and handsomest yellow woods were there, and they were described to me as, "stink-wood, breeze-wood and sneeze-wood." The rich yellow of the wood is veined by handsome dark streaks, with "1876" inlaid in large black figures in the centre. The spade was just a common spade, and could not by any possibility be called anything else. But there is no time to linger and laugh any longer beneath all these fluttering

streamers and waving boughs, for here are the Natal Carbineers, a plucky little handful of light horse clad in blue and silver, who have marched, at their own charges, all the way down from Maritzburg to help keep the ground this fine New Year's Day. Next come a strong body of Kafir police, trudging along through the dust with odd shuffling gait, bended knees, bare legs, bodies leaning forward, and keeping step and time by means of a queer sort of barbaric hum and grunt. Policemen are no more necessary than my best bonnet: they are only there for the same reason —for the honor and glory of the thing. The crowd is kept in order by somebody here and there with a ribboned wand, for it is the most orderly and respectable crowd you ever saw. In fact, such a crowd would be an impossibility in England or any highly-civilized country. There are no dodging vagrants, no slatternly women, no squalid, starving babies. In fact, our civilization has not yet mounted to effervescence, so we have no dregs. Every white person on the ground was well clad, well fed, and apparently well-to-do. The "lower orders" were represented by a bright fringe of coolies and Kafirs, sleek, grinning and as fat as ortolans, especially the babies. Most of the Kâfirs were dressed in snow-white knickerbockers and shirts bordered by gay bands of color, with fillets of scarlet ribbon tied round their heads, while as for the coolies, they shone out like a shifting bed of tulips, so bright were the women's *chuddahs* and the men's jackets. All looked smiling, healthy and happy, and the public enthusiasm rose to its height when to the sound of a vigorous band (it is early yet in the day, remember, O flute and trombone!) a perfect liliputian mob of toddling children came on the ground. These little people were all in their cleanest white frocks and prettiest hats: they clung to each other and to their garlands and staves of flowers until the tangled mob reminded one of a May-Day fête. Not that any English May Day of my acquaintance could produce such a lavish profusion of roses and buds and blossoms of every hue and tint, to say nothing of such a sun and sky. The children's corner was literally like a garden, and nothing could be prettier than the effect of their little voices shrilling up through the summer air, as, obedient to a lifted wand, they burst into the chorus of the national anthem when the governor and mayor drove up. Cheers from white throats; gruff, loud shouts all together of *Bayete!* (the royal salute) and *Inkosi!* ("chieftain") from black throats; yells, expressive of excitement and general good-fellowship, from throats of all colors. Then a moment's solemn pause, a hushed silence, bared heads, and the loud, clear tones of a very old pastor in the land were heard imploring the blessing of Almighty God on this our undertaking. Again the sweet childish trebles rose into the sunshine in a chanted Amen, and then there were salutes from cannon, feux-de-joie from carbines, and more shoutings, and all the cocked hats were to be seen bowing; and then one more tremendous burst of cheering told that *the* sod was cut and turned and trundled, and finally pitched out of the new barrow back again upon the dusty soil—all in the most artistic and satisfactory fashion. "There are the Kafir navvies: they are *really* going to work now." (This latter with great surprise, for a Kafir *really* working, now or ever, would indeed have been the raree-show of the day.) But this natural phenomenon was left to develop itself in solitude, for the crowd began to reassemble into processions, and generally to find its way under shelter from sun and dust. The five hundred children were heralded and marched off to the tune of one of their own pretty hymns to where unlimited buns and tea awaited them, and we elders betook ourselves to the grateful shade and coolness of the flower-decked new market-hall, open to-day for the first time, and turned by flags and ferns and lavish wealth of what in England are costliest hot-house flowers into a charming banqueting-hall. All these exquisite ferns and blossoms cost far less than the string and nails which fastened them against the walls, and their fresh fragrance and greenery struck gratefully on our sun-baked eyes as we found our way into the big room.

Nothing could be more creditable to a young colony than the way everything was arranged, for the difficulties in one's culinary path in Natal are hardly to be appreciated by English housekeepers. At one time there threatened to be almost a famine in D'Urban, for besides the pressure of all these extra mouths of visitors to feed, there was this enormous luncheon, with some five hundred hungry people to be provided for. It seems so strange that with every facility for rearing poultry all around it should be scarce and dear, and when brought to market as thin as possible. The same may be said of vegetables: they need no culture beyond being put in the ground, and yet unless you have a garden of your own it is very difficult to get anything like a proper supply. I heard nothing but wails from distracted housekeepers about the price and scarcity of food that week. However, *the* luncheon showed no sign of scarcity, and I was much amused at the substantial and homely character of the *menu*, which included cold baked sucking pig among its delicacies. A favorite specimen of the confectioner's art that day consisted of a sort of solid brick of plum pudding, with, for legend, " The First Sod " tastefully picked out in white almonds on its dark surface. But it was a capital luncheon, and so soon as the mayor had succeeded in impressing on the band that they were not expected to play all the time the speeches were being made, everything went on very well. Some of the speeches were short, but oh! far, far too many were long, terribly long, and the whole affair was not over before five o'clock. The only real want of the entertainment was ice. It seems so hard not to have it in a climate which can produce such burning days, for those tiresome cheap little ice-machines with crystals are of no use whatever. I got one which made ice (under pressure of much turning) in the ship, but it has never made any here, and my experience is that of everybody else. Why there should not be an ice-making or an ice-importing company no one knows, except that there is so little energy or enterprise here that everything is dawdly and uncomfortable because it seems too much trouble to take pains to supply wants. It is the same everywhere throughout the colony : sandy roads with plenty of excellent materials for hardening them close by ; no fish to be bought because no one will take the trouble of going out to catch them. But I had better stop scribbling, for I am evidently getting tired after my long day of unwonted festivity. It is partly the oppression of my best bonnet, and partly the length of the speeches, which have wearied me out so thoroughly.

MARITZBURG, January 6.

Nothing could afford a greater contrast than our return journey. It was the other extreme of discomfort and misery, and must surely have been sent to make us appreciate and long for the completion of this very railway. We waited a day beyond that fixed for our return, in order to give the effects of a most terrific thunderstorm time to pass away, but it was succeeded by a perfect deluge of rain. Rain is not supposed to last long at this season of the year, but all I can say is that this rain did last. When the third day came and brought no sign of clearing up with it, and very little down to speak of, we agreed to delay no longer ; besides which our places in the post-cart could not be again exchanged, as had previously been done, for the stream of returning visitors was setting strongly toward Maritzburg, and we might be detained for a week longer if we did not go at once. Accordingly, we presented ourselves at the D'Urban post-office a few minutes before noon and took our places in the post-cart. My seat was on the box, and as I flattered myself that I was well wrapped up, I did not feel at all alarmed at the prospect of a cold, wet drive. Who would believe that twenty-four hours ago one could hardly endure a white muslin dressing-gown ? Who would believe that twenty-four hours ago a lace shawl was an oppressive wrap, and that the

serious object of my envy and admiration all these hot days on the Berea has been a fat Abyssinian baby, as black as a coal, and the strongest and biggest child one ever saw. That sleek and grinning infant's toilette consisted of a string of blue beads round its neck, and in this cool and airy costume it used to pervade the house, walking about on all fours exactly like a monkey, for of course it could not stand. Yet, how cold that baby must be to-day ! But if it is, its mother has probably tied it behind her in an old shawl, and it is nestling close to her fat broad back fast asleep.

But the baby is certainly a most unwarrantable digression, and we must return to our post-cart. The discouraging part of it was that the vehicle itself had been in all the storm and rain of yesterday. Of course no one had dreamed of washing or wiping it out in any fashion, so we had to sit upon wet cushions and put our feet into a pool of red mud and water. Now, if I must confess the truth, I, an old traveler, had done a very stupid thing. I had been lured by the deceitful beauty of the weather when we started into leaving behind me everything except the thinnest and coolest garments I possessed, and I therefore had to set out on this journey in the teeth of a cold wind and driving rain clad in a white gown. It is true, I had my beloved and most useful ulster, but it was a light waterproof one, and just about half enough in the way of warmth. Still, as I had another wrap, a big Scotch plaid, I should have got along very well if it had not been for the still greater stupidity of the only other female fellow-passenger, who calmly took her place in the open postcart behind me in a brown holland gown, without scarf or wrap or anything whatever to shelter her from the weather, except a white calico sunshade. She was a Frenchwoman too, and looked so piteous and forlorn in her neat toilette, already drenched through, that of course I could do nothing less than lend her my Scotch shawl, and trust to the driver's friendly promises of empty corn-bags at some future stage. By the time the bags came—or rather by the time we got to the bags—I was indeed wet and cold. The ulster did its best, and all that could be expected of it, but no garment manufactured in a London shop could possibly cope with such wild weather, tropical in the vehemence of its pouring rain, wintry in its cutting blasts. The wind seemed to blow from every quarter of the heavens at once, the rain came down in sheets, but I minded the mud more than either wind or rain: it was more demoralizing. On the box-seat I got my full share and more, but yet I was better off there than inside, where twelve people were squeezed into the places of eight. The horses' feet got balled with the stiff red clay exactly as though it had been snow, and from time to time as they galloped along, six fresh ones at every stage, I received a good lump of clay, as big and nearly as solid as a croquet-ball, full in my face. It was bitterly cold, and the night was closing in when we drove up to the door of the best hotel in Maritzburg, at long past eight instead of six o'clock. It was impossible to get out to our own place that night, so there was nothing for it but to stay where we were, and get what food and rest could be coaxed out of an indifferent bill of fare and a bed of stony hardness, to say nothing of the bites of numerous mosquitoes. The morning light revealed the melancholy state of my unhappy white gown in its full horror. All the rivers of Natal will never make it white again, I fear. Certainly there is much to be said in favor of railway-traveling, after all, especially in wet weather.

JANUARY 10.

Surely, I have been doing something else lately besides turning this first sod? Well, not much. You see, no one can undertake anything in the way of expeditions or excursions, or even sight-seeing, in summer, partly on account of the heat, and partly because of the thunderstorms. We have had a few very severe ones lately, but we hail them with joy on account of the cool clear atmosphere which succeeds to a display of electrical vehemence. We walked home from church a few evenings ago on a very wild and threatening night, and I never shall forget the weird beauty of the scene. We had started to go to church about six o'clock: the walk was only two miles, and the afternoon was calm and cloudless. The day had been oppressively hot, but there were no immediate signs of a storm. While we were in church, however, a fresh breeze sprang up and drove the clouds rapidly before it. The glare of the lightning made every corner of the church as bright as day, and the crash of the thunder shook the wooden roof over our heads. But there was no rain yet, and when we came out—in fear and trembling, I confess, as to how we were to get home—we could see that the violence of the storm had either passed over or not yet reached the valley in which Maritzburg nestles, and was expending itself somewhere else. So F—— decided that we might venture. As for vehicles to be hired in the streets, there are no such things, and by the time we could have persuaded one to turn out for us — a very doubtful contingency, and only to be procured at the cost of a sovereign or so — the full fury of the storm would probably be upon us. There was nothing for it, therefore, but to walk, and so we set out as soon as possible to climb our very steep hill. Instead of the soft, balmy twilight on which we had counted, the sky was of an inky blackness, but for all that we had light enough and to spare. I never saw such lightning. The flashes came literally every second, and lit up the whole heavens and earth with a blinding glare far brighter than any sunshine. So great was the contrast, and so much more intense the darkness after each flash of dazzling light, that we could only venture to walk on *during* the flashes, though one's instinct was rather to stand still, awestricken and mute. The thunder growled and cracked incessantly, but far away, toward the Inchanga Valley. If the wind had shifted ever so little and brought the storm back again, our plight would be poor indeed; and with this dread upon us we trudged bravely on and breasted the hillside with what haste and courage we could. During the rare momentary intervals of darkness we could perceive that the whole place was ablaze with fireflies. Every blade of grass held a tiny sparkle of its own, but when the lightning shone out with its yellow and violet glare the modest light of the poor little fireflies seemed to be quite extinguished. As for the frogs, the clamorous noise they kept up sounded absolutely deafening, and so did the shrill, incessant cry of the cicalas. We reached home safely and before the rain fell, but found all our servants in the verandah in the last stage of dismay and uncertainty what to do for the best. They had collected waterproofs, umbrellas and lanterns ; but as it was not actually raining yet, and we certainly did not require light on our path—for they said that each flash showed them our climbing, trudging figures as plainly as possible—it was difficult to know what to do, especially as the Kafirs have, very naturally, an intense horror and dislike to going out in a thunderstorm. This storm was not really overhead at all, and scarcely deserves mention except as the precursor of a severe one of which our valley got the full benefit. It was quite curious to see the numbers of dead butterflies on the garden-paths after that second storm. Their beautiful plumage was not dimmed or smirched nor their wings broken : they would have been in perfect order for a naturalist's collection ; yet they were quite dead and stiff. The natives declare it is the lightning which kills them thus.

My own private dread — to return to that walk home for a moment—was of stepping on a snake, as there are a great many about, and one especial variety, a small poisonous brown adder, is of so torpid and lazy a nature that it will not glide out of your way, as other snakes do, but lets you tread on it and then bites you. It is very marvelous, considering how many snakes there are, that one hears of so few bad accidents. G—— is always poking about in likely places for them, as his supreme ambition is to see one. I fully expect a catastrophe some day, and keep stores of ammonia and brandy handy. Never was such a fearless little monkey. He is always scampering about on his old Basuto pony, and

of course tumbles off now and then ; but he does not mind it in the least. When he is not trying to break his neck in this fashion he is down by himself at the river fishing, or he is climbing trees, or down a well which is being dug here, or in some piece of mischief or other. The sun and the fruit are my *bêtes noires*, but neither seems to hurt him, though I really don't believe that any other child in the world has ever eaten so many apricots at one time as he has been doing lately. This temptation has just been removed, however, for during our short absence at D'Urban every fruit tree has been stripped to the bark—every peach and plum, every apple and apricot, clean gone. Of course, no one has done it, but it is very provoking all the same, for it used to be so nice to take the baby out very early, and pick up the fallen apricots for breakfast. The peaches are nearly all pale and rather tasteless, but the apricots are excellent in flavor, of a large size and in extraordinary abundance. There was also a large and promising crop of apples, but they have all been taken in their unripe state. As a rule, the Kafirs are scrupulously honest, and we left plate and jewelry in the house under Charlie's care whilst we were away, without the least risk, for such things they would never touch ; but fruit or mealies they cannot be brought to regard as personal property, and they gather the former and waste the latter without scruple. It is a great objection to the imported coolies, who make very clean and capital servants, that they have inveterate habits of pilfering and are hopelessly dishonest about trifles. For this reason they are sure to get on badly with Kafir fellow-servants, who are generally quite above any temptation of that kind.

JANUARY 14.

A few days ago we took G—— to see the annual swimming sports in the small river which runs through the park. It was a beautiful afternoon, for a wonder, with no lowering thunder-clouds over the hills, so the banks of the river were thronged for half a mile and more with spectators. It made a very pretty picture, the large willow trees drooping into the water on either shore, the gay concourse of people, the bright patch of color made by the red coats of the band of the regiment stationed across the stream, the tents for the competitors to change in, the dark wondering faces of Kafirs and coolies, who cannot comprehend *why* white people should take so much trouble and run so much risk to amuse themselves. We certainly must appear to them to be possessed by a restless demon of energy, both in our work and our play, and never more so than on this hot afternoon, when, amid much shouting and laughing, the various water-races came off. The steeplechase amused us a great deal, where the competitors had to swim over and under various barriers across the river; and so did the race for very little boys, which was a full and excellent one. The monkeys took to the water as naturally as fishes, and evidently enjoyed the fun more than any one. Indeed, the difficulty was to get them out of the water and into the tents to change their swimming costume after the race was over. But the most interesting event was one meant to teach volunteers how to swim rivers in case of field service, and the palm lay between the Natal Carbineers and a smart body of mounted police. At a given signal they all plunged on horseback into the muddy water, and from a very difficult part of the bank too, and swam, fully accoutred and carrying their carbines, across the river. It was very interesting to watch how clever the horses were, and how some of their riders slipped off their backs the moment they had fairly entered the stream and swam side by side with their steeds until the opposite bank was reached; and then how the horses paused to allow their dripping masters to mount again— no easy task in heavy boots and saturated clothes, with a carbine in the left hand which had to be kept dry at all risks and hazards. When I asked little G——— which part he liked best, he answered without hesitation, "The assidents" (anglicè, accidents), and I am not sure that

he was not right; for, as no one was hurt, the crowd mightily enjoyed seeing some stalwart citizen in his best clothes suddenly topple from his place of vantage on the deceitfully secure-looking but rotten branch of a tree and take an involuntary bath in his own despite. When that citizen further chanced to be clad in a suit of bright-colored velveteen the effect was much enhanced. It is my private opinion that G——— was longing to distinguish himself in a similar fashion, for I constantly saw him "lying out" on most frail branches, but try as he might, he could not accomplish a tumble.

JANUARY 17.

I have had an opportunity lately of attending a Kafir *lit de justice*, and I can only say that if we civilized people managed our legal difficulties in the same way it would be an uncommonly good thing for everybody except the lawyers. Cows are at the bottom of nearly all the native disputes, and the Kafirs always take their grievance soberly to the nearest magistrate, who arbitrates to the best of his ability between the disputants. They are generally satisfied with his award, but if the case is an intricate one, or they consider that the question is not really solved, then they have the right of appeal, and it is this court of appeal which I have been attending lately. It is held in the newly-built office of the minister for native affairs— the prettiest and most respectable-looking public office which I have seen in Maritzburg, by the way. Before the erection of this modest but comfortable building the court used to be held out in the open air under the shade of some large trees—a more picturesque method of doing business, certainly, but subject to inconveniences on account of the weather. It is altogether the most primitive and patriarchal style of business one ever saw, but all the more delightful on that account.

It is inexpressibly touching to see with one's own eyes the wonderfully deep personal devotion and affection of the Kafirs for the kindly English gentleman who for thirty years and more has been their real ruler and their wise and judicious friend. Not a friend to pamper their vices and give way to their great fault of idleness, but a true friend to protect their interests, and yet to labor incessantly for their social advancement and for their admission into the great field of civilized workers. The Kafirs know little and care less for all the imposing and elaborate machinery of British rule; the queen on her throne is but a fair and distant dream-woman to them; Sir Garnet himself, that great inkosi, was as nobody in their eyes compared to their own chieftain, their king of hearts, the one white man to whom of their own free will and accord they give the royal salute whenever they see him. I have stood in magnificent halls and seen king and kaiser pass through crowds of bowing courtiers, but I never saw anything which impressed me so strongly as the simultaneous springing to the feet, the loud shout of *Bayete!* given with the right hand upraised (a higher form of salutation than *Inkosi!* and only accorded to Kafir royalty), the look of love and rapture and satisfied expectation in all those keen black faces, as the minister, quite unattended, without pomp or circumstance of any sort or kind, quietly walked into the large room and sat himself down at his desk with some papers before him. There was no clerk, no official of any sort: no one stood between the people and the fountain of justice. The extraordinary simplicity of the trial which commenced was only to be equaled by the decorum and dignity with which it was conducted. First of all, everybody sat down upon the floor, the plaintiff and defendant amicably side by side opposite to the minister's desk, and the other natives, about a hundred in number, squatted in various groups. Then, as there was evidently a slight feeling of surprise at my sitting myself down in the only other chair—they probably considered me a new-fashioned clerk—the minister explained that I was the wife of another inkosi, and that I wanted to see and hear how Kafirmen stated their case when anything went wrong with their affairs. This explana-

tion was perfectly satisfactory to all parties, and they regarded me no more, but immediately set to work on the subject in hand. A sort of *précis* of each case had been previously prepared from the magistrate's report for Mr. S——'s information by his clerk, and these documents greatly helped me to understand what was going on. No language can be more beautiful to listen to than either the Kafir or Zulu tongue: it is soft and liquid as Italian, with just the same gentle accentuation on the penultimate and antepenultimate syllables. The clicks which are made with the tongue every now and then, and are part of the language, give it a very quaint sound, and the proper names are excessively harmonious.

In the first cause which was taken the plaintiff, as I said before, was not quite satisfied with the decision of his own local magistrate, and had therefore come here to restate his case. The story was slightly complicated by the plaintiff having two distinct names by which he had been known at different times of his life. "Tevula," he averred, was the name of his boyhood, and the other, "Mazumba," the name of his manhood. The natives have an unconquerable aversion to giving their real names, and will offer half a dozen different aliases, making it very difficult to trace them if they are "wanted," and still more difficult to get at the rights of any story they may have to tell. However, if they are ever frank and open to anybody, it is to their own minister, who speaks their language as well as they do themselves, and who fully understands their mode of reasoning and their habits of mind.

Tevula told his story extremely well, I must say—quietly, but earnestly, and with the most perfectly respectful though manly bearing. He sometimes used graceful and natural gesticulation, but not a bit more than was needed to give emphasis to his oratory. He was a strongly-built, tall man, about thirty-five years of age, dressed in a soldier's greatcoat—for it was a damp and drizzling day—had bare legs and feet, and wore nothing on his head except the curious ring into which the men weave their hair.

So soon as a youth is considered old enough to assume the duties and responsibilities of manhood he begins to weave his short crisp hair over a ring of grass which exactly fits the head, keeping the woolly hair in its place by means of wax. In time the hair grows perfectly smooth and shining and regular over this firm foundation, and the effect is as though it were a ring of jet or polished ebony worn round the brows. Different tribes slightly vary the size and form of the ring; and in this case it was easy to see that the defendant belonged to a different tribe, for his ring was half the size, and worn at the summit of a cone of combed-back hair which was as thick and close as a cap, and indeed looked very like a grizzled fez. Anybody in court may ask any questions he pleases, and in fact what we should call "cross-examine" a witness, but no one did so whilst I was present. Every one listened attentively, giving a grunt of interest whenever Tevula made a point; and this manifestation and sympathy always seemed to gratify him immensely. But it was plain that, whatever might be the decision of the minister, who listened closely to every word, asking now and then a short question—which evidently hit some logical nail right on the head—they would abide by it, and be satisfied that it was the fairest and most equitable solution of the subject.

Here is a *résumé* of the first case, and it is a fair sample of the intricacies of a Kafir lawsuit: Our friend Tevula possesses an aged relative, a certain aunt, called Mamusa, who at the present time appears to be in her dotage, and consequently her evidence is of very little value. But once upon a time — long, long ago—Mamusa was young and generous: Mamusa had cows, and she *gave* or *lent*—there was the difficulty—a couple of heifers to the defendant, whose name I can't possibly spell on account of the clicks. Nobody denies that of her own free will these heifers had been bestowed by Mamusa on the withered-looking little old man squatting opposite, but the question is, Were they a loan or a gift? For many years nothing was done about these heifers, but one fine day Tevula gets wind of the story, is immediately seized with a fit of affection for his aged relative, and takes her to live in his kraal, proclaiming himself her protector and heir. So far so good: all this was in accordance with Kafir custom, and the narration of this part of the story was received with grunts of asseveration and approval by the audience. Indeed, Kafirs are as a rule to be depended upon, and their minds, though full of odd prejudices and quirks, have a natural bias toward truth. Two or three years ago Tevula began by claiming, as heir-at-law, though the old woman still lives, twenty cows from the defendant as the increase of these heifers: *now* he demands between thirty and forty. When asked why he only claimed twenty, as nobody denies that the produce of the heifers has increased to double that number, he says naïvely, but without hesitation, that there is a fee to be paid of a shilling a head on such a claim if established, and that he only had twenty shillings in the world; so, as he remarked with a knowing twinkle in his eye, "What was the use of my claiming more cows than I had money to pay the fee for?" But times have improved with Tevula since then, and he is now in a position to claim the poor defendant's whole herd, though he generously says he will not insist on his refunding those cows which do not resemble the original heifers, and are not, as they were, dun and red and white. This sounded magnanimous, and met with grunts of approval until the blear-eyed defendant remarked, hopelessly, "They are all of those colors," which changed the sympathies of the audience once more. Tevula saw this at a glance, and hastened to improve his position by narrating an anecdote. No words of mine could reproduce the dramatic talent that man displayed in his narration. I did not understand a syllable of his language, and yet I could gather from his gestures, his intonation, and above all from the expression of his hearers' faces, the sort of story he was telling them. After he had finished, Mr. S—— turned to me and briefly translated the episode with which Tevula had sought to rivet the attention and sympathy of the court. Tevula's tale, much condensed, was this: Years ago, when his attention had first been directed to the matter, he went with the defendant out on the veldt to look at the herd. No sooner did the cattle see them approaching than a beautiful little dun-colored heifer, the exact counterpart of her grandmother (Mamusa's cow), left the others and ran up to him, Tevula, lowing and rubbing her head against his shoulder, and following him all about like a dog. In vain did her reputed owner try to drive her away: she persisted in following Tevula all the way back to his kraal, right up to the entrance of his hut. "I was her master, and the inkomokazi knew it," cried Tevula triumphantly, looking round at the defendant with a knowing nod, as much as to say, "Beat that, if you can!" Not knowing what answer to make, the defendant took his snuff-box out of his left ear and solaced himself with three or four huge pinches. I started the hypothesis that Mamusa might once have had a *tendresse* for the old gentleman, and might have bestowed these cows upon him as a love-gift; but this idea was scouted, even by the defendant, who said gravely, "Kafir women don't buy lovers or husbands: we buy the wife we want." A Kafir girl is exceedingly proud of being bought, and the more she costs the prouder she is. She pities English women, whose bridegrooms expect to receive money instead of paying it, and considers a dowry as a most humiliating arrangement.

I wish I could tell you how Mamusa's cows have finally been disposed of, but, although it has occupied three days, the case is by no means over yet. I envy and admire Mr. S——'s untiring patience and unfailing good-temper, but it is just these qualities which make his Kafir subjects (for they really consider him as their ruler) so certain that their affairs will not be neglected or their interests suffer in his hands.

Whilst I was listening to Tevula's oratory my eyes and my mind sometimes wandered to the eager and silent audience, and I amused myself by studying their strange head-dresses. In most instances the men wore their hair in the woven rings to which I have alluded, but there were several young men present who indulged in purely fancy head-dresses. One stalwart youth had got hold of the round cardboard lid of a collar-box, to which he had affixed two bits of string, and tied it firmly but jauntily on one side of his head. Another lad had invented a most extraordinary decoration for his wool-covered pate, and one which it is exceedingly difficult to describe in delicate language. He had procured the intestines of some small animal, a lamb or a kid, and had cleaned and scraped them and tied them tightly, at intervals of an inch or two, with string. This series of small clear bladders he had then inflated, and arranged them in a sort of bouquet on the top of his head, skewering tufts of his crisp hair between, so that the effect resembled a bunch of bubbles, if there could be such a thing. Another very favorite adornment for the head consisted of a strip of gay cloth or ribbon, or of even a few bright threads, bound tightly like a fillet across the brows and confining a tuft of feathers over one ear; but I suspect all these fanciful arrangements were only worn by the gilded youth of a lower class, because I noticed that the chieftains and *indunas*, or headmen of the villages, never wore such frivolities. They wore indeed numerous slender rings of brass or silver wire on their straight, shapely legs, and also necklaces of lions' or tigers' claws and teeth round their throats, but these were trophies of the chase as well as personal ornaments.

PART V.

MARITZBURG, February 10, 1876.

IN the South African calendar this is set down as the first of the autumnal months, but the half dozen hours about mid-day are still quite as close and oppressive as any we have had. I am, however, bound to say that the nights—at all events, up here—are cooler, and I begin even to think of a light shawl for my solitary walks in the verandah just before bedtime. When the moon shines these walks are pleasant enough, but when only the "common people of the skies" are trying to filter down their feebler light through the misty atmosphere, I have a lurking fear and distrust of the reptiles and bugs who may also have a fancy for promenading at the same time and in the same place. I say nothing of bats, frogs and toads, mantis or even huge moths: to these we are quite accustomed. But although I have never seen a live snake in this country myself, still one hears such unpleasant stories about them that it is just as well to what the Scotch call "mak siccar" with a candle before beginning a constitutional in the dark.

It is not a week ago since a lady of my acquaintance, being surprised at her little dog's refusal to follow her into her bedroom one night, instituted a search for the reason of the poor little creature's terror and dismay, and discovered a snake coiled up under her chest of drawers. At this moment, too, the local papers are full of recipes for the prevention and cure of snake-bites, public attention being much attracted to the subject on account of an Englishman having been bitten by a black "mamba" (a very venomous adder) a short time since, and having died of the wound in a few hours. In his case, poor man! there does not seem to have been a chance from the first, for he was obliged to walk some distance to the nearest house, and as they had no proper remedies there,

he had to be taken on a farther journey of some miles to a hospital. All this exercise and motion caused the poison to circulate freely through the veins, and was the worst possible thing for him. The doctors here seem agreed that the treatment of ammonia and brandy is the safest, and many instances are adduced to show how successful it has been, though one party of practitioners admits the ammonia, but denies the brandy. On the other hand, one hears of a child bitten by a snake and swallowing half a large bottle of raw brandy in half an hour without its head being at all affected, and, what is more, recovering from the bite and living happy ever after. I keep quantities of both remedies close at hand, for three or four venomous snakes have been killed within a dozen yards of the house, and little G—— is perpetually exploring the long grass all around or hunting for a stray cricket-ball or a pegtop in one of those beautiful fern-filled ditches whose tangle of creepers and plumy ferns is exactly the favorite haunt of snakes. As yet he has brought back from these forbidden raids nothing more than a few ticks and millions of burs.

As for the ticks, I am getting over my horror at having to dislodge them from among the baby's soft curls by means of a sharp needle, and even G—— only shouts with laughter at discovering a great swollen monster hanging on by its forceps to his leg. They torment the poor horses and dogs dreadfully; and if the said horses were not the very quietest, meekest, most underbred and depressed animals in the world, we should certainly hear of more accidents. As it is, they confine their efforts to get rid of their tormentors to rubbing all the hair off their tails and sides in patches against the stable walls or the trunk of a tree. Indeed, the clever way G——'s miserable little Basuto pony actually climbs inside a good-sized bush, and sways him-

46

self about in it with his legs off the ground until the whole thing comes with a crash to the ground, is edifying to behold to every one except the owner of the tree. Tom, the Kafir boy, tried hard to persuade me the other day that the pony was to blame for the destruction of a peach tree, but as the only broken-down branches were those which had been laden with fruit, I am inclined to acquit the pony. Carbolic soap is an excellent thing to wash both dogs and horses with, as it not only keeps away flies and ticks from the skin, which is constantly rubbed off by incessant scratching, but helps to heal the tendency to a sore place. Indeed, nothing frightened me so much as what I heard when I first arrived about Natal sores and Natal boils. Everybody told me that ever so slight a cut or abrasion went on slowly festering, and that sores on children's faces were quite common. This sounded very dreadful, but I am beginning to hope it was an exaggeration, for whenever G—— cuts or knocks himself (which is every day or so), or scratches an insect's bite into a bad place, I wash the part with a little carbolic soap (there are two sorts—one for animals and a more refined preparation for the human skin), and it is quite well the next day. We have all had a threatening of those horrid boils, but they have passed off.

In town the mosquitoes are plentiful and lively, devoting their attentions chiefly to new-comers, but up here—I write as though we were five thousand feet instead of only fifty above Maritzburg—it is rare to see one. I think "fillies" are more in our line, and that in spite of every floor in the house being scrubbed daily with strong soda and water. "Fillies," you must know, is our black groom's (Charlie's) way of pronouncing *fleas*, and I find it ever so much prettier. Charlie and I are having a daily discussion just now touching sundry moneys he expended during my week's absence at D'Urban for the kittens' food. Charlie calls them the "lil' catties," and declares that the two small animals consumed three shillings and ninepence worth of meat in a week. I laughingly say, "But,

Charlie, that would be nearly nine pounds of meat in six days, and they couldn't eat that, you know." Charlie grins and shows all his beautiful even white teeth: then he bashfully turns his head aside and says, "I doan know, ma': I buy six' meat dree time." "Very well, Charlie, that would be one shilling and sixpence." "I doan know, ma';" and we've not got any further than that yet.

But G—— and I are picking up many words of Kafir, and it is quite mortifying to see how much more easily the little monkey learns than I do. I forget my phrases or confuse them, whereas when he learns two or three sentences he appears to remember them always. It is a very melodious and beautiful language, and, except for the clicks, not very difficult to learn. Almost everybody here speaks it a little, and it is the first thing necessary for a new-comer to endeavor to acquire; only, unfortunately, there are no teachers, as in India, and consequently you pick up a wretched, debased kind of patois, interlarded with Dutch phrases. Indeed, I am assured there are two words, *el hashi* ("the horse"), of unmistakable Moorish origin, though no one knows how they got into the language. Many of the Kafirs about town speak a little English, and they are exceedingly sharp, when they choose, about understanding what is meant, even if they do not quite catch the meaning of the words used. There is one genius of my acquaintance, called "Sixpence," who is not only a capital cook, but an accomplished English scholar, having spent some months in England. Generally, to Cape Town and back is the extent of their journeyings, for they are a home-loving people; but Sixpence went to England with his master, and brought back a shivering recollection of an English winter and a deep-rooted amazement at the boys of the Shoe Brigade, who wanted to clean his boots. That astonished him more than anything else, he says.

The Kafirs are very fond of attending their own schools and church services, of which there are several in the town; and I find one of my greatest difficulties in living out here consists in getting Kafirs to come out of town, for by doing so they miss their regular attendance at chapel and school. A few Sundays ago I went to one of these Kafir schools, and was much struck by the intently-absorbed air of the pupils, almost all of whom were youths about twenty years of age. They were learning to read the Bible in Kafir during my visit, sitting in couples, and helping each other on with immense diligence and earnestness. No looking about, no wandering, inattentive glances, did I see. I might as well have "had the receipt of fern-seed and walked invisible" for all the attention I excited. Presently the pupil-teacher, a young black man, who had charge of this class, asked me if I would like to hear them sing a hymn, and on my assenting he read out a verse of "Hold the Fort," and they all stood up and sang it, or rather its Kafir translation, lustily and with good courage, though without much tune. The chorus was especially fine, the words "Inkanye kanye" ringing through the room with great fervor. This is not a literal translation of the words "Hold the Fort," but it is difficult, as the teacher explained to me, for the translator to avail himself of the usual word for "hold," as it conveys more the idea of "take hold," "seize," and the young Kafir missionary thoroughly understood all the nicety of the idiom. There was another class for women and children, but it was a small one. Certainly, the young men seemed much in earnest, and the rapt expression of their faces was most striking, especially during the short prayer which followed the hymn and ended the school for the afternoon.

I have had constantly impressed upon my mind since my arrival the advice *not* to take Christian Kafirs into my service, but I am at a loss to know in what way the prejudice against them can have arisen. "Take a Kafir green from his kraal if you wish to have a good servant," is what every one tells me. It so happens that we have two of each—two Christians and two heathens—about the place, and there is no doubt whatever which is the best. Indeed, I have some-

times conversations with the one who speaks English, and I can assure you we might all learn from him with advantage. His simple creed is just what came from the Saviour's lips two thousand years ago, and comprises His teaching of the whole duty of man—to love God, the great "En' Kos," and his neighbor as himself. He speaks always with real delight of his privileges, and is very anxious to go to Cape Town to attend some school there of which he talks a great deal, and where he says he should learn to read the Bible in English. At present he is spelling it out with great difficulty in Kafir. This man often talks to me in the most respectful and civil manner imaginable about the customs of his tribe, and he constantly alludes to the narrow escape he had of being murdered directly after his birth for the crime of being a twin. His people have a fixed belief that unless one of a pair of babies be killed at once, either the father or mother will die within the year; and they argue that as in any case one child will be sure to die in its infancy, twins being proverbially difficult to rear, it is only both kind and natural to kill the weakly one at once. This young man is very small and quiet and gentle, with an ugly face, but a sweet, intelligent expression and a very nice manner. I find him and the other Christian in our employment very trustworthy and reliable. If they tell me anything which has occurred, I know I can believe their version of it, and they are absolutely honest. Now, the other lads have very loose ideas on the subject of sugar, and make shifty excuses for everything, from the cat breaking a heavy stone filter up to half the marketing being dropped on the road.

I don't think I have made it sufficiently clear that besides the Sunday-schools and services I have mentioned there are night-schools every evening in the week, which are fully attended by Kafir servants, and where they are first taught to read their own language, which is an enormous difficulty to them. They always tell me it is so much easier to learn to read English than Kafir; and if one studies the two languages, it is plain to see how much simpler the new tongue must appear to a learner than the intricate construction, the varying patois and the necessarily phonetic spelling of a language compounded of so many dialects as the Zulu-Kafir.

FEBRUARY 12.

In some respects I consider this climate has been rather over-praised. Of course it is a great deal—a very great deal—better than our English one, but that, after all, is not saying much in its praise. Then we must remember that in England we have the fear and dread of the climate ever before our eyes, and consequently are always, so to speak, on our guard against it. Here, and in other places where civilization is in its infancy, we are at the mercy of dust and sun, wind and rain, and all the eccentric elements which go to make up weather. Consequently, when the balance of comfort and convenience has to be struck, it is surprising how small an advantage a really better climate gives when you take away watering-carts and shady streets for hot weather, and sheltered railway-stations and hansom cabs for wet weather, and roads and servants and civility and general convenience everywhere. This particular climate is both depressing and trying in spite of the sunny skies we are ever boasting about, because it has a strong tinge of the tropical element in it; and yet people live in much the same kind of houses (only that they are very small), and wear much the same sort of clothes (only that they are very ugly), and lead much the same sort of lives (only that it is a thousand times duller than the dullest country village), as they do in England. Some small concession is made to the thermometer in the matter of puggeries and matted floors, but even then carpets are used wherever it is practicable, because this matting never looks clean and nice after the first week it is put down. All the houses are built on the ground floor, with the utmost economy of building material and labor, and consequently there are no passages : every room is, in fact, a passage and leads to its neighbor. So the perpetually dirty bare feet, or, still worse, boots fresh from the mud or dust of the streets, soon wear out the matting. Few houses are at all prettily decorated or furnished, partly from the difficulty of procuring anything pretty here, the cost and risk of its carriage up from D'Urban if you send to England for it, and partly from the want of servants accustomed to anything but the roughest and coarsest articles of household use. A lady soon begins to take her drawing-room ornaments *en guignon* if she has to dust them herself every day in a very dusty climate. I speak feelingly and with authority, for that is my case at this moment, and applies to every other part of the house as well.

I must say I like Kafir servants in some respects. They require, I acknowledge, constant supervision ; they require to be told to do the same thing over and over again every day; and, what is more, besides telling, you have to stand by and see that they do the thing. They are also very slow. But still, with all these disadvantages, they are far better than the generality of European servants out here, who make their luckless employers' lives a burden to them by reason of their tempers and caprices. It is much better, I am convinced, to face the evil boldly and to make up one's mind to have none but Kafir servants. Of course one immediately turns into a sort of overseer and upper servant one's self; but at all events you feel master or mistress of your own house, and you have faithful and good-tempered domestics, who do their best, however awkwardly, to please you. Where there are children, then indeed a good English nurse is a great boon; and in this one respect I am fortunate. Kafirs are also much easier to manage when the orders come direct from the master or mistress, and they work far more willingly for them than for white servants. Tom, the nurse-boy, confided to me yesterday that he hoped to stop in my employment for forty moons. After that space of time he considered that he should be in a position to buy plenty of wives, who would work for him and support him for the rest of his life. But how Tom or Jack, or any of the boys in fact, are to save money I know not, for every shilling of their wages, except a small margin for coarse snuff, goes to their parents, who fleece them without mercy. If they are fined for breakages or misconduct (the only punishment a Kafir cares for), they have to account for the deficient money to the stern parents; and both Tom and Jack went through a most graphic pantomime with a stick of the consequences to themselves, adding that their father said both the beating from him and the fine from us served them right for their carelessness. It seemed so hard they should suffer both ways, and they were so good-tempered and uncomplaining about it, that I fear I shall find it very difficult to stop any threepenny pieces out of their wages in future. A Kafir servant usually gets one pound a month, his clothes and food. The former consists of a shirt and short trousers of coarse check cotton, a soldier's old great-coat for winter, and plenty of mealy-meal for "scoff." If he is a good servant and worth making comfortable, you give him a trifle every week to buy meat. Kafirs are very fond of going to their kraals, and you have to make them sign an agreement to remain with you so many months, generally six. By the time you have just taught them, with infinite pains and trouble, how to do their work, they depart, and you have to begin it all over again.

I frequently see the chiefs or indunas of chiefs passing here on their way to some kraals which lie just over the hills. These kraals consist of half a dozen or more large huts, exactly like so many huge beehives, on the slope of a hill. There is a rude attempt at sod-fencing round them; a few head of cattle graze in the neighborhood; lower down, the hillside is roughly scratched by the women with crooked hoes to form a mealy-ground. (Cows and mealies are all they require except snuff or tobacco, which they smoke out of a cow's horn.) They seem a very gay and cheerful people, to judge by the laughter and jests I hear from the groups returning to these kraals

every day by the road just outside our fence. Sometimes one of the party carries an umbrella; and I assure you the effect of a tall, stalwart Kafir, clad either in nothing at all or else in a sack, carefully guarding his bare head with a tattered Gamp, is very ridiculous. Often some one walks along playing upon a rude pipe, whilst the others jog before and after him, laughing and capering like boys let loose from school, and all chattering loudly. You never meet a man carrying a burden unless he is a white settler's servant. When a chief or the induna of a kraal passes this way, I see him, clad in a motley garb of red regimentals with his bare "ringed" head, riding a sorry nag, only the point of his great toe resting in his stirrup. He is followed closely and with great *empressement* by his "tail," all "ringed" men also —that is, men of some substance and weight in the community. They carry bundles of sticks, and keep up with the ambling nag, and are closely followed by some of his wives bearing heavy loads on their heads, but stepping out bravely with beautiful erect carriage, shapely bare arms and legs, and some sort of coarse drapery worn across their bodies, covering them from shoulder to knee in folds which would delight an artist's eye and be the despair of a sculptor's chisel. They don't look either oppressed or discontented. Happy, healthy and jolly are the words by which they would be most truthfully described. Still, they are lazy, and slow to appreciate any benefit from civilization except the money, but then savages always seem to me as keen and sordid about money as the most civilized mercantile community anywhere.

FEBRUARY 14.

I am often asked by people who are thinking of coming here, or who want to send presents to friends here, what to bring or send. Of course it is difficult to say, because my experience is limited and confined to one spot at present: therefore I give my opinion very guardedly, and acknowledge it is derived in great part from the experience of others who have been here a long time. Amongst other wraps, I brought a sealskin jacket and muff which I happened to have. These, I am assured, will be absolutely useless, and already they are a great anxiety to me on account of the swarms of fish-tail moths which I see scuttling about in every direction if I move a box or look behind a picture. In fact, there are destructive moths everywhere, and every drawer is redolent of camphor. The only things I can venture to recommend as necessaries are things which no one advised me to bring, and which were only random shots. One was a light waterproof ulster, and the other was a lot of those outside blinds for windows which come, I believe, from Japan, and are made of grass—green, painted with gay figures. I picked up these latter by the merest accident at the Baker-street bazaar for a few shillings : they are the comfort of my life, keeping out glare and dust in the day and moths and insects of all kinds at night. As for the waterproof, I do not know what I should have done without it ; and little G——'s has also been most useful. It is the necessary of necessaries here—a *real*, good substantial waterproof. A man cannot do better than get a regular military waterproof which will cover him from chin to heel on horseback ; and even waterproof hats and caps are a comfort in this treacherous summer season, where a storm bursts over your head out of a blue dome of sky, and drenches you even whilst the sun is shining brightly.

A worse climate and country for clothes of every kind and description cannot be imagined. When I first arrived I thought I had never seen such ugly toilettes in all my life; and I should have been less than woman (or more—which is it ?) if I had not derived some secret satisfaction from the possession of at least prettier garments. What I was vain of in my secret heart was my store of cotton gowns. One can't very well wear cotton gowns in London ; and, as I am particularly fond of them, I indemnify myself for going abroad by rushing wildly into extensive purchases in cambrics and print dresses. They are so pretty and so cheap, and when charmingly made, as

mine *were* (alas, they are already things of the past!), nothing can be so satisfactory in the way of summer country garb. Well, it has been precisely in the matter of cotton gowns that I have been punished for my vanity. For a day or two each gown in turn looked charming. Then came a flounce or bordering of bright red earth on the lower skirt and a general impression of red dust and dirt all over it. That was after a drive into Maritzburg along a road ploughed up by ox-wagons. Still, I felt no uneasiness. What is a cotton gown made for if not to be washed ? Away it goes to the wash ! What is this limp, discolored rag which returns to me iron-moulded, blued until it is nearly black, rough-dried, starched in patches, with the fringe of red earth only more firmly fixed than before ? Behold my favorite ivory cotton ! My white gowns are even in a worse plight, for there are no two yards of them the same, and the grotesque mixture of extreme yellowness, extreme blueness and a pervading tinge of the red mud they have been washed in renders them a piteous example of misplaced confidence. Other things fare rather better—not much—but my poor gowns are only hopeless wrecks, and I am reduced to some old yachting dresses of ticking and serge. The price of washing, as this spoiling process is pleasantly called, is enormous, and I exhaust my faculties in devising more economical arrangements. We can't wash at home, for the simple reason that we have no water, no proper appliances of any sort, and to build and buy such would cost a small fortune. But a tall, white-aproned Kafir, with a badge upon his arm, comes now at daylight every Monday morning and takes away a huge sackful of linen, which is placed, with sundry pieces of soap and blue in its mouth, all ready for him. He brings it back in the afternoon full of clean and dry linen, for which he receives three shillings and sixpence. But this is only the first stage. The things to be starched have to be sorted and sent to one woman, and those to be mangled to another, and both lots have to be fetched home again by Tom and Jack. (I have forgotten to tell you that Jack's real name, elicited with great difficulty, as there is a click somewhere in it, is "Umpashong-wana," whilst the pickle Tom is known among his own people as "Umkabang-wana." You will admit that our substitutes for these five-syllabled appellations are easier to pronounce in a hurry. Jack is a favorite name: I know half a dozen black Jacks myself.) To return, however, to the washing. I spend my time in this uncertain weather watching the clouds on the days when the clothes are to come home, for it would be altogether *too* great a trial if one's starched garments, borne aloft on Jack's head, were to be caught in a thunder-shower. If the washerwoman takes pains with anything, it is with gentlemen's shirts, though even then she insists on ironing the collars into strange and fearful shapes.

Let not men think, however, that they have it all their own way in the matter of clothes. White jackets and trousers are commonly worn here in summer, and it is very soothing, I am told, to try to put them on in a hurry when the arms and legs are firmly glued together by several pounds of starch. Then as to boots and shoes: they get so mildewed if laid aside for even a few days as to be absolutely offensive; and these, with hats, wear out at the most astonishing rate. The sun and dust and rain finish up the hats in less than no time.

But I have not done with my clothes yet. A lady must keep a warm dress and jacket close at hand all through the most broiling summer weather, for a couple of hours will bring the thermometer down ten or twenty degrees, and I have often been gasping in a white dressing-gown at noon and shivering in a serge dress at three o'clock on the same day. I am making up my mind that serge and ticking are likely to be the most useful material for dresses, and, as one must have something very cool for these burning months, tussore or foulard, which get themselves better washed than my poor dear cottons. Silks are next to useless—too smart, too hot, too entirely out of place in such a life as this, except perhaps one or two of tried principles,

which won't spot or fade or misbehave themselves in any way. One goes out of a warm, dry afternoon with a tulle veil on to keep off the flies, or a feather in one's hat, and returns with the one a limp, wet rag and the other quite out of curl. I only wish any milliner could see my feathers now! All straight, rigidly straight as a carpenter's rule, and tinged with red dust besides. As for tulle or crêpe-lisse frilling, or any of those soft pretty adjuncts to a simple toilette, they are five minutes' wear—no more, I solemnly declare.

I love telling a story against myself, and here is one. In spite of repeated experiences of the injurious effect of alternate damp and dust upon finery, the old Eve is occasionally too strong for my prudence, and I can't resist, on the rare occasions which offer themselves, the temptation of wearing pretty things. Especially weak am I in the matter of caps, and this is what befell me. Imagine a lovely, soft summer evening, broad daylight, though it is half-past seven (it will be dark directly, however): a dinner-party to be reached a couple of miles away. The little open carriage is at the door, and into this I step, swathing my gown carefully up in a huge shawl. This precaution is especially necessary, for during the afternoon there has been a terrific thunderstorm and a sudden sharp deluge of rain. Besides a swamp or two to be ploughed through as best we may, there are those two miles of deep red muddy road full of ruts and big stones and pitfalls of all sorts. The drive home in the dark will be nervous work, but now in daylight let us enjoy whilst we may. Of course I *ought* to have taken my cap in a box or bag, or something of the sort; but that seemed too much trouble, especially as it was so small it needed to be firmly pinned on in its place. It consisted of a centre or crown of white crêpe, a little frill of the same, and a close-fitting wreath of deep red feathers all round. Very neat and tidy it looked as I took my last glance at it whilst I hastily knotted a light black lace veil over my head by way of protection during my drive When

I got to my destination there was no look-ing-glass to be seen anywhere, no maid, no anything or anybody to warn me. Into the dining-room I marched in hap-py unconsciousness that the extreme dampness of the evening had flattened the crown of my cap, and that it and its frill were mere unconsidered limp rags, whilst the unpretending circlet of feath-ers had started into undue prominence, and struck straight out like a red nimbus all round my unconscious head. How my fellow-guests managed to keep their countenances I cannot tell. I am cer-tain *I* never could have sat opposite to any one with such an Ojibbeway Indian's head-dress on without giggling. But no one gave me the least hint of my mis-fortune, and it only burst upon me sud-denly when I returned to my own room and my own glass. Still, there was a ay of hope left: it *might* have been the dampness of the drive home which had worked me this woe. I rushed into F——'s dressing-room and demanded quite fiercely whether my cap had been like that all the time.

"Why, yes," F—— admitted; adding by way of consolation, "In fact, it is a good deal subdued now: it was very wild all dinner-time. I can't say I ad-mired it, but I supposed it was all right."

Did ever any one hear such shocking apathy? In answer to my reproaches for not telling me, he only said, "Why, what could you have done with it if you *had* known? Taken it off and put it in your pocket, or what?"

I don't know, but anything would have been better than sitting at table with a thing only fit for a May-Day sweep on one's head. It makes me hot and angry with myself even to think of it now.

F——'s clothes could also relate some curious experiences which they have had to go through, not only at the hands of his washerwoman, but at those of his temporary valet, Jack (I beg his pardon, Umpashongwana) the Zulu, whose zeal exceeds anything one can imagine. For instance, when he sets to work to brush F——'s clothes of a morning he is by no means content to brush the cloth clothes. Oh dear, no! He brushes the socks,

putting each carefully on his hand like a glove and brushing vigorously away. As they are necessarily very thin socks for this hot weather, they are apt to melt away entirely under the process. I say nothing of his blacking the boots inside as well as out, or of his laboriously scrub-bing holes in a serge coat with a scrub-bing-brush, for these are errors of judg-ment dictated by a kindly heart. But when Jack puts a saucepan on the fire without any water and burns holes in it, or tries whether plates and dishes can support their own weight in the air with-out a table beneath them, then, I con-fess, my patience runs short. But Jack is so imperturbable, so perfectly and genuinely astonished at the untoward result of his experiments, and so grieved that the *inkosacasa* (I have not an idea how the word ought to be spelt) should be vexed, that I am obliged to leave off shaking my head at him, which is the only way I have of expressing my dis-pleasure. He keeps on saying, "Ja, oui, yaas," alternately, all the time, and I have to go away to laugh.

FEBRUARY 16.

I was much amused the other day at receiving a letter of introduction from a mutual friend in England, warmly rec-ommending a newly-arrived bride and bridegroom to my acquaintance, and especially begging me to take pains to introduce the new-comers into the "best society." To appreciate the joke thor-oughly you must understand that there is no society here at all — absolutely none. We are not proud, we Maritz-burgians, nor are we inhospitable, nor exclusive, nor unsociable. Not a bit. We are as anxious as any community can be to have society or sociable ga-therings, or whatever you like to call the way people manage to meet togeth-er; but circumstances are altogether too strong for us, and we all in turn are forced to abandon the attempt in despair. First of all, the weather is against us. It is maddeningly uncertain, and the best-ar-ranged entertainment cannot be consid-ered a success if the guests have to strug-gle through rain and tempest and streets ankle-deep in water and pitchy darkness to assist at it. People are hardly likely to make themselves pleasant at a party when their return home through storm and darkness is on their minds all the time: at least, I know *I* cannot do so. But the weather is only one of the lets and hinderances to society in Natal. We are all exceedingly poor, and necessary food is very dear: luxuries are enormously expensive, but they are generally not to be had at all, so one is not tempted by them. Servants, particularly cooks, are few and far between, and I doubt if even any one calling himself a cook could send up what would be considered a fairly good dish elsewhere. Kafirs can be taught to do one or two things pretty well, but even then they could not be trusted to do them for a party. In fact, if I stated that there were no good servants—in the ordinary acceptation of the word—here at all, I should not be guilty of exaggeration. If there are, all I can say is, I have neither heard of nor seen them. On the contrary, I have been overwhelmed by lamentations on that score in which I can heartily join. Besides the want of means of conveyance (for there are no cabs, and very few *remises*) and good food and attendance, any one wanting to entertain would almost need to build a house, so impossible is it to collect more than half a dozen people inside an ordinary-sized house here. For my part, my verandah is the comfort of my life. When more than four or five people at a time chance to come to afternoon tea, we overflow into the verandah. It runs round three sides of the four rooms called a house, and is at once my day-nursery, my lumber-room, my summer-parlor, my place of exercise—everything, in fact. And it is an incessant occupation to train the creepers and wage war against the legions of brilliantly-colored grasshoppers which infest and devour the honeysuckles and roses. Never was there such a place for insects! They eat up everything in the kitchen-garden, devour every leaf off my peach and orange trees, scarring and spoiling the fruit as well. It is no comfort whatever that they are wonderfully beautiful creatures, striped and ringed with a thousand colors in a thousand various ways: one has only to see the riddled appearance of every leaf and flower to harden one's heart. Just now they have cleared off every blossom out of the garden except my zinnias, which grow magnificently and make the devastated flower-bed still gay with every hue and tint a zinnia can put on—salmon-color, rose, scarlet, pink, maroon, and fifty shades besides. On the veldt too the flowers have passed by, but their place is taken by the grasses, which are all in seed. People say the grass is rank and poor, and of not much account as food for stock, but it has an astonishing variety of beautiful seeds. In one patch it is like miniature pampas-grass, only a couple of inches long each seed-pod, but white and fluffy. Again, there will be tall stems laden with rich purple grains or delicate tufts of rose-colored seed. One of the prettiest, however, is like wee green harebells hanging all down a tall and slender stalk, and hiding within their cups the seed. Unfortunately, the weeds and burs seed just as freely, and there is one especial torment to the garden in the shape of an innocent-looking little plant something like an alpine strawberry in leaf and blossom, bearing a most aggravating tuft of little black spines which lose no opportunity of sticking to one's petticoats in myriads. They are familiarly known as "black jacks," and can hold their own as pests with any weed of my acquaintance.

But the most beautiful tree I have seen in Natal was an *Acacia flamboyante*. I saw it at D'Urban, and I shall never forget the contrast of its vivid green, bright as the spring foliage of a young oak, and the crown of rich crimson flowers on its topmost branches, tossing their brilliant blossoms against a background of gleaming sea and sky. It was really splendid, like a bit of Italian coloring among the sombre tangle of tropical verdure. It is too cold up here for this glorious tree, which properly belongs to a far more tropical temperature than even D'Urban can mount up to.

I am looking forward to next month

and the following ones to make some little excursions into the country, or to go "trekking," as the local expression is. I hear on all sides how much that is interesting lies a little way beyond the reach of a ride, but it is difficult for the mistress—who is at the same time the general servant—of an establishment out here to get away from home for even a few days, especially when there is a couple of small children to be left behind. No one travels now who can possibly help it, for the sudden violent rains which come down nearly every afternoon swell the rivers and make even the spruits impassable; so a traveler may be detained for days within a few miles of his destination. Now, in winter the roads will be hard, and dust will be the only inconvenience. At least, that is what I am promised.

PART VI.

I DON'T think I like a climate which produces a thunderstorm *every* afternoon. One disadvantage of this electric excitement is that I hardly ever get out for a walk or drive. All day it is burning hot: if there is a breath of air, it is sultry, and adds to the oppression of the atmosphere instead of refreshing it. Then about midday great fleecy banks of cloud begin to steal up behind the ridge of hills to the south-west. Gradually they creep round the horizon, stretching their soft gray folds farther and farther to every point of the compass, until they have shrouded the dazzling blue sky and dropped a cool, filmy veil of mist between the sun's fierce, steady blaze and the baked earth below. That is always my nervous moment. F—— declares I am exactly like an old hen with her chickens; and I acknowledge that I should like to cluck and call everything and everybody into shelter and safety. If little G—— is out on his pony alone, as is generally the case—for he returns from school early in the afternoon — and I think of the great open veldt, the rough, broken track and the treacherous swamp, what wonder is it that I cannot rest in-doors, but am always making bareheaded expeditions every five minutes to the brow of the hill to see if I can discern the tiny figure tearing along the open, with its floating white puggery streaming behind? The pony may safely be trusted not to loiter, for horse and cow, bird and beast, know what that rapidly-darkening shadow means, and what sudden death lurks within those patches of inky clouds, from which a deep and rolling murmur comes from time to time. I am uneasy even if F—— has not returned, for the little river, the noisy Umsindusi, thinks nothing of suddenly spreading itself far and wide over its banks, turning the low-lying ground into a lake for miles.

It is true that this may only last for a few hours, or even moments, but five minutes is quite enough to do a great deal of mischief when a river is rising at the rate of two feet a minute—mischief not only to human beings, but to bridges, roads and drains, as well as plantations and fields. Yet that tropical downpour, where the clouds let loose the imprisoned moisture suddenly in solid sheets of water instead of by the more slow and civilized method of drops, is a relief to my mind, for there are worse possibilities than a wet jacket behind those lurid, low-hanging vapors. There are hailstorms, like one yesterday morning which rattled on the red tile roof like a discharge of musketry, and with nearly as damaging an effect, for several tiles were broken and tumbled down, leaving melancholy gaps, like missing teeth, in the eaves. There are thunderbolts, which strike the tallest trees, leaving them in an instant gaunt and bare and shriveled, as though centuries had suddenly passed over their green and waving heads. There are flashes of lightning which dart through a verandah or room, and leave every living thing in it struck down dead —peals of thunder which seem to shake the very earth to its centre. There are all these meteorological possibilities — nay, probabilities — following fast upon a burning, hot, still morning; and what wonder is it that I am anxious and nervous until everybody belonging to me is under shelter, though shelter can only be from the driving rain or tearing gusts of wind? No wall or window, no bolt or bar, can keep out the dazzling death which swoops down in a violet glare and snatches its victims anywhere and everywhere. A Kafir washerman, talking yesterday morning to his employer in her verandah, was in the act of saying, "I will be *sure* to come to-morrow," when he fell forward on his face, dead from a blinding flash out of a passing thundercloud. An old settler, a little way up-

56

country, was reading prayers to his household the other night, and in a second half the little kneeling circle were struck dead alongside of the patriarchal reader —dead on their knees. Two young men were playing a game of billiards quietly enough: one was leaning forward to make a stroke when there came a crash and a crackle, and he dropped dead with his cue in his hand. The local papers are full every day of a long list of casualties, but it is not from these sources I have drawn the preceding examples: I only chanced to hear them yesterday, and they all happened quite close by.

As for cattle or trees being killed, that is an every-day occurrence in summer, and even a hailstorm, so long as it does not utterly bombard the town and leave the houses roofless and open to wind and weather, is not thought anything of. The hail - shower of yesterday, though, bombarded my creepers and reduced them to a pitiful state in five minutes. So soon as it was possible to venture outside the house, F—— called me to see the ruin of leaf and bud which strewed the cemented floor of the verandah. It is difficult to describe, and still more difficult to believe, the state to which the foliage had been reduced. On the weather side of the house every leaf was torn off, and not only torn, but riddled through and through as though by a charge of swanshot. All my young rose-shoots, climbing so swiftly up to the roof of the verandah, were snapped off and stripped of their tender leaves and pretty buds. The honeysuckles' luxuriant foliage was all gone, lying in a wet, forlorn mass of beaten green leaves around each pillar, and there was not a leaf left on the vines. But a much more serious trouble came out of that storm. Though it has passed with the passing fury of wind and rain, still, it will always leave a feeling of insecurity in my mind during similar outbursts. The great hailstones were forced by the driving wind in immense quantities beneath the tiles, and deposited on the rude planking which, painted white, forms the ceiling. This planking has the boards wide apart, so it is not difficult to see that so soon as the warmth of the house melted the hailstones — that is, in five minutes—the water trickled down as through a sieve. It was not to be dealt with like an ordinary leak: it was here, there and everywhere, on sofas and chairs, beds and writing-tables; and the moment the sun shone out again, bright and hot as ever, the contents of the house had to be turned out of doors to dry. Drying meant, however, warping of writing-tables, and in fact of all woodwork, and fading of chintzes, beneath the broiling glare of a midday sun. Such are a few of the difficulties of existence in South Africa—difficulties, however, which must be met and got over as best they may, and laughed at once they are past and over, as I am really doing in spite of my affectation of grumbling.

A very pleasant adventure came to us the other evening, however, through one of these sudden thunderstorms. Imagine a little tea-table, with straw chairs all around it, standing in the verandah. A fair and pleasant view lies before us of green rises and still greener hollows, with dark dots of plantations from which peep red roofs or white gables. Beyond, again, lies Maritzburg under the lee of higher hills, which cast a deeper shadow over the picturesque little town. We are six in all, and four horses are being led up and down by Kafir grooms, for their riders have come out for a breath of air after a long, burning day of semi-tropical heat, and also for a cup of tea and a chat. We were exactly even, three ladies and three gentlemen; and we grumbled at the weather and complained of our servants according to the usual style of South-African conversation.

Presently, some one said, "It's much cooler now."

"Yes," was the answer, "but look at those clouds; and is that a river rolling down the hillside?"

Up to that moment there had not been a drop of rain, but even as the words passed the speaker's lips a blinding flash of light, a sullen growl and a warning drop of rain, making a splash as big as half a crown at our feet, told their own story. In less time than it takes me to write or you to read the horses had been hastily led up to the stable and stuffed into stalls only meant for two, and already occupied. But Natalian horses are generally meek, underbred, spiritless creatures, with sense enough to munch their mealies in peace and quiet, no matter how closely they are packed. As for me, I snatched up my tea-tray and fled into the wee drawing-room. Some one else caught up the table; the straw chairs were left as usual to be buffeted by the wind and weather, and we retreated to the comparative shelter of the house. But no doors or windows could keep out the torrent of rain which burst like a waterspout over our heads, forcing its way under the tiles, beneath the badly-fitting doors and windows, sweeping and eddying all around like the true tropical tempest it was. Claps of thunder shook the nursery, where we three ladies had taken refuge, ostensibly to encourage and cheer the nurse, but really to huddle together like sheep with the children in our midst. Flash after flash lit up the fast-gathering darkness as the storm rolled away, to end in an hour or so as suddenly as it began. By this time it was not much past six, and though the twilight is early in these parts, there was enough daylight still left for our guests to see their way home. So the horses were brought, adieux were made, and our guests set forth, to return, however, in half an hour asking whether there was any other road into town, for the river was sweeping like a maelstrom for half a mile on either side of the frail wooden bridge by which they had crossed a couple of hours earlier. Now, the only other road into town is across a ford, or "drift," as it is called here, of the same river a mile higher up. Of course, it was of no use thinking of *this* way for even a moment; but as they were really anxious to get home if possible, F—— volunteered to go back and see if it was practicable to get across by the bridge. I listened and waited anxiously enough in the verandah, for I could hear the roar of the rushing river down below —a river which is ordinarily as sluggish as a brook in midsummer—and I was

so afraid that F—— or one of the other gentlemen would rashly venture across. But it was not to be attempted by any one who valued his life that evening, and F—— returned joyously, bringing our guests home as captives. It was great fun, for, in true colonial fashion, we had no servants to speak of except the nurse, the rest being Kafirs, one more ignorant than the other. And fancy stowing four extra people into a house with four rooms already full to overflowing! But it was done, and done successfully too, amid peals of laughter and absurd contrivances and arrangements, reminding us of the dear old New Zealand days.

The triumph of condensation was due, however, to Charlie, the Kafir groom, who ruthlessly turned my poor little pony carriage out into the open air to make room for some of his extra horses, saying, "It wash it, ma'—make it clean: carriage no can get horse-sickness." And he was right, for it is certain death to turn a horse unaccustomed to the open out of his stable at night, especially at this time of year. We were all up very early next morning, and I had an anxious moment or two until I knew whether my market-Kafir could get out to me with bread, etc.; but soon after seven I saw him trudging gayly along with his bare legs, red tunic and long wand or stick, without which no Kafir stirs a yard away from home. Apropos of that red tunic, it was bought and given to him to prevent him from *wearing* the small piece of waterproof canvas I gave him to wrap up my bread, flour, sugar, etc. in on a wet morning. I used to notice that these perishable commodities arrived as often quite sopped through and spoiled *after* this arrangement about the waterproof as before, but the mystery was solved by seeing "Ufan" (otherwise John) with my basket poised on his head, the rain pelting down upon its contents, and the small square of waterproof tied with a string at each corner over his own back. That reminds me of a hat I saw worn in Maritzburg two days ago in surely the most eccentric fashion hat was ever yet put on. It was a large, soft gray felt, and, as far as I could judge, in pretty good condition. The Kafir who sported it had fastened a stout rope to the brim, at the extreme edge of the two sides. He had then turned the hat upside down, and wore it thus securely moored by these ropes behind his ears and under his chin. There were sundry trifles of polished bone, skewers and feathers stuck about his head as well, but the inverted hat sat serenely on the top of all, the soft crown being further secured to its owner's woolly pate by soda-water wire. I never saw anything so absurd in my life; but Charlie, who was holding my horse, gazed at it with rapture, and putting both hands together murmured in his best English and in the most insinuating manner, "Inkosi have old hat, ma'? Like dat?" He evidently meant to imitate the fashion if he could.

Poor Charlie has lost his savings—three pounds. He has been in great trouble about it, as he was saving up his money carefully to buy a wife. It has been stolen, I fear, by one of his fellow-servants, and suspicion points strongly to Tom the Pickle, who cannot be made to respect the rights of property in any shape, from my sugar upward. The machinery of the law has been set in motion to find these three pounds, with no good results, however; and now Charlie avows his intention of bringing a "witch-finder" (that is, a witch who finds) up to tell him where the money is. I am invited to be present at the performance, but I only hope she won't say *I* have got poor Charlie's money, for the etiquette is that whoever she accuses has to produce the missing sum at once, no matter whether he knows anything about its disappearance or not.

Before I quite leave the subject of thunderstorms — of which I devoutly hope this is the last month—I must observe that it seems a cruel arrangement that the only available material for metaling the roads should be iron-stone, of which there is an immense quantity in the immediate neighborhood of Maritzburg. It answers the purpose admirably so far as changing the dismal swamps of the streets into tolerably hard high-

roads goes; but in such an electric climate as this it is really very dangerous. Since the principal street has been thus improved, I am assured that during a thunderstorm it is exceedingly dangerous to pass down it. Several oxen and Kafirs have been struck down in it, and the lightning seems to be attracted to the ground, and runs along it in lambent sheets of flame. Yet I fancy it is a case of iron-stone or nothing, for the only other stone I see is a flaky substance which is very friable and closely resembles slate, and would be perfectly unmanageable for road-making purposes.

Speaking of roads, I only wish anybody who grumbles at rates and taxes, which at all events keep him supplied with water and roads, could come here for a month. First, he should see the red mud in scanty quantities which represents our available water-supply (except actually *in* the town); and next he should walk or ride or drive—for each is equally perilous—down to the town, a mile or two off, with me of a dark night. I say, "with me," because I should make it a point to call the grumbler's attention to the various pitfalls on the way. I think I should like him to drive about seven o'clock, say to dinner, when one does not like the idea of having to struggle with a broken carriage or to go the remainder of the way on foot. About 7 P. M. the light is peculiarly treacherous and uncertain, and is worse than the darkness later on. Very well, then, we will start, first looking carefully to the harness, lest Charlie should have omitted to fasten some important strap or buckle. There is a track—in fact, there are three tracks—all the way down to the main road, but each track has its own dangers. Down the centre of one runs a ridge like a backbone, with a deep furrow on either hand. If we were to attempt this, the bed of the pony carriage would rest on the ridge, to the speedy destruction of the axles. To the right there is a grassy track, which is as uneven as a ploughed field, and has a couple of tremendous holes, to begin with, entirely concealed by waving grass. The secret of these constant holes is that a nocturnal animal called an ant-bear makes raids upon the ant-hills, which are like mole-hills, only bigger, destroys them, and scoops down to the new foundation in its search for the eggs, an especial dainty hard to get at. So one day there is a little brown hillock to be seen among the grass, and the next only a scratched-up hole. The tiny city is destroyed, the fortress taken and razed to the ground. All the ingenious galleries and large halls are laid low and the precious nurseries crumbled to the dust. If we get into one of these, we shall go no farther (a horse broke his neck in one last week). But we will suppose them safely passed; and also the swamp. To avoid this we must take a good sweep to the left over perfectly unknown ground, and we shall be sure to disturb a good many Kafir cranes —birds who are so ludicrously like the black-headed, red-legged, white-bodied cranes in a "Noah's ark" that they seem old friends at once. Now, there is one deep, deep ravine right across the road, and then a steep hill, halfway down which comes a very pretty bit of driving in doubtful light. You've got to turn abruptly to the left on the shoulder of the hill. Exactly where you turn is a crevasse of unknown depth, originally some sort of rude drain. The rains have washed away the hoarding, made havoc around the drain, and left a hole which it is not pleasant to look into on foot and in broad daylight. But, whatever you do, don't, in trying to avoid this hole, keep too much to the right, for there is what was once intended for a reasonable ditch, but furious torrents of water racing along have seized upon it as a channel and turned it into a river-course. After that, at the foot of the hill, lies a quarter of a mile of mud and heavy sand, with alternate big projecting boulders and deep holes made by unhappy wagons having stuck therein. Then you reach—always supposing you have not yet broken a spring—the willow bridge, a little frail wooden structure, prettily shaded and sheltered by luxuriant weeping willows drooping their trailing green plumes into the muddy Umsindusi; and so on to the main road into Pieter-Maritzburg. Such

a bit of road as this is! It ought to be photographed. I suppose it is a couple of dozen yards wide (for land is of little value hereabouts, and we can afford wide margins to our highways), and there certainly is not more than a strip a yard wide which is anything like safe driving. In two or three places it is deeply furrowed for fifty yards or so by the heavy summer rains. Here and there are standing pools of water in holes whose depth is unknown, and everywhere the surface is deeply seamed and scarred by wagon-wheels. Fortunately for my nerves, there are but few and rare occasions on which we are tempted to confront these perils by night, and hitherto we have been tolerably fortunate.

MARCH 10.

You will think this letter is nothing but a jumble of grumbles if, after complaining of the roads, I complain of my hens; but, really, if the case were fairly stated, I am quite sure that Mr. Tetmegeier or any of the great authorities on poultry-keeping would consider I had some ground for bemoaning myself. In the first place, as I think I have mentioned before, there is a sudden and mysterious disease among poultry which breaks out like an epidemic, and is vaguely called "fowl-sickness." That possibility alone is an anxiety to one, and naturally makes the poultry-fancier desirous of rearing as many chickens as possible, so as to leave a margin for disaster. In spite of all my incessant care and trouble, and a vast expenditure of mealies, to say nothing of crusts and scraps, I only manage to rear about twenty-five per cent. of my chickens. Even this is accomplished in the face of such unparalleled stupidity on the part of my hens that I wonder any chickens survive at all. Nothing will induce the hens to avail themselves of any sort of shelter for their broods. They just squat down in the middle of a path or anywhere, and go to sleep there. I hear sleepy "squawks" in the middle of the night, and find next morning that a cat or owl or snake has been supping off half my baby-chickens. Besides this sort of nocturnal fatalism, they perpetrate wholesale infanticide during the day by dragging the poor little wretches about among weeds and grass five feet high, all wet and full of thorns and burs. But it is perhaps in the hen-house that the worst and most idiotic part of their nature shows itself. Some few weeks ago I took three hens who were worrying us all to death by clucking entreaties to be given eggs to sit upon, and established them in three empty boxes, with seven or eight eggs under each. What do you think these hens have done? They have contrived, in the first place, to push and roll all the eggs into one nest. Then they appear to have invited every laying hen in the place into that box, for I counted forty-eight eggs in it last week. Upon these *one* hen sits, in the very centre. Of course, there are many eggs outside her wings, although she habitually keeps every feather fluffed out to the utmost; which must in itself be a fatigue. Around her, standing, but still sitting vigorously, were three other hens covering, or attempting to cover, this enormous nestful of eggs. Every now and then they appear to give a party, for I find several eggs kicked out into the middle of the hen-house, and strange fowls feeding on them amid immense cackling. Nothing ever seems to result from this pyramid of feathers. It (the pyramid) has been there just five weeks now, and at distant intervals a couple of chickens have appeared which none of the hens will acknowledge. Sitting appears to be their one idea. They look upon chickens as an interruption to their more serious duties, and utterly disregard them. It is quite heartbreaking to see these unhappy chickens seeking for a mother, and meeting with nothing but pecks and squalls, which plainly express, "Go along, *do!*" One hen I have left, as advised, to her own devices, and she has shown her instinct by laying ten eggs on a rafter over the stable, upon which she can barely balance herself and them. Upon these eggs she is now sitting with great diligence, but as each chicken is hatched there is no possible fate for it but to tumble off the rafter and be killed. There is no ladder or any means of as-

cent, or of descent except a drop of a dozen feet. Another hen has turned a pigeon off her nest, and insisted on sitting upon the two eggs herself. Great was her dismay, however, when she found that her babies required to be fed every five minutes, and that no amount of pecking could induce them to come out for a walk the day they were hatched. She deserted them, of course, and the poor little pigeons died of neglect. Now, do you not think Kafir hens are a handful for a poor woman, who has quantities of other things to do, to have to manage?

Part of my regular occupation at this time of year, when nearly every blade of grass carries a tick at its extreme tip, is to extract these pertinacious little beasties from the children's legs and arms. I can understand how it is that G—— is constantly coming to me saying, "A needle, mumsy, if you please: here is such a big tick!" because he is always in the grass helping Charlie to stuff what he has cut for the horses into a sack or assisting some one else to burn a large patch of rank vegetation, and dislodging snakes, centipedes and all sorts of venomous things in the process,—I can understand, I say, how this mischievous little imp, who is always in the front of whatever is going on, should gather unto himself ticks, mosquitoes, and even "fillies;" but I cannot comprehend why the baby, who, from lack of physical possibilities, leads a comparatively harmless and innocent existence, should also attract ticks to his fat arms and legs. I thought perhaps they might come from a certain puppy which gets a good deal of hugging up, but I am assured that a tick never leaves an animal. They will come off the grass upon any live thing passing, but they never move once they have taken hold of flesh with their cruel pincers. It is quite a dreadful thing to see the oxen "out-spanned" when they come down to the "spruit" to drink. Their dewlaps, and indeed their whole bodies, seem a mass of these horrible, swollen, bloated insects, as big as a large pea already, but sucking away with all their might, and resisting all efforts the unhappy animals can make with tail or head to get rid of them. Whenever I see the baby restless and fidgety, I undress him, and I am pretty sure to find a tick or two lazily moving about looking for a comfortable place to settle. G—— gave me quite a fright the other day. He was nicely dressed, for a wonder, to go for a drive with me in the carriage, and was standing before my looking-glass attempting to brush his hair. Suddenly I saw a stream of blood pouring down his neck, and on examination I found that he must have dislodged the great bloated tick lying on his collar, and which had settled on a vein just above his ear. The creature had made quite a wound as it was being torn away by the brush, and the blood was pouring freely from it, and would not be staunched. No cold water or plaster or anything would stop it, and the end was that poor little G—— had to give up his drive and remain at home with wet cloths on his head. He was rather proud of it, all the same, considering it quite an adventure, especially as he declared it did not hurt at all. Both the children keep very well here, although they do not look so rosy as they used to in England; but I am assured that the apple-cheeks will come back in the winter. They have enormous appetites, and certainly enjoy the free, unconventional life amazingly; only Baby will *not* take to a Kafir nurse-boy. He condescends to smile when Charlie or any of the servants (for they all pet him a great deal) executes a war-dance for his amusement or sings him a song, but he does not like being carried about in their arms. I have now got a Kafir nurse-girl, a Christian. She is a fat, good-tempered and very docile girl of about fifteen, who looks at least twenty-five years old. Baby only goes to her to pluck off the gay 'kerchief she wears on her head. When that is removed he shrieks to get away from her.

It is so absurd to see an English child falling into colonial ways. G—— talks to all the animals in Kafir, for they evidently don't understand English. If one wants to get rid of a dog, it is of no use saying "Get out!" ever so crossly; but when G—— yells "Foot-sack!" (this is pure phonetic spelling, out of my own head) the cur retreats precipitately. So to a horse: you must tell him to go on in Kafir, and he will not stop for any sound except a long low whistle. G—— even plays at games of the country. Sometimes I come upon the shady side of the verandah, taken up with chairs arranged in pairs along all its length and a sort of tent of rugs and shawls at one end, which is the wagon. "I am playing at trekking, mumsy dear: would you like to wait and see me out-span? There is a nice place with water for the bullocks, and wood for my fire. Look at the brake of my wagon; and here's such a jolly real bullock-whip Charlie made me out of a bamboo and strips of bullock-hide." G—— can't believe he ever played at railways or horses or civilized games, and it is very certain that the baby will trek and out-span so soon as he can toddle.

We grown-up people catch violent colds here; and it is no wonder, considering the changes of weather, far beyond what even you, with your fickle climate, have to bear. Twenty-four hours ago it was so cold that I was glad of my sealskin jacket at six o'clock in the evening, and it was really bitterly cold at night. The next morning there was a hot wind, and it has been like living at the mouth of a furnace ever since. What wonder is it that I hear of bronchitis or croup in almost every house, and that we have all got bad colds in our throats and chests? I heard the climate defined the other day as one in which sick people get well, and well people get sick, and I begin to think it is rather a true way of looking at it. People are always complaining, and the doctors (of whom there are a great many in proportion to the population) seem always very busy. Everybody says, "Wait till the winter," but I have been here four months now, three of which have certainly been the most trying and disagreeable, as to climate and weather, I have ever experienced; nor have I ever felt more generally unhinged and unwell in my life. This seems a hard thing to say of a climate with so good a reputation as this, but I am obliged to write of things as I find them. I used to hear the climate immensely praised in England, but I don't hear much said in its favor here. The most encouraging remark one meets with is, "Oh, you'll get used to it."

HOWICK, March 13.

It is difficult to imagine that so cool and charming a spot as this is only a dozen miles from Maritzburg, of which one gets so tired. It must be acknowledged that each mile might fairly count for six English ones if the difficulty of getting over it were reckoned. The journey occupied three hours of a really beautiful afternoon, which had the first crisp freshness of autumn in its balmy breath, and the road climbed a series of hills, with, from the top of each, a wide and charming prospect. We traveled in a sort of double dog-cart of a solidity and strength of construction which filled me with amazement until I saw the nature of the ground it had to go over. Then I was fain to confess it might have been— if such were possible — twice as strong with advantage, for in spite of care and an exceeding slow pace we bent our axles. This road is actually the first stage of the great overland journey to the diamond-fields, and it is difficult to imagine how there can be any transport service at all in the face of such difficulties. I have said so much about bad roads already that I feel more than half ashamed to dilate upon this one; yet roads, next to servants, are the standing grievance of Natal. To see a road-party at work — and you must bear in mind that thousands are spent annually on roads—is to understand in a great measure how so many miles come to be mere quagmires and pitfalls for man and beast. A few tents by the roadside here and there, a little group of lazy, three-parts-naked Kafirs, a white man in command who probably knows as little of the first principles of roadmaking as his dog, and a feeble scratching up of the surrounding mud, transferring it from one hole to the other,—that is roadmaking in Natal, so far as it has presented itself to me. On this particular route the fixed idea of the road-parties—of which we passed three—was to dig a broad, wide ditch a couple of feet below the level of the surrounding country, and to pick up the earth all over it, so that the first shower of rain might turn it into a hopeless, sticky mass of mud. As for any idea of making the middle of the road higher than the sides, that appears to be considered a preposterous one, and is not, at all events, acted upon in any place I have seen. It was useless to think of availing ourselves of the ditch, for the mud looked too serious after last night's heavy rain; so we kept to an older track, where we bumped in and out of holes in a surprising and bruising fashion. It took four tolerably stout and large horses to get us along at all; and if they had not been steadily and carefully driven, we should have been still more black and blue and stiff and aching than we were. I wonder if you will believe me when I say that I was assured that many of the holes were six feet deep? I don't think our wheels went into any hole more than three feet below the rough surface. I found, however, that the boulders were worse than the holes. One goes, to a certain extent, quietly in and out of a hole, but the wheel slips very suddenly off the top of a high boulder, and comes to the ground with a cruel jerk. There was plenty of rock in the hillside, so every now and then the holes would be filled up by boulders, and we crawled for some yards over ground which had the effect of an exceedingly rough wall having tumbled down over it. If one could imagine Mr. MacAdam's idea carried out in Brobdingnag, one would have some faint notion of the gigantic proportions of the hardening material on that road.

It was—as is often the case where an almost tropical sun draws up the moisture from the earth—a misty evening, and the distant view was too vague and vaporous to leave any distinct picture on my memory. Round Howick itself are several little plantations in the clefts of the nearest downs, and each plantation shelters a little farm or homestead. We can only just discern in more distant hollows deep blue-black shadows made by patches of real native forest, the first I have seen ; but close at hand the park-like country is absolutely bare of timber save for these sheltering groups of gum trees, beneath whose protection other trees can take root and flourish. Gum trees seem the nurses of all vegetation in a colony : they drain a marshy soil and make it fit for a human dwelling-place wherever they grow. There you see also willows with their delicate tender leaves, and sentinel poplars whose lightly-poised foliage keeps up a cool rustle always. But now the road is getting a trifle better, and we are beginning to drop down hill. Hitherto it has been all stiff collar-work, and we have climbed a thousand feet or more above Maritzburg. It is closing in quite a cold evening, welcome to our sun-baked energies, as we drive across quite an imposing bridge (as well it may be, for it cost a good many thousand pounds) which spans the Umgeni River, and so round a sharp turn and up a steepish hill to where the hotel stands amid sheltering trees and a beautiful undergrowth of ferns and arum lilies. Howick appears to be all hotel, for two have already been built, and a third is in progress. A small store and a pretty wee church are all the other component parts of the place. Our hotel is delightful, with an enchanting view of the Umgeni widening out as it approaches the broad cliff from which it leaps a few hundred yards farther on.

Now, ever since I arrived in Natal I have been pining to see a real mountain and a real river—not a big hill or a capricious spruit, sometimes a ditch and sometimes a lake, but a respectable river, too deep to be muddy. Here it is before me at last, the splendid Umgeni, curving among the hills, wide and tranquil, yet with a rushing sound suggestive of its immense volume. We can't waste a moment in-doors : not even the really nice fresh butter—and what a treat that is you must taste Maritzburg butter to understand—nor the warm tea can detain us for long. We snatch up our shawls and run out in the gloaming to follow the

river's sound and find out the spot where it leaps down. It is not difficult, once we are in the open air, to decide in which direction we must go, and for once we brave ticks, and even snakes, and go straight across country through the long grass. There it is. Quite suddenly we have come upon it, so beautiful in its simplicity and grandeur, no ripple or break to confuse the eye and take away the sense of unity and consolidation. The river widens, and yet hurries, gathering up strength and volume until it reaches that great cliff of iron-stone. You could drop a plumb-line over it, so absolutely straight is it for three hundred and fifty feet. I have seen other waterfalls in other parts of the world, but I never saw anything much more imposing than this great perpendicular sheet of water broken into a cloud of spray and foam so soon as it touches the deep, silent basin below. The water is discolored where it flings itself over the cliff, and there are tinges and stains of murky yellow on it there, but the spray which rises up from below is purer and whiter than driven snow, and keeps a great bank of lycopodium moss at the foot of the cliff, over which it is driven by every breath of air, fresh and young and vividly green. Many rare ferns and fantastic bushes droop on either side of the great fall—droop as if they too were giddy with the noise of the water rushing past them, and were going to fling themselves into the dark pools below. But kindly Nature holds them back, for she needs the contrast of branch and stem to give effect to the purity of the falling water. Just one last gleam of reflected sunlight gilded the water's edge where it dashed over the cliff, and a pale crescent moon hung low over it in a soft "daffodil sky." It was all ineffably beautiful and poetic, and the roar of the falling river seemed only to bring out with greater intensity the absolute silence of the desolate spot and the starlight hour.

MARCH 15.

If the fall was beautiful in the mysterious gloaming, it looks a thousand times more fair in its morning splendor of sunshine. The air here is pleasant—almost cold, and yet deliciously balmy. It is certainly an enchanting change from Pieter - Maritzburg, were it not for the road which lies between. It is not, however, a road at all. What is the antithesis of a road, I wonder—the opposite of a road? That is what the intervening space should be called. After the river takes its leap it moves quietly away among hills and valleys, a wide sheet of placid water, as though there was nothing more needed in the way of exertion. I hear there are some other falls, quite as characteristic in their way, a few miles farther in the interior, but as the difficulty of getting to them is very great they must wait until we can spare a longer time here. To-day we drove across frightful places until we got on a hill just opposite the fall. I am not generally nervous, but I confess to a very bad five minutes as we approached the edge of the cliff. The brake of the dog-cart was hard down, but the horses had their ears pricked well forward and were leaning back almost on their haunches as we moved slowly down the grassy incline. Every step seemed as if it would take us right over the edge, and the roar and rush of the falling water opposite appeared to attract and draw us toward itself in a frightful and mysterious manner. I was never more thankful in my life than when the horses stood stark still, planted their fore feet firmly forward, and refused, trembling all over, to move an inch nearer. We were not really so very close to the edge, but the incline was steep and the long grass concealed that there was any ground beyond. After all, I liked better returning to a cliff a good deal nearer to the falls, where a rude seat of stones had been arranged on a projecting point from whence there was an excellent view. I asked, as one always does, whether there had ever been any accidents, and among other narratives of peril and disaster I heard this one.

Some years ago—nothing would induce the person who told me the story to commit himself to any fixed period or any nearer date than this—a wagon drawn by a long team of oxen was attempting to cross the "drift," or ford, which used to exist a very short way above the falls. I saw the spot afterward, and it really looked little short of madness to have attempted to establish a ford so near the place where the river falls over this great cliff. They tried to build a bridge, even, at the same spot, but it was swept away over and over again, and some of the buttresses remain standing to this day. One of them rests on a small islet between the river and the cliff, only a few yards away from the brink of the precipice. It is a sort of rudimentary island, formed by great blocks of stone and some wind-blown earth in which a few rank tufts of grass have taken root, binding it all together. But this island does not divide the volume of water as it tumbles headlong over the cliff, for the river is only parted by it for a brief moment. It sweeps rapidly round on either side of the frail obstacle, and then unites itself again into a broad sheet just before its leap. The old boers used to imagine that this island broke the force of the current, and would protect them from being carried over the falls by it. In winter, when the water is low and scarce, this may be so, but in summer it is madness to trust to it. Anyway, the Dutchman got his team halfway across, a Kafir sitting in the wagon and driving, another lad acting as "forelooper" and guiding the "span" (as a team is called here). The boer prudently rode, and had no sooner reached the midstream than he perceived the current to be of unusual depth and swiftness. He managed, however, to struggle across to the opposite bank, and from thence he beheld his wagon overturn, his goods wash out of it and sweep like straws over the precipice : as for the poor little forelooper, nobody knows what became of him. The overturned wagon, with the struggling oxen still yoked to it and the Kafir driver clinging on, swept to the edge of the falls. There a lucky promontory of this miniature island caught and held it fast, drowning some of the poor bullocks indeed, but saving the wagon. Doubtless, the Kafir might easily have saved himself, for he had hold of the wagon when it was checked in its rapid rush. But instead of grasping at bush or rock, at a wheel or the horn of a bullock, he stood straight up, holding his whip erect in his right hand, and with one loud defiant whoop of exultation jumped straight over the fearful ledge. His master said the fright must have driven him mad, for he rode furiously along the bank shouting words of help and encouragement, which probably the poor Kafir never heard, for he believed his last hour had come and sprang to meet the death before him with that dauntless bravery which savages so often show in the face of the inevitable. As one sat in safety and looked at the rushing, irresistible water, one could easily picture to one's self the struggling pile of wagon and oxen in the water just caught back at the edge, the frantic horseman by the river-side gesticulating wildly, and the ebony figure erect and fearless, with the long streaming whip held out, taking that desperate leap as though of his own free will.

I think we spent the greater part of the day at the fall, looking at it under every effect of passing cloud-shadow or sunny sky, beneath the midday brilliancy of an almost tropical sun and in the soft pearly-gray tints of the short twilight. The young moon set almost as soon as she rose, and gave no light to speak of: it was therefore no use stumbling in the dark to the edge of so dangerous a cleft when we could see nothing except the ghostly shimmer of spray down below, and only hear the ceaseless roar of the water. So how do you think we amused ourselves after our late dinner? We went to a traveling circus advertised to play at Howick "for one night only." That is to say, it was not there at all, because the wagons had all stuck fast in some of the holes in that fearful road. But the performing dogs and ponies had not stuck, nor the "boneless boy. "*He* could not stick anywhere," as G—— remarked, and they held a little performance of their own in a room at the other hotel. Thither we stumbled through pitchy darkness at nine o'clock, G—— insisting on being taken out of bed and dressed again to come with us. There was a good deal of difference between the behavior and demeanor of the black and white spectators of that small performance. The Kafirs sat silent, dignified and attentive, gazing with wide-open eyes at the "boneless boy," who turned himself upside down and inside out in the most perplexing fashion. "What do you think of it?" I asked a Kafir who spoke English. "Him master take all him bone out 'fore him begin, inkosa-casa: when him finish, put 'em all back again inside him;" and indeed that was what our pliable friend looked like. We two ladies—for I had the rare treat of a charming companion of my own "sect" on this occasion—could not remain long, however, on account of our white neighbors. Many were drunk, all were uproarious. They lighted their cigars with delightful colonial courtesy and independence, and called freely for more liquor; so we were obliged to leave the boneless one in the precise attitude of one of those porcelain grotesque monsters one sees, his feet held tightly in his hands on either side of his little grinning Japanese face, and his body disposed comfortably in an arch over his head. Even G—— had to give up and come away, for he was stifled by smoke and frightened by the noise. The second rank of colonists here do not seem to me to be drawn from so respectable and self-respecting a class as those I came across in New Zealand and Australia. Perhaps it is demoralizing to them to find themselves, as it were, over the black population whom they affect to despise and yet cannot do without. They do not seem to desire contact with the larger world outside, nor to receive or welcome the idea of progress which is the life-blood of a young colony. Natal resembles an overgrown child with very bad manners and a magnificent ignorance of its own shortcomings.

At daylight next morning we were up betimes and made an early start, so as to avoid the heat of the morning sun. A dense mist lay close to the earth as far as the eye could reach, and out of its soft white billows only the highest of the hilltops peeped like islands in a lake of fleecy clouds. We bumped along in our usual style, here a hole, there a boulder, slipping now on a steep cutting — for this damp mist makes the hillsides very "greasy," as our driver remarked—climbing painfully over ridge after ridge, until we came to the highest point of the road between us and Maritzburg. Here we paused for a few moments to breathe our panting team and to enjoy the magnificent view. I have at last seen a river worthy of the name, and now I see mountains — not the incessant rising hills which have opened out before me in each fresh ascent, but a splendid chain of lofty mountains—not peaks, for they are nearly all cut quite straight against the sky, but level lines far up beyond the clouds, which are just flushing red with the sunrise. The mountains are among and behind the clouds, and have not yet caught any of the light and color of the new day. They loom dimly among the growing cloud-splendors, cold and ashen and sombre, as befits their majestic outlines. These are the Drakenfels, snow-covered except in the hottest weather. I miss the serrated peaks of the Southern Alps and the grand confusion of the Himalayan range. These mountains are lofty, indeed rise far into cloudland, but except for a mighty crag or a huge notch here and there they represent a series of straight lines against the sky. This is evidently the peculiarity of the mountain - formation of South Africa. I noticed it first in Table Mountain at Cape Town: it is repeated in every little hill between D'Urban and Maritzburg, and now it is before me, carried out on a gigantic scale in this splendid range. My eye is not used to it, I suppose, for I hear better judges of outline and proportion than I am declare it is

characteristic and soothing, with all sorts of complimentary adjectives to which I listen in respectful silence, but with which I cannot agree in my secret heart. I like mountains to have peaks for summits, and not horizontal lines, no matter how lofty these lines may be. It was a beautiful scene, for from the Drakenfels down to where we stood there rolled a very ocean of green, billowy hills, softly folded over each other, with delicious purple shadows in their hollows and shining pale - green lights on their sunny slopes. We had left the Umgeni so far behind that it only showed like a broad silver ribbon here and there, while the many red roads stretching away into the background certainly derived enchantment from distance. The foreground was made lively by an encampment of wagons which were just going to "in-span" and start. The women fussed about the gypsy-like fires getting breakfast, the Kafirs shouted to the bullocks prudently grazing until the last moment, and last, not least, to the intense delight of G——, four perfectly tame ostriches were walking leisurely among the wagons eating food out of the children's hands and looking about for "digesters" among the grass. I felt inclined to point out the boulders with which the road was strewn to their favorable notice. They had come from far in the interior, from the distant borders of the Transvaal, a weary way off. These ostriches were the family pets, and were going to be sold and sent to England. The travelers — "trekkers" is the correct word — expected to get at least thirty-five pounds each for these splendid male birds in full plumage, and they were probably worth much more. We made a fresh start from this, and the best of our way into Maritzburg before the sun became too overpowering.

PART VII.

CAN you believe that we are crying out for rain already, and anxiously scanning the clouds as they bank up over the high hills to the south-west? But so it is. It would be a dreadful misfortune if the real dry weather were to set in so early, and without the usual heavy downfall of rain which fills the tanks and spruits, and wards off the evil day of a short water-supply and no grass. Besides which, everybody here faithfully promises pleasanter weather — weather more like one's preconceived idea of the climate of Natal—after a regular three days' rain. It is high time—for my temper, as well as for the tanks—that this rain should come, for the slow, dragging summer days are now only broken by constant gales of hot wind. These same hot winds are worse than anything—more exasperating and more exhausting—nor does a drop of dew fall at night to refresh the fast-browning vegetation over which they scatter a thick haze of dust. Hot winds are bad enough in India, lived through in large, airy, lofty rooms, with mats of fragrant grass kept constantly wet and hung at every door and window—with punkahs and ice, and all the necessary luxury and idle calm of Indian life. What must they be here—and remember, the wind is just as hot, only it blows for shorter intervals, instead of continuously for months—in small houses, with low rooms of eight or ten feet square, and in a country where the mistress of the house is head-cook, head-nurse, head-housemaid, and even head-coachman and gardener, and where a glass of cold water is a luxury only dreamed of in one's feverish slumbers? Nature demands that we should all be lotos-eaters and lie "propt on beds of amaranth and moly" —at all events from November to April. Necessity insists on our rising early and going to bed late, and eating the bread of carefulness during all those hot weeks.

That is to say, one must work very hard one's self if one desires to have a tolerably clean and comfortable house and to live in any sort of rational and civilized fashion. For my part, I like hard work, speaking generally, but *not* in a hot wind. Yet people seem to be pretty well, except their tempers—again speaking for myself —so I suppose the climate is disagreeable rather than actually unhealthy.

I feel it is exceedingly absurd the way I dilate incessantly upon three topics— roads (I promise faithfully not to say a word about *them* this time), weather (I have had my grumble at that, and feel all the better for it), and servants. We have lately added to our establishment a Kafir-girl who is a real comfort and help. Ma*l*ia — for Kafirs cannot pronounce the letter *r:* "red" is always "led" with them, and so on—is a short, fat, good-humored-looking damsel of fifteen years of age, but who looks thirty. Regarded as a servant, there is still much to be desired, in spite of the careful and excellent training she has enjoyed in the household of the bishop of Natal, but as a playmate for G——, who is teaching her the noble game of cricket, or as a nursemaid for the baby, she is indeed a treasure of sweet-temper and willingness. To be sure, she did race the perambulator down a steep hill the other day, upsetting the baby and breaking the small vehicle into bits, but still English nursemaids do the same, and do not tell the truth about it at once, as Malia did. It was done to amuse the two children, and answered that part of the programme excellently well, even the final upset eliciting peals of laughter from both the mischievous monkeys. It is also rather singular that in spite of the extreme slowness and deliberation of her movements she breaks quite as much crockery in a week as any one else would in a year. And she is so inexpressibly quaint about it all that one has neither

the heart nor the command of countenance requisite to scold. I handed her
a saucer last night to put down. The
next moment she remarked in her singularly sweet and gentle voice and pretty, musical accent, "Now, here is the
saucer in three pieces." So it was; and
how she broke it without dropping it
must ever be a mystery to me. It was
like a conjuring trick, but it occurs somewhat too often. Malia ought not to be a
housemaid at all, for she has a thirst for
knowledge which is very remarkable,
and a good deal of musical talent. She
speaks and reads three languages—Kafir, English and Dutch — with perfect
ease and fluency; and is trying hard to
learn to write, practicing incessantly on
a slate; she is always whistling or singing, or picking out tunes on a sort of
pipe, on which she plays some airs very
prettily. Every spare moment of her
time she is poring over a book, and her
little Kafir Bible is ever at hand. I wish
with all my heart that I had time to teach
her to write and to learn Kafir from her
myself, but except on Sunday, when I
read with her and hear her say some
hymns, I never have a moment. She is
so anxious to learn, poor girl! that she
watches her opportunity, and when I sit
down to brush my hair or lace my boots
she drops on one knee by my side, produces her book from her pocket, and
says in the most *câlinante* voice, "Sall I
lead to you a little, inkosa casa?" Who
could have the heart to say no, although
my gravity is sorely tried by some peculiarities of pronunciation? She *cannot*
say "such:" it is too harsh, and the nearest we can arrive at, after many efforts,
is "sush." Almost every word has a
vowel tacked on to the end, so as to
bring it as near to her own liquid, soft-
sounding Zulu as possible. I think what
upsets me most is to hear our first parents
perseveringly called "'Dam and Eva,"
but indeed most of the Bible names are
difficult of recognition. Yet her idioms
are perfect, and she speaks in well-
chosen, rather elegant phraseology. Every alternate Sunday, Malia goes down
to town dressed in the smartest of bright
pink cotton frocks, made very full and

very short, a clean white apron, and a
sky-blue kerchief arranged on her head
in a becoming turban. Malia's shy grins
of delight and pride as she comes thus
arrayed to make me her parting curtsey
are quite charming to behold, and display a set of teeth which it would be
hard to match for beauty anywhere out
of Kafirland. Indeed, all these people
seem to possess most exquisite teeth, and
they take great care of them, rinsing
their mouths and polishing these even,
glistening pearls at every opportunity.

The more I see of the Kafirs, the more
I like them. People tell me they are
unreliable, but I find them gay and
good-humored, docile and civil. Every
cowherd on the veldt has his pretty
"sako" bow (phonetic spelling again,
on my part) as he passes me when I am
fern or grass - seed hunting in the early
morning, and I hear incessant peals of
laughter from kitchen and stable. Of
course, laughter probably means idleness, but I have not the heart to go out
every time (as indeed I ought, I believe)
and make them, as Mr. Toots calls it,
"resume their studies." Their mirth is
very different from that of my old friends
the West Indian negroes, who are always
chattering and grinning. The true Kafirs wear a stolid expression of countenance in public, and are not easily moved
to signs of surprise or amusement, but at
home they seem to me a very merry and
sociable people. Work is always a difficulty and a disagreeable to them, and
I fear that many generations must pass
before a Kafir will do a hand's turn more
than is actually necessary to keep his
body and soul together. They are very
easily trained as domestic servants, in
spite of the drawback of not understanding half what is said to them, and they
make especially good grooms. The most
discouraging part of the training process,
however, is that it is wellnigh perpetual,
for except gypsies I don't believe there
is on the face of the earth a more restless, unsettled human being than your
true Kafir. Change he seems to crave
for, and change he will have, acknowledging half his time that he knows it
must be for the worse. He will leave a

comfortable, easy place, where he is well treated and perfectly happy, for harder work, and often blows, just for the sake of a change. No kindness can attach him, except in the rarest instances, and nothing upon earth could induce him to forego his periodical visits to his own kraal. This means a return, for the time being, to barbarism, which seems very strange when a man has had time to get accustomed to clothes and a good room and good food, and the hundred and one tastes which civilization teaches. Imagine laying aside the comforts and decencies of life to creep in at the low door of a big beehive, and squat naked round a huge fire, smoking filthy tobacco and drinking a kind of beer which is made from mealies! I've often seen this beer, and Charlie is very anxious I should taste it, bringing me some occasionally in an old biscuit-tin with assurances that "Ma'" will find it very good. But I cannot get beyond looking at it, for it is difficult to associate the idea of beer with a thick liquid resembling dirty chocolate more than anything else. So I always stave off the evil day of tasting with ingenious excuses.

Perhaps the Kafirs are more behindhand in medical faith than in any other respect. The other day one of our Kafirs had a bad bilious attack, and, declining all offers of more civilized treatment, got one of his own physicians to bleed him in the great toe, with, as he declared, the happiest effect. Certain it is that in the afternoon he reported himself as perfectly well. But the most extraordinary kind of remedy came before me quite lately. Tom had a frightful headache, which is not to be wondered at, considering how that boy smokes the strongest tobacco out of a cow's horn morning, noon and night, to say nothing of incessant snuff-taking. The first I heard of Tom's headache was when Charlie came to ask me for a remedy; which I thought very nice on his part, because he and Tom live in a chronic state of quarreling, and half my time is taken up in keeping the peace between them. However, I told Charlie that I knew of no remedy for a bad headache except going to bed, and that was what I should advise Tom to do. Charlie smiled rather contemptuously, as if pitying my ignorance, and asked if I would give him a box of wooden matches. Now, matches are a standing grievance in a Kafir establishment, and go at the rate of a box a day if not carefully locked up; so I, failing to connect wooden matches and Tom's headache together, began a reproachful catalogue of how many boxes he had asked for lately. Charlie, however, hastily cut me short by saying, "But, ma', it for make Tom well." So of course I produced a box of Bryant & May, and stood by to watch Charlie doctoring Tom. Match after match did Charlie strike, holding the flaming splinter up Tom's exceedingly wide nostrils, until the box was empty. Tom winced a good deal, but bore this singeing process with great fortitude. Every now and then he cried out, as well he might, when Charley thrust a freshly-lighted match up his nose, but on the whole he stood it bravely, and by the time the matches were all burned out he declared his headache was quite cured, and that he was ready to go and chop wood; nor would he listen to the idea of going to bed. "It very good stuff to smell, ma'," said Charlie: "it burn de sickness away." Kafirs are inexpressibly queer, too, about their domestic arrangements; and I had a long argument with a Kafir-woman only the other day, through Malia's interpretation, as to the propriety of killing one of her babies when she chanced to have twins. My dusky friend declared it was much the best plan, and one which was always followed when the whites did not interfere. If both children were kept alive, she averred they would both be wretched, puny little creatures, and would be quite sure to die eventually; so, as a Kafir looks to his children to take care of and work for him, even in his middle age, the sons by their wages, the daughters by their dowries, or rather by the prices paid for them, she declared it was very bad economy to try and rear two babies at once, and calmly recapitulated the instances in her own and her neighbors' families where one wretched twin had been killed to give the other a better chance. She confessed she had been much puzzled upon one occasion when the twins were a girl and a boy, for both would have been useful hereafter. "I thought of the cows I should get for the girl," she said, "and then I thought of the boy's wages, and I didn't know which to keep; but the girl, she cry most, so I kill her, and the boy grow up very good boy—earn plenty money." That was Malia's interpretation, for, although she speaks excellent English, when another person's words have to be reproduced her tenses get a little confused and jumbled up. But she is a capital mouthpiece, and it always amuses me to bargain, through her, for my eggs and chickens and mealies. Sorry bargaining it is, generally resulting in my paying double the market-price for these commodities. Lately I have been even more fleeced than usual, especially by my egg-man, who is an astute old Kafir, very much adorned with circlets of copper wire on his legs and arms. He brings his eggs in a bag, which he swings about so recklessly that it is a perpetual marvel to me how they escape annihilation. Every time he comes he adds threepence to the price of his eggs per dozen on account of the doubled hut-tax; and I assure him that in time it will end in my having paid the whole amount instead of him. Hitherto, the natives have paid a tax of seven shillings per annum on each hut, but this year it has been doubled; so the Kafirs very sensibly make their white customers pay a heavy percentage on the necessaries of life with which they supply them. It is exactly what it used to be in London three or four years ago, when coals were so costly: everything rose in price, from china vases down to hairpins; so now this doubled hut-tax is the excuse for a sudden rise in the value of eggs, fowls, cows, mealies and what not. I don't understand political economy myself, but it always seems to me a curious fact that although every article of food or clothing is only too ready to jump up in price on the smallest excuse, it *never comes down again.* I try to chaff

my old Kafir egg-merchant, and show him by figures that his extra charge for eggs pays his extra seven shillings in about six weeks. I endeavor to persuade him, after this increased tax is thus provided for, to go back to his original price, but he smiles knowingly and shakes his head, murmuring, "Ka, ka," which appears to mean "No."

All this time, however, I am longing to tell you of a famous tea-party I have had here lately—a regular "drum," only it beat all the London teas hollow, even with dear little "Minas"* thrown into the bargain, because in the corner of *my* cards were the words "Tea and witches." Now, I ask you, could any one wish for a greater excitement than that to enliven a summer afternoon? Attractive as was the bait, it was a blunder or a fib—which you choose—for, so far from being witches, my five extraordinary performers were the sworn enemies of witches, being, in fact, "witch-finders," or "witch-doctors," as they are just as often called. I am quite sure that no one has ever suffered so much anxiety about a small entertainment as I did about that tea-party. Of course, there was the usual thunderstorm due that afternoon, and not until the last moment, when the clouds rolled off toward the Umgeni valley, leaving us a glorious sky and a pleasant breeze, did I cease to fear that the whole thing might prove a *fiasco.* By the time I had begun to have confidence in the weather came a distracted message from the obliging neighbor who supplies me with milk, to say that, as ill-luck would have it, her cows had selected this particular afternoon of all the year to stray away and get themselves impounded, and that consequently the delivery of sundry bottles (everything is sold in bottles here) of new milk was as uncertain as—what shall I say?—Natal weather, for nothing can be more uncertain than *that.* Imagine my dismay! No one even dared to suggest preserved milk to me, so well known is my antipathy to that miserable makeshift. I should have sat me down and wept if at

* A wonderful performing dog exhibited by Madame Häger, and much in request last season.

tnat moment I had not discovered a small herd of cattle wending their way across the veldt to my neighbor's gate. Oh joy! the milk and the weather were all right! But what was that enormous mob of shouting, singing Kafirs clamoring outside my garden fence? They were my witch-finders, escorted by nearly the whole black population of Maritzburg: they had arrived about three hours before the proper time, and were asking for some place to dress in, not from any fastidiousness, but simply because they didn't want profane eyes to witness the details of assuming their professional decorations. Remember, there was not a white man nearer than Maritzburg, and there was nothing upon earth to prevent any number of these excited, shouting men and boys from walking into my little house, or at least helping themselves to anything off the tea-tables, which the servants were beginning to arrange in the verandah. But they were as docile and obedient as possible, readily acceding to my desire that they should remain outside the fence, and asking for nothing except copious draughts of water. Certainly, I was armed with a talisman, for I went out to them myself, with one of my numerous "Jacks" as an interpreter, and told them they must all sit down and wait patiently until Mr. S—— (their own beloved inkosi) came, adding that he would be there immediately. That was a fib, for he could not come until late, but an excellent substitute very soon appeared and set my mind partly at rest. I say, only "partly," because I had been so teased about my party. F—— had been especially aggravating, observing from time to time that my proceedings were at once illegal and improper, adding that "he was surprised at me." Can you imagine anything more trying? And yet I knew quite well all the time that he was just as anxious to see these people as we were, only he persisted in being semi-official and disagreeable. Never mind: I triumphed over him afterward, when it all went off so well. When I had leisure to think of anything but whether there would be a riot or not, I had horrible misgivings about the com-

pulsory scantiness of my invitations. I should have liked to ask all my acquaintances, as well as the few friends I had invited, but what is one to do with a doll's house and a dozen tea-cups? Those were my resources, and I taxed them to the uttermost as it was. One cannot hire things here, and I had no place to put them if I could; but it is horrid to feel, as I did, that heaps of people must have wondered why they were left out.

At last five o'clock came, bringing with it a regiment of riders, thirsting for tea and clamorous to see the witches, wanting their fortunes told, their lost trinkets found, and Heaven knows what besides. "They are not witches at all," I said gravely: "they are witch-finders, and I believe the whole thing is very wrong." There was a depressing announcement for one's hostess to make! But it had a good effect for the moment, and sent my guests quietly off to console themselves with their tea: *that*, at least, could not be wrong, especially as the milk had arrived, new and delicious. In the mean time, kind Mr. F—— had gone off to fetch the witches, as everybody persisted in calling them, and presently they appeared in full official dress, walking along in a measured, stately step, keeping time and tune to the chanting of a body-guard of girls and women who sang continuously, in a sort of undertone, a montonous kind of march. They made an excellent stage-entrance—grave, composed, erect of carriage and dauntless of mien. These Amazonian women walked past the verandah, raising their hand, as the men do, with the low cry of "Inkosi!" in salutation. Their pride is to be looked upon *as* men when once they take up this dread profession, which is also shared with them by men. They are permitted to bear shield and spear as warriors, and they hunt and kill with their own hands the wild beasts and reptiles whose skins they wear. Their day is over and ended, however, for the cruelties practiced under their auspices had risen to a great height, and it is now against the law to seek out a witch by means of these pitiless women. It is not difficult to understand—bearing in mind the superstition and cruelty which existed in remote parts of England not so very long ago—how powerful such women became among a savage people, or how tempting an opportunity they could furnish of getting rid of an enemy. Of course, they are exceptional individuals, more observant, more shrewd and more dauntless than the average fat, hardworking Kafir-women, besides possessing the contradictory mixture of great physical powers and strong hysterical tendencies. They work themselves up to a pitch of frenzy, and get to believe as firmly in their own supernatural discernment as any individual among the trembling circle of Zulus to whom a touch from the whisk they carry in their hands is a sentence of instant death. It gave a certain grim interest to what a Scotch friend called the "ploy" to know that it had once been true, and I begged Mr. F——to explain to them before they began that the only reason I had wanted to see them arose from pure curiosity to know what they looked like, how they were dressed, and so forth, and that I quite understood that it was all nonsense and very wrong and against the law to do, *really*, but that this was only a play and pretence. Shall I confess that I felt rather ashamed at making this public avowal? But my conscience demanded it clamorously, and I felt many misgivings lest I should indeed be causing any "weak brother to offend." However, it was too late now for scruples, and a sort of shout came up from the good-humored, well-behaved crowd outside, assuring me they knew it was only for fun and that it was quite right, and they were glad for the English "inkosa-casa" and her friends to see an old custom which it was a good thing to have done with. This little speech, so full of true tact, put me at my ease at once, and we all took up our position at one side of the little semi-circular lawn, where the dance-crescent was already formed, supplying ourselves the place of the supposed ring of spectators and victims. I wish I could make you see the scene as I saw it, and shall ever see it when I look back upon it.

The first original "tail" of my witch-finders had been supplemented by a crowd of people who formed a background, keeping perfectly quiet, and, though uninvited and unexpected, giving not the slightest trouble. That is the odd part of a colony: individuals are rougher, less polite and more brusque and overbearing than the people one is accustomed to see in England, but the moment it comes to a great concourse of people, then the absolute respectability of class asserts itself, and the crowd—the "rough" element being conspicuous by its absence—is far more orderly than any assemblage of a dozen people elsewhere. Imagine a villa at Wimbledon or Putney, and some four or five hundred uninvited people calmly walking into the grounds to look at something they wished to see, without a ghost of a policeman or authority in charge! Yet that was our predicament for an hour or two, and not a leaf or rosebud or blade of grass was touched or injured in any way, nor was there a sound to be heard to mar the tranquil beauty of that summer evening. It was indeed "a beauteous evening, calm and free"—in spite of my chronic state of grumbling at the climate and weather, I must acknowledge *that*—an evening which might have been made to order. Recent rains had washed the surrounding hills, brightened the dust-laden grass to green once more, and freshened up everything. The amphitheatre of rising ground which surrounds Maritzburg had never looked more beautiful, with purple and blue shadows passing over it from the slow-sailing clouds above. Toward the west the sky was gently taking that peculiar amethystic glow which precedes a fine sunset, and the sun itself laid long, parting lances of pure golden light across hill and dale around. A fresh air came up from the south, blowing softly across the downs, and sleepy, picturesque little Maritzburg —empty for the afternoon of its inhabitants, I should fancy—nestled cozily up against the undulating ground opposite. Then, to come nearer home, just outside our sod-fence a line of dusky faces rose above the ferns and waving grasses—

faces whose gleaming eyes were riveted on the performers within. The little drive and garden-paths were crowded with strangers, white and colored—all, as I said before, perfectly quiet and orderly, but evidently interested and amused. A semicircle of girls and women—some in gay civilized garb, some in coarsest drapery, some with drowsy babies hung at their backs, some with bright beads on wrist and neck, but all earnest and intent on their part—stood like the chorus of a Greek play, beating their hands together and singing a low monotonous chant, the measure and rhythm of which changed every now and again with a stamp and a swing. A pace or two in front of these singers were the witch-finders in full ceremonial dress. Collectively, they are known by the name of the "Izinyanga" or "Abangoma," but each had of course her distinctive name, and each belonged to a separate tribe. Conspicuous from her great height, Nozinyanga first caught my eye, her floating, helmet-like plume of the tail-feathers of the saka-bula bird shading her fierce face, made still more gruesome by wafers of red paint on cheek and brow. In her right hand she held a light sheaf of assegais or lances, and on her left arm was slung a small pretty shield of dappled ox hide. Her petti-coat was less characteristic than that of her sister-performers, being made of a couple of large gay handkerchiefs worn kiltwise. But she made up for the short-comings of characteristic decoration in her skirts by the splendor of the bead necklaces and armlets, fringes of goat's hair and scarlet tassels, with which she was covered from throat to waist. A baldric of leopard skin was fastened across her capacious chest, and down her back hung a beautifully dried and flat-tened skin of an enormous boa constrict-or. This creature must have been of a prodigious length, for, whilst its hooded head was fastened at the broad nape of Nozinyanga's neck, its tail dragged some two feet or so on the ground behind her. Now, Nozinyanga stood something like six feet two inches on her bare feet, but although I first looked at her, attracted

by her tall stature and defiant pose, the proceedings were really opened by a small, lithe woman with a wonderfully pathetic, wistful face, who seemed more in earnest than her big sisters, and who in her day must doubtless have brushed away many a man's life with the quag-ga's tail she brandished so lightly.

To make you understand the terrible in-terest attaching to these women, I ought to explain to you here that it used to be the custom whenever anything went wrong, either politically or socially, among the Zulus and other tribes, to attribute the shortcomings to witch-agency. The next step to be taken, after coming to this res-olution, was to seek out and destroy the witch or witches; and for this purpose a great meeting would be summoned by order of the king and under his super-intendence, and a large ring of natives would sit trembling and in fear of their lives on the ground. In the centre of these danced the witch-finders or witch-doctors; and as they gradually lashed themselves up to a frantic state of frenzy —bordering, in fact, on demoniacal pos-session—they lightly switched with their quagga tail one or other of the quivering spectators. No sooner had the fatal brush passed over the victim than he was drag-ged away and butchered on the spot; and not only he, but all the live things in his hut—wives and children, dogs and cats —not a stick left standing or a living creature breathing. Sometimes a whole kraal was exterminated in this fashion; and it need not be told what a method it became of gratifying private revenge and paying off old scores. Of all the blessings, so unwillingly and grudgingly admitted, which ever so partial a civiliza-tion has brought to these difficult, lazy, and yet pugnacious Kafir people, none can be greater, surely, than the rule which strictly forbids this sort of Lynch law from being carried out anywhere, under any circumstances, by these priest-esses of a cruel faith. Now, perhaps, you see why there was such a strong under-current of interest and excitement be-neath the light laughter and frolic of our summer-afternoon tea-party.

Nozilwane was the name of this terrible little sorceress, who frightened more than one of us more thoroughly than we should like to acknowledge, peering up in our faces, as she hung about the group of guests, with a weird and wistful glance which was both uncanny and uncomfortable. She was really beautifully dressed for her part in lynx skins folded over and cver from waist to knee, and the upper part of her body covered by strings of wild beasts' teeth and fangs, skeins of brilliantly-hued yarn, beads, strips of snake skin and fringes of Angora goat fleece. This was a singularly effective and graceful decoration, worn round the body and above each elbow, and falling in soft white flakes among the gay coloring and against the dusky skin. Lynx tails hung down like lappets on each side of her face, which was overshadowed, almost hidden, by the profusion of sakabula feathers. This bird has a very beautiful plumage, and is sufficiently rare for the natives to attach a peculiar value and charm to the tail-feathers. They are like those of a young cock, curved and slender, and of a dark-chestnut color, with a white eye at the extreme tip of each feather. Among this floating, thick plumage small bladders were interspersed, and skewers and pins fashioned out of tusks. All the witch-finders wear their own hair (or rather wool) alike; that is, highly greased and twisted up with twine until it loses the appearance of hair completely, and hangs around their faces like a thick fringe dyed deep red.

Nozilwane stepped out with a creeping, cat-like gesture, bent double, as if she were seeking out a trail. Every movement of her undulating body kept time to the beat of the girls' hands and the low, crooning chant. Presently, she affected to find the clew she sought, and sprang aloft with a series of wild pirouettes, shaking her spears and brandishing her little shield in a frenzied fashion. But Nomaruso, albeit much taller and in less good condition than the lady of the lynx skins, was determined that she should not remain the cynosure of our eyes; and she too, with a yell and a caper, cut into the dance to the sound of louder grunts and faster hand-claps.

Nomaruso turned her back to us a good deal in her performances, conscious of a magnificent snake skin, studded besides in a regular pattern with brass-headed nails, which floated like a streamer down her back. She wore a magnificent *jupon* of leopard skins decorated with red rosettes, and her toilette was altogether more recherché and artistic than any of the others. Her bangles were brighter, her goat fringes whiter, and her face more carefully painted. Yet Nozilwane held her own gallantly in virtue of being a mere bag of bones, and also having youth and a firm belief in herself on her side. The others, though they all joined in hunting out a phantom foe, and triumphed over his discovery in turn, were soon breathless and exhausted, and glad to be led away by some of the attendant women to be anointed and to drink water. Besides which, they were all of a certain age, and less inclined to frisk about than the agile Nozilwane. As for great big Nozinyanga, *she* danced like Queen Elizabeth, "high and disposedly;" and no wonder, for I should think she weighed at least fifteen stone. Umgiteni, in a petticoat of white Angora skin and a corsage of bladders and teeth, beads and viper skins, was nothing remarkable; nor was Umànonjazzla, a melancholy-looking woman with an enormous wig-like coiffure of red woolen ringlets and white skewers. Her physiognomy, too, was a trifle more stolid and commonplace than that of her comrades; and altogether she gave me the impression of being a sensible, respectable woman who was very much ashamed of herself for playing such antics. However, she brandished her divining-brush with the rest, and cut in now and then to "keep the flure" with the untiring Nozilwane.

All this time the chanting and hand-beating never ceased, the babies dozed placidly behind their mothers' backs, and we all began to think fondly of a second cup of tea. The sun had now quite dropped behind the high hills to the west, and was sending long rays right up across the tranquil sky. We felt we had enough of imaginary witch-finding, and looked about for some means of ending the affair. "Let us test their powers of finding things," said one of the party: "I have lost a silver pipestem, which I value much." So the five wise women were bidden to discover what was lost, and where it was to be found. They set about this in a curious and interesting way, which reminded one of the children's game of "magic music." In the first place, it was a relief to know there were not any ghastly recollections attached to this performance; and in the next, one could better understand by the pantomime what they were about. In front of us squatted on heels and haunches a semicircle of about a dozen men, who were supposed to have invoked the aid of the sisterhood to find some lost property. These men, however, did not in the least know what was asked for, and were told to go on with their part until a signal was given that the article had been named. They were all highly respectable head-men — "indunas," in fact — each worth a good herd of cows at least, and much portable property. In everyday life it would have been hard to beat them for shrewd common sense. Yet it was easy to perceive that the old savage instincts and beliefs were there strong as ever, and that though they affected to take it all, as we did, as an afternoon's frolic, they were firm believers in the mystic power of the Abangoma, else they never could have played their parts so well, so eagerly and with such vivid interest.

"What is it the inkosi has lost?" they cried. "Discover, reveal make plain to us."

It was a good moment in which to try the experiment, because all the singing and dancing had worked the Izinyanga up to a high pitch of enthusiasm and excitement, and the inspiration was held to be complete; so, without hesitation, Nomaruso accepted the men's challenge and cried, "Sing for me: make a cadence for me." Then, after a moment's hesitation, she went on in rapid, broken utterance, "Is this real? is it a test? is it but a show? do the white chiefs want to laugh at our pretensions? Has the white lady called us only to show other white people that we can do nothing? Is anything really lost? is it not hidden? No, it *is* lost. Is it lost by a black person? No, a white person has lost it. Is it lost by the great white chief?" (meaning their own King of Hearts, their native minister). "No, it is lost by an ordinary white man. Let me see what it is that is lost. Is it money? No. Is it a weighty thing? No, it can be always carried about: it is not heavy. All people like to carry it, especially the white inkosi. It is made of the same metal as money. I could tell you more, but there is no earnestness in all this: it is only a spectacle."

Between each of these short sentences the seeress made a pause and eagerly scanned the faces of the men before her. For safe reply they gave a loud, simultaneous snap of their finger and thumb, pointing toward the ground as they did so and shouting but one word, "Y-i-z-wa!" (the first syllable tremendously accented and drawn out), "discover—reveal." That is all they can say to urge her on, for in this case they know not themselves; but the priestesses watch their countenances eagerly to see if happily there may be, consciously or unconsciously, some sign or token whether, as children say in their games, they are "hot" or not.

Nomaruso will say no more—she suspects a trick—but Nozilwane rushes about like one possessed, sobbing and quivering with excitement. "It is this—it is that." Gigantic Nozinyanga strikes her lance firmly into the ground and cries haughtily, in her own tongue, "It is his watch," looking round as though she dared us to contradict her. The other three join hands and gallopade round and round, making the most impossible suggestions; but the "inquirers," as the kneeling men are called, give them no clew or help, nothing but the rapid fingersnap, the hand pointed sternly down to the ground, as though they were to seek it there, and the fast-following cry, "Yizwa, yizwa!"

At last Nozilwane has it: "His pipe." ("Yizwa, yizwa!") "A thing which has come off his pipe;" and so it is. Nozilwane's pluck and perseverance and cunning watching of our faces at each hit she made have brought her off triumphantly. A grunt and a murmur of admiration go round. The indunas jump up and subside into ebony images of impassive respectability; the chorus, sorely weary by this time, breaks up into knots, and the weird sisterhood drop as if by one accord on their knees, sitting back on their heels, before me, raise their right hands in salutation and deliver themselves of a little speech, of which this is as close a translation as it is possible to get of so dissimilar a language: "Messages were sent to us at our kraals that an English lady wished to see us and witness our customs. When we heard these messages our hearts said, 'Go to the English lady.' So we have come, and now our hearts are filled with pleasure at having seen this lady, and ourselves heard her express her thanks to us. We would also, on our part, thank the lady for her kindness and her presents. White people do not believe in our powers, and think that we are mad; but still we know it is not so, and that we really have the powers we profess. So it comes that we are proud this day at being allowed to show ourselves before our great white chief and so many great white people. We thank the lady again; and say for us, O son of Mr. F——! that we wish her ever to dwell in peace, and we desire for her that her path may have light." It was not easy to find anything equally pretty to say in return for this, but I, in my turn, invoked the ready wit and fluent tongue of the "son of Mr. F——," and I dare say he turned out, as if from me, something very neat and creditable.

So we were all mutually pleased with each other; only I was haunted all the time of this pretty speech-making by the recollection of a quaint saying, often used by a funny old Scotch nurse we had when we were children: I don't think I have ever heard it since, but it darted into my mind with my first platitude: "When gentlefolks meet compliments pass." We were all anxious to outdo each other in politeness, but unless my *niaiseries* gained a good deal by being changed into Zulu, I fear the witch-finders did the best in that line.

The twilight, sadly short now, was fast coming on, and all the black people were anxious to get back to their homes. Already the crowd of spectators had melted away like magic, streaming down the green hillsides by many a different track: only a remnant of the body-guard lingered to escort the performers home. As they passed the corner of the verandah where the tea-table was set, I fancied they glanced wistfully at the cakes; so I rather timidly handed a substantial biscuit, as big as a saucer, to the huge Nozinyanga, who graciously accepted it as joyfully as a child would. Another little black hand was thrust out directly, and yet another, and so the end was that the tea-tables were cleared, then and there, of all the eatables; and it was not until every dish was empty that the group moved on, raising a parting cry of "Inkosa casa!" and a sort of cheer or attempt at a cheer. They were so unfeignedly delighted with this sudden "happy thought" about the cakes and biscuits that it was quite a pleasure to see them, so good-humored and docile, moving off the moment they saw I really had exhausted my store, with pretty gestures of gratitude and thanks. We had to content ourselves with bread and butter with our second cups of tea, but we were so tired and thirsty, and so glad of a little rest and quiet, that I don't think we missed the cakes.

As we sat there enjoying the last lovely gleams of daylight and chatting over the strange, weird scene, we could just hear the distant song of the escort as they took the tired priestesses home, and we all fell to talking of the custom when it was in all its savage force. Many of the friends present had seen or heard terrible instances of the wholesale massacre which would have followed just such an exhibition as this had it been in earnest. But I will repeat for you some of the less ghastly stories. One shall be modern and one ancient — as ancient as half a century ago, which *is* ancient for modern tradition. The modern one is the tamest, so it shall come first.

Before the law was passed making it wrong to consult these Izinyanga or witch-doctors a servant belonging to one of the English settlers lost his savings, some three or four pounds. He suspected one of his fellow-servants of being the thief, summoned the Izinyanga, and requested his master to "assist" at the ceremony. All the other servants were bidden to assemble themselves, and to do exactly what the witch-finder bade them. She had them seated in a row in front of her, and ordered them, one and all, to bare their throats and chests, for, you must remember, they were clothed as the law obliges them to be in the towns — in a shirt and knickerbockers. This they did, the guilty one with much trepidation, you may be sure, and she fixed her eyes on that little hollow in the neck where the throat joins the body, watching carefully the accelerated pulsation: "It is thou: no, it is not. It must then be you;" and so on, dodging about, pointing first to one, and then rapidly wheeling round to fix on another, until the wretched criminal was so nervous that when she made one of her sudden descents upon him, guided by the bewraying pulse, which fluttered and throbbed with anxiety and terror, he was fain to throw up his hands and confess, praying for mercy. In this case the Izinyanga was merely a shrewd, observant woman with a strong spice of the detective in her; but they are generally regarded not only as sorceresses, whose superior incantations can discover and bring to light the machinations of the ordinary witch, but as priestesses of a dark and obscure faith.

The other instance of their discernment we talked of happened some fifty years ago, when Chaka the Terrible was king of the Zulus. The political power of these Izinyanga had then reached a great height in Zululand, and they were in the habit of denouncing as witches— or rather wizards—one after the other of the king's ministers and chieftains. It was difficult to put a stop to these wholesale murders, for the sympathy of the people was always on the side of the witch-finders, cruel though they were. At last the king thought of an expedient. He killed a bullock, and with his own hands smeared its blood over the royal hut in the dead of night. Next day he summoned a council, and announced that some one had been guilty of high treason in defiling the king's hut with blood, and that, too, when it stood, apparently secure from outrage, in the very middle of the kraal. What was to be done? The Izinyanga were summoned, and commanded, on pain of death, to declare who was the criminal. This they were quite ready to do, and named without hesitation one after another the great inkosi who sat trembling around. But instead of dooming the wretched victim to death, the *dénouement* closely resembled that of the famous elegy: "The dog it was that died." In other words, the witch-finders who named an inkosi heard to their astonishment that *they* were to be executed and the denounced victim kept alive. This went on for some time, until one, cleverer than the rest, and yet afraid of committing himself too much, rose up and said oracularly, "I smell the heavens above." Chaka took this as a compliment, as well as a guess in the right direction, ordered all the remaining Izinyanga to be slain on the spot, and appointed the fortunate oracle to be his one and only witch-finder for ever after.

Chaka's name will be remembered for many and many a day in Zululand and the provinces which border it by both black and white. In the first decade of this century, when Napoleon was mapping out Europe afresh with the bayonet for a stylus, and we were pouring out blood and money like water to check him here and there—at that very time Ranpehera in New Zealand and Chaka in Zululand were playing a precisely similar game. Here, Chaka had a wider field for his Alexander-like rage for conquest, and he and his wild warriors dashed over the land like a mountain-stream. No place was safe from him, and he was the terror of the unhappy first settlers. Even now his name brings a sense of uneasiness with it, for it is still a spell to rouse the warrior-spirit, which only sleeps in the breasts of his wild subjects across the border.

PART VIII.

MARITZBURG, May 10, 1876.

N O, I will *not* begin about the weather
this time. It is a great temptation
to do so, because this is the commence-
ment of the winter, and it is upon the
strength of the coming four months that
the reputation of Natal, as possessing the
finest climate in the world, is built. Before I came here meteorologists used to
tell me that the "average" temperature
of Maritzburg was so and so, mentioning something very equable and pleasant; but then, you see, there is this little
difference between weather-theories and
the practice of the weather itself: it is
sadly apt to rush into extremes, and degrees of heat and cold are very different
when totted up and neatly spread over
many weeks, from the same thing bolted
in lumps. Then you don't catch cold on
paper, nor live in doubt whether to have
a fire or open windows and doors. To
keep at all on a level with the thermometer here, one needs to dress three or four
times a day; and it is quite on the cards
that a muslin gown and sealskin jacket
may both be pleasant wear on the same
day. We have all got colds, and, what
is worse, we have all had colds more
or less badly for some time past; and I
hear that everybody else has them too.
Of course, this news is an immense consolation, else why should it invariably
be mentioned as a compensation for
one's own paroxysms of sneezing and
coughing?

It is certainly cooler, at times quite
cold, but the sudden spasms of fierce
hot winds and the blazing sun during
the midday hours appear the more with-
ering and scorching for the contrast with
the lower temperature of morning and
evening. Still, we all keep saying (I
yet protest against the formula, but I've
no doubt I shall come round presently
and join heart and soul in it), " Natal has
the finest climate in the world," although
we have to go about like the man in the

fable, and either wrap our cloaks tightly
around us or throw them wide open to
breathe. But there! I said I would not
go off into a meteorological report, and
I will not be beguiled by the attractions
of a grievance—for there is no such satisfactory grievance as weather—into breaking so good a resolution. Rather let me
graft upon this monotonous weather-
grumble a laugh at the expense of poor
Zulu Jack, whom I found the other morning in a state of nervous anxiety over the
butter, which steadily refused to be spread
on a slice of bread for little G——'s con-
sumption. "Have you such a thing as a
charm about you, lady-chief?" Jack demanded in fluent Zulu; "for this butter
is assuredly bewitched. Last night I
could make slices of buttered bread
quite easily: this morning, behold it!"
and he exhibited his ill-used slice of
bread, with obstinate and isolated dabs
of butter sticking about it. So, you see,
it *must* be cooler; and so it is, I acknowledge, except of a morning on which a hot
wind sets in before sunrise.

To show you how perfectly impartial
and unprejudiced even a woman can be,
I am going to admit that the day last
week on which I took a long ride to
Edendale—a mission-station some half
dozen miles away—was as absolutely delightful as a day could well be. It was a
gray, shady day, very rare beneath these
sunny skies, for clouds generally mean
rain or fog, but this day they meant nothing worse than the tiniest sprinkle at
sundown—just a few big drops flirted in
our faces from the ragged edge of a swift-
ly-sailing thundercloud. There was no
wind to stir up the dust, and yet air
enough to be quite delicious: now and
then the sun came out from behind the
friendly clouds, creating exquisite effects
of light and shadow among the hills
through which our road wound. Across
many a little tributary of the Umsindusi,
by many a still green valley and round

79

many a rocky hill-shoulder, our road lay —a road which for me was most pleasantly beguiled by stories of Natal as it was five-and-twenty years ago, when lions came down to drink at these streams, when these very plains were thickly studded with buck and eland, buffalo and big game whose names would be a treasure of puzzledom to a spelling bee. In those days no man's hand ever left for an instant the lock of his trusty gun, sleeping or waking, standing or sitting, eating or riding.

The great want of ever so fair a landscape in these parts is timber. Here and there a deeper shadow in the distant hill-clefts may mean a patch of scrub, but when once you pass the belt of farms which girdle Maritzburg for some four or five miles in every direction, and leave behind their plantations of gums and poplars, oaks and willows, then there is nothing more to be seen but rolling hill-slopes bare of bush or shrub, until the eye is caught by the trees around the settlement we are on our way to visit. It stands quite far back among the hills— too much under their lee, in fact, to be quite healthy, I should fancy, for a layer of chilly, vaporous air always lurks at the bottom of these folded-away valleys, and breeds colds and fever and ague. Still, it is all inexpressibly homelike and fertile as it lies there nestling up against the high, rising ground, with patches of mealies spread in a green fan around and following the course of the winding river in tall green rustling brakes like sugar-cane. The road, a fairly good one for Natal, was strangely still and silent, and bereft of sight or sound of animal life. At one of the spruits a couple of timber-wagons were outspanned, and the jaded, tick-covered bullocks gave but little animation to the scene. Farther on, whilst we cantered easily along over a wide plain still rich in grass, a beautiful little falcon swept across our path. Slow and low was its flight, quite as though it neither feared nor cared for us, and I had ample time to admire its exquisite plumage and its large keen eye. By and by we came upon the usual "groups from the antique" in bronze and ebony working

at the road, and, as usual, doing rather more harm than good. But when we had crossed the last streamlet and turned into a sort of avenue which led to the main street of the settlement, then there was life and mövement enough and to spare. Forth upon the calm air rang the merry voices of children, of women carrying on laughing dialogues across the street, and of men's deeper-toned but quite as fluent jabber. And here are the speakers themselves as we leave the shade of the trees and come out upon the wide street rising up before us toward the mountain-slope which ends its vista.

Sitting at the doors of their houses are tidy, comfortable-looking men and women, the former busy plaiting with deft and rapid movement of their little fingers neat baskets and mats of reeds and rushes—the latter either cooking mealies, shelling them or crushing them for the market. Everywhere are mealies and children. Fat black babies squat happily in the dust, munching the boiled husk before it is shelled; older children are equally happy cleaning with finger and tongue a big wooden spoon just out of the porridge-pot; whilst this same familiar pot, of every conceivable size, but always of the same three-legged shape, something like a gypsy-kettle, lurks more or less *en évidence* in the neighborhood of every house. No grass-thatched huts are here, but thoroughly nice, respectable little houses, nearly all of the same simple pattern, with vermilion or yellow-ochre doors, and half covered with creepers. Whoever despairs of civilizing the Kafir need only look here and at other similar stations to see how easily he adapts himself to comfortable ways and customs, and in what a decent, orderly fashion he can be trained to live with his fellows.

Edendale is a Wesleyan mission-station, and the history of its settlement is rather a curious one—curious from its being the result of no costly organization, no elaborate system of proselytism, but the work of one man originally, and the evident result and effect of a perception on the part of the natives of the benefits of association and civilization.

And here I feel it incumbent on me to bear testimony—not only in this instance and in this colony — to the enormous amount of real, tangible, common-sense good accomplished among the black races all over the world by both Wesleyan Methodist and Baptist missions and missionaries. I am a staunch Churchwoman myself, and yield to no one in pure love and reverence for my own form of worship; but I do not see why that should hinder me from acknowledging facts which I have noticed all my life. Long ago in Jamaica, how often in our girlish rambles and rides have my sister and I come suddenly upon a little clearing in the midst of the deep silence and green gloom of a tropical forest! In the centre of the clearing would be a rude thatched barn, with felled trees for seats, and neither door nor window. "What is that?" we would ask of the negro lad who always rode on a mule behind us to open gates or tell us the right road home again after an excursion in search of rare orchids or parrots' nests. "Dat Baptist chapel, missis. Wesleyan, him hab chapel too ober dere. Sunday good man come preach — tell us poor niggers all good tings. Oder days same good gempleman teach pickaninnies." That was the answer, and in those few words would lie the history of much patient, humble planting of good seed, unnoticed by the more pompous world around. The minister works perhaps during the week at some means of support, but devotes even his scant leisure moments to teaching the little black children. I am so ignorant of the details on which dissenters differ from us that I dare not go into the subject, but I only know it was the same thing in India. Up in the Himalayas I have come across just the same story scores of times. Whilst our more costly and elaborate system of organization is compelled to wait for grants and certified teachers, and desks and benches, and Heaven knows what, the Methodist or Baptist missionary fells a few trees, uses them as walls and seats, thatches the roof of his shelter, and begins then and there to teach the people around him something of the sweet charities and decencies of a Christian life.

Doubtless, Edendale had once upon a time as humble a beginning, but when I saw it that soft autumn day it was difficult to recall such a chrysalis stage of its existence. On our right hand rose a neat brick chapel, substantial and handsome enough in its way, with proper seats and good woodwork within. This plain structure, however, cost something over a thousand pounds, nearly every penny of which has been contributed by Kafirs, who twenty-five years ago had probably never seen a brick or a bench, and were in every respect as utter savages as you could find anywhere. Nor is this the only place of worship or instruction on the estate, although it is the largest and most expensive, for within the limits of the settlement, or "location," as it is called —only embracing, remember, some thirty-five hundred acres under cultivation —there is another chapel, a third a few miles farther off at a sort of out-station, and no less than four day-schools with two hundred scholars, and three Sunday-schools at which two hundred and eighty children assemble weekly. All the necessary buildings for these purposes have been created entirely by and at the expense of the natives, who only number eight hundred residents in the village itself. On Sundays, however, I heard with much pleasure that more than a hundred natives from neighboring kraals attend the services at the chapels, attracted no doubt in the first instance by the singing. But still, one cannot have a better beginning, and the Kafir is quite shrewd enough to contrast his squalid hut, his scanty covering and monotonous food with the well-clad, well-housed, well-fed members of the little community of whom he catches this weekly glimpse, and every one of whom, save their pastor, is as black as himself.

But I promised to tell you briefly how the little settlement first originated. Its founder and organizer was the Rev. James Allison, a Wesleyan missionary who labored long and successfully among the Basuto and Amaswazi tribes in the interior, far away. Circumstances, external as well as private, into which I need not enter, led to his purchasing from Pretorius, the old Dutch president of Natal, this "location" or estate of some sixty-five hundred acres in extent, and settling himself upon it. He was followed by a great many of his original flock, who were warmly and personally attached to him, and had faithfully shared his fortunes in the past. In this way the nucleus of a settlement lay ready to his hand, and he seems to have been a man of great business talents and practical turn of mind, as well as a spiritual teacher of no mean ability. The little village I saw the other day was quickly laid out, and the small freehold lots—or "craen," as they are called still by their old Dutch name—were readily bought by the native settlers. This was only in 1851, and probably the actual tillage of the soil was not commenced for a year or two later. As we walked through the fertile fields with their rich and abundant crops standing ready for the sickle, and looked down into the sheltered nooks where luxuriant gardens full of vegetables flourished, it was difficult to believe that ever since the first blade of grass or corn was put in till now those fields had never known any artificial dressing or manuring of any sort. For more than twenty years the soil had yielded abundantly without an hour's rest, or any further cultivation than a very light plough could give. The advantages of irrigation, so shamefully overlooked elsewhere, were here abundantly recognized, and every few yards brought one to a diminutive channel, made by a hoe in a few minutes, bearing from the hill above a bright trickle down to the gardens and houses. I confess I often thought during that pleasant ramble of the old saying about God helping those who help themselves, for all the comfort and well-to-do-ness which met my eyes every moment was entirely from within. The people had done everything with their own hands, and during the past year had, besides, contributed over two hundred pounds to their minister's support. There have been three or four pastoral successors to Mr. Allison, who left the settlement about a dozen years ago, and the minister, who offered me, a complete stranger, a most cordial and kindly welcome, showing me everything which could interest me, and readily falling in with my desire to understand it all, was the Rev. Daniel Eva, who has only been in charge of this mission for eighteen months. I was much struck by his report of the cleverness of the native children ; only it made one regret still more that they had not better and greater opportunities all over the colony of being taught and trained. In the girls' school I saw a bright-eyed little Kafir maiden, neatly dressed and with the most charming graceful carriage and manner, who was only twelve years old, and the most wonderful arithmetician. She had passed her teacher long ago, and was getting through her "fractions" with the ease and rapidity of Babbage's calculating - machine. Nothing short of Euclid was at all likely to satisfy her appetite for figures. She and her slate were inseparable, and she liked nothing better than helping the other children with their sums. But, indeed, they were all very forward with their learning, and did their native teachers great credit. What I longed for, more than anything else, was to see a regular training-school established in this and similar stations where these clever little monkeys could be trained as future domestic servants for us whites, and as good, knowledgeable wives for their own people. There was for some years an industrial school here, and I was dreadfully sorry to hear it had been given up, but not before it had turned out some very creditable artisans among the boys, all of whom are doing well at their respective trades and earning their five or six shillings a day as skilled workmen. This school used to receive a yearly grant from the local government of one hundred pounds, but when, from private reasons, it was given up, the grant was of course withdrawn. The existing schools only get a government grant of fifty pounds a year ; and, small as the sum seems, it is yet difficult to expect more from a heavily-taxed white population who are at this moment busy in preparing a better and more costly scheme of education than they possess at present for their own children. Still, I confess my heart was much drawn to this cheerful, struggling little community ; and not only to it, but to its numerous offshoots scattered here and there far away. The Edendale people already look forward to the days when they shall have outgrown their present limits, and have purchased two very large farms a hundred miles farther in the interior, to which several of the original settlers of the parent mission have migrated, and so formed a fresh example of thrift and industry and a fresh nucleus of civilization in another wild part.

There were a hundred houses in the village (it is called George Town, after Sir George Grey), and into some of these houses I went by special and eager invitation of the owners. You have no idea how clean and comfortable they were, nor what a good notion of decoration civilized Kafirs have. In fact, there was rather too much decoration, as you will admit if I describe one dwelling to you. This particular house stood on high ground, just where the mountain slopes abruptly, so it had a little terrace in front to make the ground level. Below the terrace was a kind of yard, in which quantities of fowls scratched and clucked, and beyond that, again, an acre of garden-ground, every part of which was planted with potatoes, pumpkins, green peas and other things. A couple of somewhat steep and rough steps helped us to mount up on the terrace, and then we were ushered—with such a natural pride and delight in a white lady visitor—into a little flagged passage. On one side was the kitchen and living-room, a fair-sized place enough, with substantial tables and chairs, and a large open hearth, on which a wood-fire was cooking the savory contents of a big pot. As for the walls, they were simply the gayest I ever beheld. Originally whitewashed, they had been absolutely covered with brilliant designs in vermilion, cobalt and yellow ochre, most correctly and symmetrically drawn in geometrical figures. A many-colored star within a circle was

a favorite pattern. The effect was as dazzling as though a kaleidoscope had been suddenly flung against a wall and its gay shapes fixed on it. But, grand as was this apartment, it faded into insignificance compared to the drawing-room and the "English bedroom," both of which were exhibited to me with much complacency by the smiling owner. Now, these rooms had originally been one, and were only divided by a slender partition-wall. When the door of the drawing-room was thrown open, I must say I almost jumped back in alarm at the size of the roses and lilies which seemed about to assault me. I never before saw such a wall-paper—never. It would have been a large pattern for, say, St. James's Hall, and there it was, flaunting on walls about seven feet by eight. A brilliant crimson flock formed the ground, and these alarming flowers, far larger than life, bloomed and nodded all over it. The chairs and sofa were gay with an equally remarkable chintz, and brilliant mats of beads and wool adorned the tables. China ornaments and pictures were in profusion, though it took time to get accustomed to those roses and lilies, so as to be able to perceive anything else. In one part of the tiny room some bricks had been taken out of the wall and a recess formed, fitted up with shelves on which stood more vases and statuettes, the whole being framed and draped with pink calico cut in large vandykes. I must say, my black hostess and her numerous female friends, who came flocking to see me, stood out well against this magnificent background. We all sat for some time exchanging compliments and personal remarks through the medium of an interpreter. But one smiling sable understood English, and it was she who proposed that the "lady-chief" should now be shown the bedroom, which was English fashion. We all flocked into it, gentlemen and all, for it was too amusing to be left out. Sure enough, there was a gay iron bedstead, a chest of drawers, and, crowning glory of all, a real dressing-table, complete with pink and white petticoat and toilette-glass. The glass might have been six inches square—I don't think it was more—but there was a great deal of wooden frame to it, and it stood among half a dozen breakfast cups and saucers which were symmetrically arranged, upside down, on the toilette-table.

"What are these for?" I asked innocently.

"Dat English fashion, missis : all white ladies hab cup-saucers on deir tables like dat."

It would have been the worst possible taste to throw any doubt on this assertion, which we all accepted with perfect gravity and good faith, and so returned to the drawing-room, much impressed, apparently, by the grandeur of the bedroom.

Of course, the babies came swarming round, and very fat and jolly they all looked in their nice cotton frocks or shirt-blouses. I did not see a single ragged or squalid or poverty-stricken person in the whole settlement, except one poor mad boy, who followed us about, darting behind some shelter whenever he fancied himself observed. Poor fellow! he was quite harmless—a lucky circumstance, for he was of enormous stature and strength. Over his pleasant countenance came a puzzled, vacant look every now and then, but nothing repulsive, though his shaggy locks hung about his face like a water-spaniel's ears, and he was only wrapped in a coarse blanket. I was sorry to notice a good deal of ophthalmia among the children, and heard that it was often prevalent here.

In another house, not quite so gay, I was specially invited to look at the contents of the good wife's wardrobe, hung out to air in the garden. She was hugely delighted at my declaring that I should like to borrow some of her smart gowns, especially when I assured her, with perfect truth, that I did not possess anything half so fine. Sundry silk dresses of hues like the rainbow waved from the pomegranate bushes, and there were mantles and jackets enough to have started a second-hand clothes' shop on the spot. This young woman—who was quite pretty, by the way—was the second wife of a rich elderly man, and I wondered what her slight, *petite* figure would look like when buried in those large and heavy garments. It chanced to be Saturday, and there was quite as much cleaning and general furbishing up of everything going on inside and outside the little houses as in an English country village, and far less shrewishness over the process.

I wanted to have one more look at the principal school-room, whose scholars were just breaking up for a long play ; so we returned, but only in time for the outburst of liberated children, whooping and singing and noisily joyful at the ending of the week's lessons. The little girls dropped their pretty curtsies shyly, but the boys kept to the charming Kafir salutation of throwing up the right hand with its two fingers extended, and crying "Inkosi!" It is a good deal prettier and more graceful than the complicated wave and bow in one which our village children accomplish so awkwardly.

Oh, how I should like to "do up" that school-room, and hang gay prints and picture-lessons on its walls, for those bright little creatures to go wild with delight at! There has been so much needed in the settlement that no money has been or can be forthcoming just yet for anything beyond bare necessaries. But the school-room wanted "doing up" very much. It was perfectly sweet and clean, and there was no occasion for any inspector to measure out so many cubic feet of air to each child, for the breeze from the mountains was whistling·in at every crevice and among the rafters, and the floor was well scrubbed daily ; but it wanted new stands and desks and forms—everything, in short—most sadly. Then just think what a boon it would be if the most intelligent and promising among the girls could be drafted from this school when twelve years old into a training-school, where they could be taught sewing and cooking and other homely accomplishments! There is no place in the colony where one can turn for a good female servant, and yet here were all these nice sharp little girls only wanting the opportunity of learning to grow up into capital servants and good future wives, above merely picking mealies or hoeing the ground.

As I have said before, I am no political economist, and the very combination of words frightens me, but still I can't help observing how we are wasting the good material which lies ready to our hands. When one first arrives one is told, as a frightful piece of news, that there are three hundred thousand Kafirs in Natal, and only seventeen thousand whites. The next remark is that immigration is the cure for all the evils of the country, and that we want more white people. Now, it seems to me that is just what we *don't* want— at least, white people of what is called the lower classes. Of course, every colony is the better for the introduction of skilled labor and intelligence of every kind, no matter how impecunious it may be. But the first thing a white person of any class at all does here is to set up Kafirs under him, whom he knocks about as much as he dares, complaining all the time of their ignorance and stupidity. Every man turns at once into a master and an independent gentleman, with black servants under him; and the result is, that it is impossible to get the simplest thing properly done, for the white people are too fine to do it, and the black ones either too ignorant or too lazy. Then there is an outcry at the chronic state of muddle and discomfort we all live in. English servants directly expect two or three Kafirs under them to do their work; and really no one except ladies and gentlemen seem to do anything save by deputy. Now, if we were only to import a small number of teachers and trained artisans of the highest procurable degree of efficiency, we could establish training-schools in connection with the missions which are scattered all over the country, and which have been doing an immense amount of good silently all these years. In this way we might gradually use up the material we have all ready to our hand in these swarming black people; and it appears to me as if it would be more likely to succeed than bringing shiploads of ignorant, idle whites into the colony. There is no doubt about

it: Natal will never be an attractive country to European immigrants; and if it is not to be fairly crowded out of the list of progressive English colonies by its population of blacks, we must devise some scheme for bringing them into the great brotherhood of civilization. They are undoubtedly an intelligent people, good - humored and easy to manage. Their laziness is their great drawback, but at such a settlement as Edendale I heard no complaints, and certainly there were no signs of it. No one learns more readily than a savage how good are clothes and shelter and the thousand comforts of civilized people. Unhappily, he learns the evil with the good, especially in the towns, but that is our own fault. In a climate with so many cold days as this the want of clothing is severely felt by the Kafirs, and it is one of the first inducements to work. Then they very soon learn to appreciate the comfort of a better dwelling than their dark huts, and a wish for more nourishing food follows next. It is easier to get at the children and form their habits and ideas than to change those of the grown - up men, for the women scarcely count for anything at present in a scheme of improvement: they are mere hewers of wood and drawers of water. So the end of it all is, that I want a little money from some of you rich people to encourage the Edendale settlers by helping them with their existing schools, and if possible setting up training-schools where boys could be taught carpentering and other trades, and the girls housewifery; and I want the same idea taken up and enlarged, and gradually carried out on a grand scale all over the country.

There are several Norwegian missions established on the borders of Zululand, presided over by Bishop Schreuder; and I have been so immensely interested in the bishop's report of a visit he paid last year to Cetywayo (there is a click in the C), the Zulu king, that I have copied some of it out of a *Blue Book* for you. Do you know there is a very wrong impression abroad about blue books? They contain the most interesting reading possible, full of details of colonial difficulties and dangers which are not to be met with anywhere else, and I have never been better entertained than by turning over the leaves of one whenever it is my good fortune to come across it. I remember one in particular upon Japan, beautifully written, and as thrillingly sensational as any of Miss Braddon's novels. However, you shall judge for yourself of the bishop's narrative. I will only mention what he is too modest to cause to appear here—and which was told me by other people—that he is one of the most zealous and fearless of the great band of missionaries, beloved and respected by black and white. In fact, my informant managed to convey a very good impression of the bishop's character to me when he summed up his panegyric in true colonial phraseology, though I quite admit that it does not sound sufficiently respectful when applied to a bishop: "He is a first-rate fellow, all round."

This document, which I have shortened a little, was addressed as a letter to our minister for native affairs, and has thus become public property, read and re-read with deep interest by us here, and likely, I am sure, to please a wider circle:

Untunjambili, August 20, 1875.

Dear Sir : I beg to send you a short sketch of my last trip to and interview with the Zulu king, in order to present to him your report of your embassy, 1873, and leave it to your discretion to lay before His Excellency the whole or a part of this sketch, got up in a language foreign to me.

After an irksome traveling right across the Tugela from here to Undi, I arrived the fifth day (August 5) at the king's head kraal sufficiently early to have a preliminary interview with the headmen then present—viz., Umnjamana, Usegetwayo, Uganze, Uzetzalusa, Untzingwayo, etc.—and, according to Zulu etiquette, lay before them the substance of my message in the main points, the same as I, the day after (6th August), told the king.

(N. B. In the course of the evening one of the headmen hinted to me that as regards the killing of people, all was not as it ought to be, and that I ought to press the matter when I had the interview with the king, as he needed to have his memory (I would rather say his conscience, for his memory is still very good—even remarkably good) stirred up, and that the present occasion was the very time to do that. The result proved this to be a very safe and timely hint.)

They spent the forenoon communicating in their bulky way this news to the king, so it was midday before I got an interview with the king, when I opened the interview verbatim, thus :

"My arrival here to-day is not on my own account. I have come at the request of the chiefs across (the Tugela) to cause you to receive by hand and by mouth a book which has come from Victoria, the queen of the English—the book of the new laws of this ˴Zulu country, which Somtseu (Mr. Shepstone) proclaimed publicly at Umlambongwenya the day he, being called to do so, set you apart to be king of the Zulus. Victoria, queen of the English, says : ' I and my great headmen (ministers) have read the new laws of the Zulu country, which you, king, and all the Zulus, agreed to with Somtseu ; and as we adhere to our words, so also I wish you, chief of the Zulus, to hold fast to these words of yours of this law which you agreed to adhere to the day you were made king by Mr. Shepstone, who was sent to do that by the government of Natal.' I have now finished : this is the only word I have brought with me from the chiefs across (the Tugela)."

The royal inscription of the copy was of course literally translated.

After having thus delivered the government message entrusted to me, I added, in the way of explaining to the king and his councilors the merits of the case at issue, by saying :

"You have heard the government word, but that you may clearly see the line of this book of the new laws, I wish to explain to you as follows : The day the Zulu nation brought the head of the king, laid low, four oxen, to the government, the Zulu nation asked that Mr.

Shepstone might come and proclaim the new laws of Zululand, and set apart the real royal child, because they no longer had power of themselves to set apart for themselves a king. Mr. Shepstone came, and began by consulting you, the Zulu nation, at Umlambongwenya on the fifth day of the week, on all the points of the new law which he had been sent for to proclaim; and he conversed with you until the sun went down, having begun early in the day. He then left you Zulus to consult together and investigate the new laws on the last day of the week and on the Sunday; and when Mr. Shepstone returned to the wagons (camp) he wrote in a book all the points of the new law; and on Monday he again came with all his attendants, and it was in accordance with his previous arrangement with you; and he came to the Umlambongwenya, the residence appointed for the purpose, that he might set apart in becoming manner the young king. We all were present: we heard him, standing publicly, holding in his hand a paper, and pointing to it, saying, ' That forgetfulness may never, never happen, I have written in this paper all the points of the new laws of the country which we agreed upon, two days ago and to-day, in the presence of all the Zulu nation, the royal children and the nobles;' and he then handed that paper to his son, that it might be accessible and speak when he himself is no more; and this proclamation of the new laws was confirmed by the English custom of firing cannons seventeen times, and according to the Zulu by the striking of shields. On the second day of the week Mr. Shepstone returned to the Umlambongwenya to take his leave of the king, and again the points of the new law were explained; and Uttamn (Cetywayo's brother) explained to Mr. Shepstone the history of this house; and on the third day the nobles all went to the wagons (camp), being sent to the king to take leave, and Mr. Shepstone went home satisfied; and when he returned to the colony he wrote this book of the narrative of his journey and his work in Zululand; and, as is done (in the colony), then he sent it to the governor,

and the governor read it, and read it all, and said the work of Somtseu is good, and the new laws of the Zulu country are good; and, as is done there too, he sent it forward to Victoria, the queen of the English; and Victoria sent back this book of the new laws by the same way to the governor, and the governor returned it to Somtseu, and here it is come back to its work (discharge its function) in Zululand, where it was set up to rule over you. And as Victoria binds herself by her words, so are you also, king, and you, the Zulu nation, bound by this new law made for you here by Somtseu at Umlambongwenya. And this is the generation of this book of the new law: It was born an infant; it went across (the water), the child of a king, to seek for kingship, and it found it; it was made king far away, and here it is returned with its rank to its own country, Zululand; therefore do not say it is only the book that speaks. No, I tell you, Zulus, of a truth, that this book has to-day rank: it took that rank beyond (the water): it has come back a king, and is supreme in this country.

"The words of the governor are finished, and my explanation is finished; but there are small items of news which I wish to tell you in your ears, which the authorities (in Natal) did not tell me, but which I speak for myself because I wish to see for you and reprove you gently, that you may understand."

Uganze then commenced in his usual tattling way to make some remarks, that they, as black people, did not understand books and the value of such written documents; whereupon I said to him, "That won't do, Ganze, that you, after having applied, as in the present case, to people who transact business through written documents, now afterward say you do not understand the value of books. You all know very well that book-rules are supreme with white people: it is therefore of no use that you, after having obtained what you wanted from the white people, now come and plead ignorance about book. If you don't know yourselves to read book, there is nothing else for you to be done but to get a trustworthy person to read for you, or learn to read yourselves."

By these remarks I stopped effectually all further talk of that kind; and, evidently displeased at Uganze's talk, the king repeated very correctly all I had endeavored to say. (You know the king has a good memory.)

While I was translating, the king and his nobles often expressed their astonishment, uttering occasionally that it was as if they were living the thing over again, and that what was translated was exactly what was spoken and transacted in your way to and under your stay at the place of encampment; and, having finished, I told them that the fullness and correctness of the details of the report was a natural result of the habit of white people under such circumstances, daily to take down in writing what transpired, in order not to forget it itself long time afterward.

As the king and his nobles now entered upon a discussion of the merits of the new laws as set forth in your report, and this discussion evidently would take the turn of being an answer to the message delivered, I found it necessary to tell them that I had received no commission to bring back any answer to the government message; and stated my own private opinion about not having received such commission by saying most explicitly, " My opinion is that the chiefs across the Tugela did not tell me to take back to them your answer, because your right words to adhere to the new law are completed. They are many: no more are necessary. The thing wanted now is your acts in accordance with the law."

Here, again, Uganze asked what I meant by *acts ;* and the answer was, "That you rule and manage this Zululand in accordance with the new law, and never overstep it;" and I explained this further by telling them frankly that many reports circulated in Natal of the extensive killing of people all over the Zululand; that from the time I this year had crossed the Tugela, Natal people had with one mouth asked me if the killing of people in Zululand now really was carried on to such an extent as reported, in spite of the new

law; that I had not with my own eyes seen any corpse, and personally only knew of them said to have been killed; that I myself had my information principally from the same sources as people in Natal, and often from Natal newspapers; that I myself personally believed that there were some, and perhaps too much, foundation for said reports : there were many who pretended having seen corpses of people killed both with guns and spears. And, after having lectured my Zulu audience very earnestly upon this vital point, I concluded, saying, " Well-wishers of the Zulus are very sorry to hear of such things, as they certainly had hoped that the new constitution would have remedied this sad shedding of blood; while, on the other hand, people who did not care whether the Zulu nation was ruined or not, merely laughed at the idea that any one ever could have entertained the hope of altering or amending the old-cherished Zulu practice of bloodshed, as the Zulus were such an irrecoverable set of man-butchers. Further, I tell you seriously, king, your reputation is bad among the whites; and, although it is not as yet officially reported to the government, still it has come to its ears, all these bloody rumors, and nobody can tell what may be the consequences hereafter—to-morrow."

The king and his izinduna seemed wonderfully tame—even conscience-smitten all along—while the rumors were mentioned, for I had expected some of their usual unruly excitement; but nothing of that kind was seen. But, although the king and his nobles present had, as mentioned above, with astonishment uttered that your report had reported exactly everything done and said there and then, he now tried to point out that you, in your report, had left out to inform the queen that he, in his transactions with you, had reserved to himself the right of killing people who kill others, who lie with the king's girls, who sin against or steal the king's property—that it is the royal Zulu prerogative "from time immemorial," at the accession to the throne, to make raid on neighboring tribes. I went into details of both questions, and proved by plain words of your report, as well as by logical conclusion therefrom, the fallacy of both complaints ; and especially as to the pretended "from time immemorial," that this was nonsense, as that bloody system of raid only was from yesterday (*chaka*), and therefore there were no reasons why it should not be broken off to-morrow ; and much more so as this raid - system only tended to exasperate all neighboring tribes against the Zulus, and eventually bring on their (Zulus') ruin, for it was well known that all neighboring tribes were gradually coming under the protection of the white people. The king made, in self-defence, some irrelevant remarks, and was of course supported by the izinduna in the usual Zulu-duda way, but, most remarkably, in a very tame way ; but I thought by myself, " It is easy to make an end to this support and combination, for I shall split your interest, and then combat you singly." So I turned the current of the discussion in this way, saying, " I do really believe that there is going on killing people in such a manner that the king is blamed in Natal for doings he first afterward is made aware of—viz., the grandees will, for example, kill a man of no note, take a few heads of cattle to the king in order to shut his mouth, saying, ' I found a rat spoiling my things, and struck this rat of mine, and here is the few cattle it left behind.' Then the king will—although the thing does not suit him—think by himself, ' If I stir up in this poltroon matter, my grandees will say that I trouble them ;' and so the thing is growing on, and brings on such rumors and bad names over in Natal. But was it not agreed upon, king, at your installation, that the common saying, ' My man,' or ' My people,' must not be tolerated any longer ? It must cease in the mouth of the grandees in the country. Here in the Zululand is now ' my people of the grandees, but all are people of the king. The grandees have no right to the people : the king is the owner of them all solely. And was it not agreed upon that no Zulu—male or female; old or young—could be executed without fair,

open trial and the special previous sanction of the king ? But now, by the old practice creeping into use again, and the grandees killing their so-called people, and the king killing his, it is like the real owner and the other imaginary owners killing independently cattle out of the same herd, without telling each other, till the herd is cut up. By executing people who really only belong to the king, the grandees will, in the same degree as they do so, detract from and diminish the royal power and prerogative, so that there in fact reign several kings in this same kingdom, at least as far as the authority over life and death concerns. The grandees are concealed behind their king in the bad rumors over in Natal ; so the king gains a bad name and blame for the whole, while the grandees gain the satisfaction of succeeding in killing people they dislike."

The king assented to these my remarks ; so the izinduna found themselves deserted and silenced. Umnjamana only tried to put in a few very tame remarks of his usual ones, but I quickly brought him to his senses by remembering him sharply of his sayings and doings at the installation. I now thought it high time to cut the further parlance short by saying, " I find that I am going to be dragged into an argument about matters that are no business of mine, and I will therefore talk no more of these things, for the new law-owners are still alive ; and, moreover, the new law is there invested with undeniable royalty ; so that even when Her Majesty Victoria, her present councilors and the rest of us are no more, the Umteto will be there, and numerous copies of it are in the hands of the white people, so that they at present and in future times will be able to compare whether the doings of yours (Zulu) are in accordance or at variance with that law, and take their measures accordingly. Victoria binds herself by books, and so you are bound by this book of new law that now is ruling supreme : that is the long and short of it, for this book of the law will decay with the country. . . . I have now talked myself tired, finished my verbal errand to you, king, and now I will hand over to you this splendid copy of the new law." He then said, "Lay it down here" (pointing to the mat under his feet). "No," I replied, "that won't do: the book is not at your feet, but you are at the feet of the book; and if my hands are not too good to hand it over to you, your hands ought not to be too good to receive it. Don't make any difficulty." So he received the copy with his hands, laid it himself on the mat, placed both his elbows on his knees, and holding bent over his head between his hands, uttered that peculiar native "Oh dear! oh dear! what a man this is!"

The king evidently felt himself so out of his depth that he quite forgot his usual final topics, begging for a royal cloak (the standing topic of late) or some similar thing, and dropped into begging for a dog to bark for him at night.

Lastly, in order to test him how he now was disposed toward mission-work, I told him that, as my business with him was finished, I should immediately, without sleeping that night at Undi, commence my homeward journey, for I had left much work to be done behind, having commenced a new station over in Natal, as here in Zululand is no work for us missionaries as long as he prohibited his subjects from becoming Christians; therefore it was at present quite sufficient for me in Zululand, where it, under present circumstances, was useless to get new stations only to live and not work on, while we over in Natal could buy, and from government, who approved of the mission-work, get land for stations; moreover, the people—for example, over at Untunjambili—were very anxious to be taught. With an heedful air the king asked, "Do the Kafirs really wish to be taught?" "Yes, they really do," I answered him.

Thinking that it would do them (the king and councilors) good to hear a bit of those proceedings, I inserted a few words about the contemplated and proposed federation between the colony of Natal, Cape, the Transvaal, and Orange States by mentioning that an important letter from the great people beyond the water had come and proposed a grand meeting of men chosen from these four states to deliberate of the best mode of establishing such federation among themselves, and the advantage and importance of this federation, which I tried to point out by a few practical instances. The king and his induna now insisted upon my not leaving before next morning, as the king wanted to prepare for me (get me some living beef); and in the course of the evening I got a special message from him to you to get from a doctor medicine for a complaint he had in the chest, rising at times from regions about the liver, and medicine for an induna who of late had been completely deaf. The messenger also told that the king already had sent to you for medicines, but as yet got no answer. I think that he has found out that it comes very expensive to call a dotela from Natal, and that it therefore would be cheapest to get the aid of genuine doctors through your kind unpaid assistance.

Under the conversation with the king the headman Usagetwayo (a rather stupid man, but whose assumed grandeur is so great and supercilious that he pretends never to know anybody, but always must ask somebody who this is) asked in his well-known hoarse way, "Who is he there who speaks with the king?" (meaning me). Umnjamana answered, "Bishop Schreuder, native man: he is Panda's old headman. You are joking in saying you don't know him: it was he for whom they cut off the large bit of land at Enlumeni." (One of my Christian natives present overheard this conversation getting on in a subdued tone while I was speaking with the king.)

When our interview commenced the king seemed rather sulky, but got gradually brighter, at least very tame, which hardly could have been expected after such dusky beginning, for which there were also other reasons, needless to specify here. I remain, etc.,

H. SCHREUDER.

PART IX.

DUST and the bazaar! These are the topics of the month. Perhaps I ought to put the bazaar first, for it is past and over, to the intense thankfulness of everybody, buyers and sellers included, whereas the dust abides with us for ever, and increases in volume and density and restlessness more and more. It certainly seems to me a severe penalty to pay for these three months of fine and agreeable weather to have no milk, hardly any butter, very little water, and to be smothered by dust into the bargain. But still, here is a little bit of bracing, healthy weather, and·far be it from me to depreciate it. We enjoy every moment of it, and congratulate each other upon it, and boast once more to new-comers that we possess "the finest climate in the world." This remark died out in the summer, but is again to be heard on all sides; and I am not strong-minded enough to take up lance and casque and tilt against it. Besides which, it would really be very pleasant if only the tanks were not dry, the cows giving but a teacupful of milk a day for want of grass, whilst butter is half a crown a pound, and of a rancid cheesiness trying to the consumer. Still, the weather is bright and sunny and fresh all day— too hot, indeed, in the sun, and generally bitterly cold in the evening and night. About once a week, however, we have a burning hot wind, and are obliged still to keep our summer clothes close at hand. The rapidity with which cold succeeds this hot wind is hardly to be believed. Our "season" is just over. It lasts as nearly as possible one week, and all the gayety and festivity of the year is crowded into it. During this time of revelry I drove down the hill to a garden-party one sunny afternoon, and found a muslin scarf absolutely unbearable, so intensely hot was the air. That was about three o'clock, and by five I was driving home in the darkening twilight, dusty as a mill-er and shivering in a seal-skin jacket. It is no wonder that most of us, Kafirs and all, have fearful colds and coughs, or that croup is both common and dangerous among the little ones. Still, we must never lose sight of the fact that it is "the finest climate in the world," and exceptionally favorable, or so they say, to consumptive patients.

I am more thankful than words can express that we live out of the town, though the pretty green slopes around are sere and yellow now, with here and there patches of black where the fires rage night and day among the tall grass. About this season prudent people burn strips around their fences and trees to check any vagrant fire, for there is so little timber that the few green trees are precious things, not to be shriveled up in an hour by fast-traveling flames for want of precautions. The spruits or brooks run low in their beds, the ditches are dry, the wells have only a bucketful of muddy water and a good many frogs in them, and the tanks are failing one after another. Yet this is only the beginning of winter, and I am told that I don't yet know what dust and drought mean. I begin to think affectionately of those nice heavy thunder-showers every evening, and to long to see again the familiar bank of cloud peeping up over that high hill to the west, precursor of a deluge. Well! well! there is no satisfying some people. I am ready to swallow my share of dust as uncomplainingly as may be, but I confess to horrible anxiety as to what we are all to do for milk for the babies presently. Every two or three days I get a polite note from whoever is supplying me with milk to say they are extremely sorry to state they shall be obliged to discontinue doing so, as their cows don't give a pint a day amongst them all. The little which is to be had is naturally enormously dear. F—— steadily declines to buy a cow, because he says he knows it will be just like all the rest, but I think if only I had a cow I should contrive to find food for it somewhere. I see those horrid tins of preserved milk drawing nearer and nearer day by day.

It is very wrong to pass over our great bazaar with so little notice. I dare say you who read this think that you know something about bazaars, but I assure you you do not—not about such a bazaar as this, at all events. We have been preparing for it, working for it, worrying for it, advertising it, building it, decorating it, and generally slaving at it for a year and more. When I arrived the first words I heard were about the bazaar. When I tried to get some one to help me with my stall, I was laughed at: all the young ladies in the place had been secured months before as saleswomen. I don't know what I should have done if a very charming lady had not arrived soon after I did. No sooner had she set foot on shore than I rushed at her and snapped her up before any one else knew that she had come, for I was quite desperate, and felt it was my only chance. However, luck was on my side, and my fair A. D. C. made up in energy and devotion to the cause for half a dozen less enthusiastic assistants. All this time I have never told you what the bazaar was for, or why we all threw ourselves into it with so much ardor. It was for the Natal Literary Society, which has been in existence some little time, struggling to form the nucleus of a public library and reading-room, giving lectures and so forth to provide some sort of elevating and refining influences for the more thoughtful among the Maritzburgians. It has been very up-hill work, and there is no doubt that the promoters and supporters deserve a good deal of credit. They had met with the usual fate of such pioneers of progress : they had been overwhelmed with prophecies of all kinds of disaster, but they can turn the tables now on their tormentors. The building did *not* take fire, nor was it robbed; there were no riots ; all the boxes arrived in time ; everybody was in the sweetest temper; no one died for want of fresh air (these

were among the most encouraging prognostics) ; and last, not least, after paying all expenses two thousand guineas stand at the bank to the credit of the society. I must say I was astonished at the financial result, but delighted too, for it is an excellent undertaking, and one in which I feel the warmest interest. It will be an immense boon to the public, and cannot fail to elevate the tone of thought and feeling in the town. This sum, large as it is for our slender resources, will only barely build a place suitable for a library and reading-room, and the nucleus of a museum. We want gifts of books and maps and prints, and nice things of all kinds; and I only wish any one who reads these lines, and could help us in this way, would kindly do so, for it will be a long time before we can buy such things for ourselves, and yet they are indispensable to the carrying out of the scheme.

Everybody from far and near came to the bazaar and bought liberally. The things provided were selected with a view to the wants of a community which has not a large margin for luxuries, and although they were very pretty, there was a strong element of practical usefulness in everything. It must have been a perfect carnival for the little ones. Such blowing of whistles and trumpets, such beating of drums and tossing of gay balls in the air, as were to be seen all around! Little girls walked about hugging newly-acquired dolls with an air of bewildered maternal happiness, whilst on every side you heard boys comparing notes as to the prices of cricket-bats (for your true colonial boy has always a keen sense of the value of money) or the merits of carpenters' tools. A wheelwright gave half a dozen exquisitely-finished wheelbarrows to the bazaar, made of the woods of the colony, and useful as well as exceedingly pretty. The price was high, but I shut my economical eyes tight and bought one, to the joy and delight of the boys, big and little. There were heaps of similar things, besides contributions from London and Paris, from Italy and Austria, from India and Australia, to say nothing of Kafir weapons and wooden utensils, of live-stock, vegetables and flowers. Everybody responded to our entreaties, and helped us liberally and kindly ; and this is the result with which we are all immensely delighted.

Some of our best customers were funny old Dutchmen from far up country, who had come down to the races and the agricultural show, which were all going on at the same time. They bought recklessly the most astounding things, but wisely made it a condition of purchase that they should not be required to take away the goods. In fact, they hit upon the expedient of presenting to one stall what they bought at another; and one worthy, who looked for all the world as if he had sat for his portrait in dear old Geoffrey Crayon's *Sketch-books*, brought us at our stall a large wax doll dressed as a bride, and implored us to accept it, and so rid him of its companionship. An immense glass vase was bestowed on us in a similar fashion later on in the evening, and at last we quite came to hail the sight of those huge beaver hats with their broad brims and peaked crowns as an omen of good fortune. But what I most wanted to see all the time were the heroes of the rocket practice. You do not know perhaps that delicious and veritable South African story ; so I must tell it to you, only you ought to see my dear boers or emigrant farmers to appreciate it thoroughly.

A little time ago the dwellers in a certain small settlement far away on the frontier took alarm at the threatening attitude of their black neighbors. I need not go into the rights — or rather the wrongs—of the story here, but skip all preliminary details and start fair one fine morning when a *commando* was about to march. Now, a commando means a small expedition armed to the teeth, which sets forth to do as much retaliatory mischief as it can. It had occurred to the chiefs of this warlike force that a rocket apparatus would be a very fine thing, and likely to strike awe into savage tribes, and so would a small, light cannon. The necessary funds were forthcoming, and some kind friend in England sent them out a beautiful little rocket-tube, all complete, and the most knowing and destructive of light field-pieces. They reached their destination in the very nick of time—the eve, in fact, of the departure of this valiant commando. It was deemed advisable to make trial of these new weapons before starting, and an order was issued for the commando to assemble a little earlier in the market-square and learn to handle their artillery pieces before marching. Not only did the militia assemble, but all the towns-folk, men, women and children, and clustered like bees round the rocket-tube, which had been placed near the powder magazine, so as to be handy to the ammunition. The first difficulty consisted in finding anybody who had ever seen a cannon before : as for a rocket-tube, that was indeed a new invention. The most careful search only succeeded in producing a boer who had many, many years ago made a voyage in an old tea-ship which carried a couple of small guns for firing signals, etc. This valiant artilleryman was at once elected commander-in-chief of the rocket-tube and the little cannon, whilst everybody stood by to see some smart practice. The tube was duly hung on its tripod, and the reluctant fellow-passenger of the two old cannon proceeded to load, and attempted to fire it. The loading was comparatively easy, but the firing ! I only wish I understood the technical terms of rocket-firing, but, although they have been minutely explained to me half a dozen times, I don't feel strong enough on the subject to venture to use them. The results were, that some connecting cord or other having been severed contrary to the method generally pursued by experts in letting off a rocket, *half* of the projectile took fire, could not escape from the tube on account of the other half blocking up the passage, and there was an awful internal commotion instead of an explosion. The tripod gyrated rapidly, the whizzing and fizzing became more pronounced every moment, and at last, with a whish and a bang, out rushed the ill-treated and imprisoned rocket. But there was no clear space for it. It ricochetted among the trees, zigzagging here and there, opening out a line for itself with lightning speed among the terrified and flustered crowd. There seemed no end to the progress of that blazing stick. A wild cry arose, "The powder magazine!" but before the stick could reach so far, it brought up all standing in a wagon, and made one final leap among the oxen, killing two of them and breaking the leg of a third. This was an unfortunate beginning for the new captain, but he excused himself on the ground that, after all, rockets were not guns: with those he was perfectly familiar, having smoked his pipe often and often on board the tea-ship long ago with those two cannon full in view. Yet the peaceablest cannons have a nasty trick of running back and treading on the toes of the bystanders; and to guard against such well-known habits it seemed advisable to plant the *trail* of this little fellow securely in the ground, so that he must perforce keep steady. "Volunteers to the front with spades!" was the cry, and a good-sized grave was made for the trail of the gun, which was then lightly covered up with earth. There was now no fear in loading him, and instead of one, two charges of powder were carefully rammed home, and two shells put in. There was some hitch also about applying the fuse to this weapon, fuses not having been known on board the tea-ship; but at last something was ignited, and out jumped *one* shell right into the middle of the market-square, and buried itself in the ground. But, alas and alas! the cannon now behaved in a wholly unexpected manner. It turned itself deliberately over on its back, with its muzzle pointing full among the groups of gaping Dutchmen in its rear, its wheels spun round at the rate of a thousand miles an hour, and a fearful growling and sputtering could be heard inside it. The recollection of the second shell now obtruded itself vividly on all minds, and caused a furious stampede among the spectators. The fat Dutchmen looked as if they were playing some child's game. One ran behind another, putting his hands on his shoulders, but no sooner did any person find himself the first of a file than he shook off the detaining hands of the man behind him and fled to the rear to hold on to his neighbor. However ludicrous this may have looked, it was still very natural with the muzzle of a half-loaded cannon pointing full toward you, and one is thankful to know that with such dangerous weapons around no serious harm was done. If you could only see the fellow-countrymen of these heroes, you would appreciate the story better — their wonderful diversity of height, their equally marvelous diversity of breadth, of garb and equipment. One man will be over six feet high, a giant in form and build, mounted on a splendid saddle fresh from the store, spick and span in all details. His neighbor in the ranks will be five feet nothing, and an absolute circle as to shape: he will have rolled with difficulty on to the back of a gaunt steed, and his horse furniture will consist of two old saddle-flaps sewn together with a strip of bullock-hide, and with a sheepskin thrown over all. You may imagine that a regiment thus turned out would look somewhat droll to the eyes of a martinet in such matters, even without the addition of a cannon lying on its back kicking, or a twirling rocket-tube sputtering and fizzing.

JUNE 7.

Let me see what we have been doing since I last wrote. I have had a Kafir princess to tea with me, and we have killed a snake in the baby's nursery. That is to say, Jack killed the snake. Jack does everything in the house, and is at once the most amiable and the cleverest servant I ever had. Not Zulu Jack. *He* is so deaf, poor boy! he is not of much use except to clean saucepans and wash up pots and pans. He seems to have no sense of smell either, because I have to keep a strict watch over him that he does not introduce a flavor of kerosene oil into everything by his partiality for wiping cups and plates with dirty lamp-cloths instead of his own nice clean dusters. But he is very civil and quiet, leisurely in all he does, and a strict conservative in his notions of work, resenting the least change of employment. No: the other Jack is a tiny little man, also a Zulu, but he speaks English well, and it is his pride and delight to dress as an English "boy"—that is what he calls it —even to the wearing of agonizingly tight boots on his big feet. Jack learns all I can teach him of cooking with perfect ease, and gives us capital meals. He is the bravest of the establishment, and is always to the fore in a scrimmage, generally dealing the *coup de grace* in all combats with snakes. In this instance my first thought was to call Jack. I had tried to open the nursery-door one sunny midday to see if the baby was still asleep, and could not imagine what it was pressing so hard against the door and preventing my opening it. I determined to see, and lo! round the edge darted the head of a large snake, held well up in air, with the forked tongue out. He must have been trying to get out of the room, but I shut the door in his face and called for Jack, arming myself with my riding-whip. Jack came running up instantly, but declined all offers of walking-sticks from the hall, having no confidence in English sticks, and preferring to trust only to his own light strong staff. Cautiously we opened the door again, but the snake was drawn up in battle-array, coiled in a corner difficult to get at, and with outstretched neck and darting head. Jack advanced boldly, and fenced a little with the creature, pretending to strike it, but when he saw a good moment he dealt one shrewd blow which proved sufficient. Then I suddenly became very courageous (after Jack had cried with a grin of modest pride, "Him dead now, inkosa-casa") and hit him several cuts with my whip, just to show my indignation at his having dared to invade the nursery and to drink up a cup of milk left for the baby. Baby woke up, and was delighted with the scrimmage, being extremely anxious to examine the dead snake, now dangling across Jack's stick. We all went about with fear and suspicion after that for some days, as the rooms all open on to the verandah, and the snakes are very fond of finding a warm, quiet corner to hibernate in. There is now a strict search instituted into all recesses—into cupboards, behind curtains, and especially into F——'s tall riding-boots—but although several snakes have been seen and killed quite close to the house, I am bound to say this is the only one which has come in-doors. Frogs hop in whenever they can, and frighten us out of our lives by jumping out upon us in the dark, as we always think it is a snake and not a frog which startles us. It requires a certain amount of persuasion and remonstrance now to induce any of us to go into a room first in the dark, and there have been many false alarms and needless shrieks caused by the lash of one of G——'s many whips, or even a boot-lace, getting trodden upon in the dark.

My Kafir princess listened courteously to a highly dramatic narrative of this snake adventure as conveyed to her through the medium of Maria. But then she listened courteously to everything, and was altogether as perfect a specimen of a well-bred young lady as you would wish to see anywhere. Dignified and self-possessed, without the slightest self-assumption or consciousness, with the walk of an empress and the smile of a child, such was Mazikali, a young widow about twenty years of age, whose husband (I can neither spell nor pronounce his name) had been chief of the Putili tribe, whose location is far away to the north-west of us, by Bushman's River, right under the shadow of the great range of the Drakensberg. This tribe came to grief in the late disturbances apropos of Langalibalele, and lost all their cattle, and what Mr. Wemmick would call their "portable property," in some unexplained way. We evidently consider that it was what the Scotch call "our blame," for every year there is a grant of money from our colonial exchequer to purchase this tribe ploughs and hoes, blankets and mealies, and so forth, but whilst the crops are growing it is rather hard times for them, and their pretty chieftainess occasionally comes down to Maritzburg to represent some particular case of suffering or hardship to their kind friend the minister for native affairs, who is always the man they fly to for help in all their troubles. Poor girl! she is going through an anxious time keeping the clanship open for her only son, a boy five years old, whom she proudly speaks of as "Captain Lucas," but whose real name is Luke.

I was drinking my afternoon tea as usual in the verandah one cold Sunday afternoon lately when Mazikali paid me this visit, so I had a good view of her as she walked up the drive attended by her maid of honor (one of whose duties is to remove stones and other obstructions from her lady's path), and closely followed by about a dozen elderly, grave "ringed" men, who never leave her, and are, as it were, her body-guard. There was something very pretty and pathetic, to any one knowing how a Kafir woman is despised by her lords and masters, in the devotion and anxious care and respect which these tall warriors and councilors paid to this gentle-eyed, grave-faced girl. Their pride and delight in my reception of her were the most touching things in the world. I went to meet her as she walked at the head of her followers with her graceful carriage and queenly gait. She gave me her hand, smiling charmingly, and I led her up the verandah steps and placed her in a large arm-chair, and two or three gentlemen who chanced to be there raised their hats to her. The delight of her people at all this knew no bounds: their keen dusky faces glowed with pride, and they raised their right hands in salutation before sitting down on the edge of the verandah, all facing their mistress, and hardly taking their eyes off her for a moment. Maria came to interpret for us, which she did very prettily, smiling sweetly; but the great success of the affair came from the baby, who toddled round the corner, and seeing this brightly-draped figure in a big chair, threw up his little hand and cried "Bayete!" It was quite a happy thought, and was rapturously received by the indunas with loud shouts of "Inkosi! inkosi!" whilst even the princess looked pleased in her composed manner. I offered her some tea, which she took without milk, managing her cup and saucer, and even spoon, as if she had been used to it all her life, though I confess to a slight feeling of nervousness, remembering the brittle nature of china as compared to calabashes or to Kafir wooden bowls. F—— gave each of her retinue a cigar, which they immediately crumbled up and took in the form of snuff with many grateful grunts of satisfaction.

Now, there is nothing in the world which palls so soon as compliments, and our conversation, being chiefly of this nature, began to languish dreadfully. Maria had conveyed to the princess several times my pleasure in receiving her, and my hope that she and her people would get over this difficult time and prosper everlastingly. To this the princess had answered that her heart rejoiced at having had its own way, and directed her up the hill which led to my house, and that even after she had descended the path again, it would eternally remember the white lady. This was indeed a figure of speech, for by dint of living in the verandah, rushing out after the children, and my generally gypsy habits, Mazikali is not very much darker than I am. All this time the little maid of honor had sat shivering close by, munching a large slice of cake and staring with her big eyes at my English nurse. She now broke silence by a fearfully distinct inquiry as to whether that other white woman was not a secondary or subsidiary wife. This question set Maria off into such fits of laughter, and covered poor little Nanna with so much confusion, that as a diversion I brought forward my gifts to the princess, consisting of a large crystal cross and a pair of ear-rings. The reason I gave her these ornaments was because I heard she had parted with everything of that sort she possessed in the world to relieve the distresses of her people. The cross hung upon a bright ribbon which I tied round her throat. All her followers sprang to their feet, waved their sticks and cried, "Hail to the chieftainess!" But, alas! there was a professional beggar attached to the party, who evidently considered the opportunity as too good to be lost, and drew Maria aside, suggesting that as the white lady was evidently enormously rich and very foolish, it would be as well to mention that the princess had only skins of wild beasts to wear (she had on a petticoat or kilt of lynx-skins, and her shoulders were wrapped in a gay striped blanket, which fell in graceful folds nearly to her feet), and suffered horribly from cold. He added that there never was such a tiresome girl, for she never *would* ask for anything; and how was she to get it without? Besides which, if she had such a dislike to asking for herself, she surely might speak about things for them: an old coat, now, or a hat, would be highly acceptable to himself, and so would a little money. But Mazikali turned quite fiercely on him, ordering him to hold his tongue, and demanding if that was tne way to receive kindness, by asking for more?

The beggar's remark, however, had the effect of drawing my attention to the princess's scanty garb. I have said it was a bitterly cold evening, and so the maid of honor pronounced it, shivering; so Nurse and I went to our boxes and had a good hunt, returning with a warm knitted petticoat, a shawl and two sets of flannel bathing-dresses. One was perfectly new, of crimson flannel trimmed with a profusion of white braid. Of course this was for the princess, and she and her maiden retired to Maria's room and equipped themselves, finding much difficulty, however, in getting into the bathing-suits, and marveling much at the perplexing fashion in which white women made their clothes. The maid of honor was careful to hang her solitary decorations, two small round bits of looking-glass, outside her skeleton suit of blue serge, and we found her an old woolen table-cover which she arranged into graceful shawl-folds with one clever twist of her skinny little arm. Just as they turned to leave the room, Maria told me, this damsel said, "Now, ma'am, if we only had a little red earth to color our foreheads, and a few brass rings, we should look very nice;" but the princess rejoined, "Whatever you do, don't ask

for anything;" which, I must say, I thought very nice. So I led her back again to her watchful followers, who hailed her improved appearance with loud shouts of delight. She then took her leave with many simple and graceful protestations of gratitude, but I confess it gave me a pang when she said with a sigh, "Ah, if all white inkosa-casas were like you, and kind to us Kafir-women!" I could not help thinking how little I had really done, and how much more we might all do.

I must mention that, by way of amusing Mazikali, I had shown her some large photographs of the queen and the royal family, explaining to her very carefully who they all were. She looked very attentively at Her Majesty's portrait, and then held it up to her followers, who rose of their own accord and saluted it with the royal greeting of "Bayete!" and as Mazikali laid it down again she remarked pensively, "I am very glad the great white chieftainess has such a kind face. I should not be at all afraid of going to tell her any of my troubles: I am sure she is a kind and good lady." Mazikali herself admired the princess of Wales' portrait immensely, and gazed at it for a long time, but I am sorry to say her followers persisted in declaring it was *only* a very pretty girl, and reserved all their grunts and shouts of respectful admiration for a portrait of the duke of Cambridge in full uniform. "Oh! the great fighting inkosi! Look at his sword and the feathers in that beautiful hat! How the hearts of his foes must melt away before his terrible and splendid face!" But indeed on each portrait they had some shrewd remark to make, tracing family likenesses with great quickness, and asking minute questions about relationship, succession, etc. They took a special interest in hearing about the prince of Wales going to India, and immediately wished His Royal Highness would come here and shoot buffalo and harte-beeste.

JUNE 15.

We had such a nice Cockney family picnic ten days ago, on Whit-Monday! F—— had been bewailing himself about this holiday beforehand, declaring he should not know what to do with himself, and regretting that holidays had ever been invented, and so on, until I felt that it was absolutely necessary to provide him with some out-door occupation for the day. There was no anxiety about the weather, for it is only too "set fair" all round, and the water shrinks away and the dust increases upon us day by day. But there was an anxiety about where to go and how to get to any place. "Such a bad road!" was the objection raised to every place I proposed, or else it was voted too far. At last all difficulties were met by a suggestion of spending a "happy day" at the falls of the lower Umgeni, only a dozen miles away, and the use of the mule-wagon. Everything was propitious, even to the materials for a cold dinner being handy, and we bundled in ever so many boys, Nurse and myself, and Maria in her brightest cotton frock and literally beaming with smiles, which every now and then broke out into a joyous, childish laugh of pure delight at nothing at all. *She* came to carry the baby, who loves her better than any one, and who understands Kafir better than English. The great thing was, that everybody had the companions they liked: as I have said, Baby had his Maria, F—— had secured a pleasant friend to ride with him, so as to be independent of the wagon, G—— had his two favorite little schoolfellows, and I—well, I had the luncheon-basket, and that was quite enough for me to think of. I kept remembering spasmodically divers omissions made in the hurry of packing it up; for, like all pleasant parties, it was quite *à l'imprévu*, and that made me rather anxious. It was really a delicious morning, sunny and yet cool, with everything around looking bright and glowing under the beautiful light. The near hills seemed to fold the little quiet town in soft round curves melting and blending into each other, whilst the ever-rising and more distant outlines showed exquisite indigo shadows and bold relief of purple and brown. The greenery of spring and summer is all parched and dried away now, but the red African soil takes in

the distance warm hues and tints which make up for the delicate coloring of young grass. Here and there, as it glows beneath the sun and a slow-sailing cloud casts a shadow, it changes from its own rich indescribable color to the purple of a heather-covered Scotch moor, but while one looks the cloud has passed away, and the violet tints die out, and it is again a bare red hillside which lies before you. A steep hillside, too, for the poor mules, but they breast it bravely at a jog trot, with their jangling bells and patient bowed heads, and we are soon at the top, looking down on the clouds of our own dust. The wind—or rather the soft air, for it is hardly a wind—blows straight in our faces as we trot on toward the south-west, and it drives the mass of finely-powdered dust raised by the heels of the six mules far behind us, to our great contentment and comfort. The two gentlemen on horseback are fain to keep clear of us and our dust, and to take a short cut whenever they can get off the highroad, which in this case and at this time of year is really a very good one. Inside the wagon, under the high hood, it is deliciously cool, but the boys are in such tearing spirits that I don't know what to do with them. Every now and then, when we are going up hill, they jump out of the wagon and search the hillside for a yellow flower, a sort of everlasting, out of the petals of which they extemporize shrill whistles; and when their invention in this line falls short, Maria steps in with a fresh suggestion. They make fearful pipes of reeds, they chirp like the grasshoppers, they all chatter and laugh together like so many magpies. When I am quite at my wits' end I produce buns, and these keep them quiet for full five minutes, but not longer.

At last, after two hours' steady up-hill pulling on the part of the mules, we have reached the great plateau from which the Umgeni takes its second leap, the first being at Howick. There, the sight of the great river rolling wide and swift between its high banks keeps the boys quiet with surprise and delight for a short space, and before they have found their tongues again the wagon has noisily crossed a resounding wooden bridge and drawn up at the door of an inn. Here the mules find rest and shelter, as well as their Hottentot drivers, whilst we are only beginning our day's work. As for the boys, their whole souls are absorbed in their fishing - rods: they grudge the idea of wasting time in eating dinner, and stipulate earnestly that they may be allowed to "eat fast." We find and charter a couple of tall Kafirs to carry the provision-baskets; F—— and his companion take careful and tender charge each of a bottle of beer; Maria shoulders the baby; I cling to my little teapot; Nurse seizes a bottle of milk, and away we all go down the dusty road again, over the bridge (the boys don't want to go a yard farther, for they see some Kafirs fishing below), across a burnt-up meadow, through scrub of terrible thorniness, and so on, guided by the rush and roar of the falling water, to our dining - room among the great boulders beneath the shade of the chief cascade. Unlike the one grand, concentrated leap of the river we saw at Howick, *here* it tumbles in a dozen places over a wide semicircular ledge of basalt. It is no joke to any one except the boys — who seem to enjoy tumbling about and grazing their elbows and chins—getting over the wet, slippery rocks which have to be crossed to get to the place we want. I tremble for the milk and the beer, and the teapot and I slip down repeatedly, but I am under no apprehension about Maria and the baby, for she plants her broad, big, bare feet firmly on the rocks, and steps over their wet, slippery surface with the ease and grace of a stout gazelle. Once, and once only, is she in danger, but it is because she is laughing so immoderately at the baby's suggestion, made in lisping Kafir when he first caught sight of the waterfall, that we should all have a bath there and then.

The falls are not in their fullest splendor to-day, for this is the dry season, and even the great Umgeni acknowledges the drain of burning sunshine day after day, and is rather more economical in her display of tumbling water and iridescent spray. Still, all is very beautiful, and in spite of our hunger—for we are all well-nigh ravenous—we climb various rocks of vantage to see the fine semicircle of cascades gleaming white among tufts of green scrub and massive boulders. In the wet season, of course, much that we see now of rock and tree is hidden by the greater volume of water, but they add greatly to the sylvan beauty of the fair scene. It is quite cold in the shade, but we have no choice, for where the sun shines invitingly there is not a foot of level rock and not an inch of soft white sand like the floor of our dining-room. Such an indignant twitter as the birds raise, hardly to be pacified by crumbs and scraps of the rapidly-vanishing bread and meat, salad and pudding! But the days are so short now that we cannot spare ourselves half the time we want either to eat or rest, or to linger and listen to the great monotonous roar of falling water, so agitating at first, so soothing after a little while. The boys have bolted their dinner, plunged their heads and hands under a tiny tricklet close by, and are off to the shallows beneath the bridge, where the river runs wide and low, where geese are cackling on the boulders, fish leaping in the pools, and Kafir lads laughing and splashing on the brink. We leave Baby and his nurse in charge of the birds' dinner until the men return for the lightened baskets, and we three "grown-ups" start for a sharp scramble up the face of the cliff, over the bed of a dry watercourse, to look at the wonderful expanse of the great river coming down from the purple hills on the horizon, sweeping across the vast, almost level, plain in a magnificent tranquil curve, wide as an inland lake, until it falls abruptly over the precipice before it. Scarcely a ripple on the calm surface, scarcely a quickening of its steady, tranquil flow, and yet it has gone, dropped clean out of sight, and that monotonous roar is the noise of its fall. I should like to see it in summer, when its stately progress is quickened and its limpid waters stained by the overflow of countless lesser streams into its broad bosom, and when its banks are fringed with tufts of tall white arum lilies — now only green folded leaves, shrunken as close to the water's edge as they can get —and when the carpet of violets beneath our feet is a sheet of blossom flecked with gayer flowers all over this great spreading veldt. To-day the wish of my heart, of all our hearts, is for a canoe apiece. Oh for the days of fairy thievery, to be able to swoop down upon Mr. Searle's yard and snatch up three perfect little canoes, paddles, sails, waterproof aprons and all, and put them down over there by that clump of lilies and crimson bushes! What a race we could have for clear eight miles up that shining reach, between banks which are never nearer than sixty or seventy feet to each other, and where the river is as smooth as glass, and free from let or hindrance to a canoe for all that distance! But, alas! there are neither roguish fairies nor stolen canoes to be seen—nothing except one's rough-and-ready fishing-rod and the everlasting mealie-meal worked into a paste for bait. We are too impatient to give it a fair trial, although the fish are leaping all around, for already the sun is traveling fast toward those high western hills, and when once he gets behind the tallest of the peaks darkness will be upon us in five minutes. We should be much more careful of our minutes even, did there not chance to be an early moon, already a silver disk in yonder bright blue sky. The homeward path is longer and easier, and leads us more circuitously back to the bridge, beneath which I am horrified to find G—— and his friends, their fishing-rods and one small fish on the bank, disporting themselves in the water, with nothing on save their hats. G—— is not at all dismayed at my shrill reproaches to him from the high bridge above, but suggests that I should throw him down my pocket handkerchief for a towel, and promises to dress and come up to the house directly. So I, with the thoughts of my tea in my mind—for we have not been able to have a fire at the falls—hurry up to the inn, and have time for a look round before the boys are ready. It is all so odd—such a strange jumble, such a thorough example of the queer upside-down fashion of colonizing which reigns here—that I cannot help describing it. A fairly good, straggling house with sufficiently good furniture, and plenty of it, and an apparent abundance of good glass and crockery. A sort of bar also, with substantial array of bottles and tins of biscuits and preserved meats and pickles of all sorts and kinds. But what I want you to bear in mind is, that all this came from England, and has finally been brought up here, nearly seventy miles from the coast, at an enormous trouble and expense. There are several young white people about the place, but a person of that class in Natal is too fine to work, and in five minutes I hear fifty complaints of want of labor and of the idleness of the Kafirs. There is no garden, no poultry - yard, no dairy. Here, with the means of irrigation at their very doors, with the possibility of food for cattle all the year round at the cost of a little personal trouble, there is neither a drop of milk nor an ounce of butter to be had. Nor an egg: "The fowls don't do so very well." I should think not, with such accommodation as they have in the way of water and food. For more than twenty years that house has stood there, a generation has grown up around it and in it, and yet it might as well have been built last year for all the signs of a homestead about it. There is somewhere a mealie-patch, and perhaps a few acres of green forage, and that is all. Now, in Australia or New Zealand, in a more rigorous climate, under far greater disadvantages, the dwellers in that house would have had farmyard and grain-fields, garden and poultry-yard, about them in five years, and all the necessary labor would have been performed by the master and mistress and their sons and daughters. Here they all sit in-doors, listless and discontented, grumbling because the Kafirs won't come and work for them. I can't make it out, and I confess I long to give all this sort of colonists a good shaking, and take away every single Kafir from them. I am sure they would get on a thousand times better. The only thing is, it is too late to shake energy and thrift into elderly or already grown-up people. They get on very well as it is, they say, and make money, which is all they care for, having no pride in neatness or order, and setting no value on the good opinion of others. They can sell their beer and pickles and tins of meat and milk at double and treble what they cost; and that is less fatiguing than digging and fencing and churning. So the tea has no milk and the bread no butter where twenty years ago cows were somewhere about five shillings apiece, and we get on as well as we can without them ; but I long, up to the very last, to shake them all round, especially the fat, pallid young people. Fortunately for Her Majesty's peace, I refrain from this expression of my opinion, and get myself and all my boys into the mule-wagon, and so off again, jogging homeward before the sun has dipped behind that great blue hill. Long ere we have gone halfway the daylight has all died away, and the boys find fresh cause for shouts of delight at the fantastic shadows the moon casts as she glides in and out of her cloud-palaces.

It would have been an enchanting drive home, wrapped up to the chin as we all were, except for the dust. What air there was came from behind us, from the same point as it had blown in the morning, but now we carried the dust along with us, and were powdered snow-white by it. Every hundred yards or so the drivers put on the brake and whistled to the mules to stop. They did not mind losing sight altogether of the leaders in a dense cloud of dust, nor even of the next pair, but when the wheelers were completely blotted out by the thick stirred-up mass of fine dust, then they thought it high time to pause and let it blow past us. But all this stopping made the return journey rather long and tedious, and all the curly little heads were nodding on our shoulders, only rousing up with a flicker of the day's animation when we came to where a grass-fire was sweeping over the veldt, and our road a dusty but wide and safe barrier against the sheets of crackling flame. All along the horizon these blazing belts showed brightly against the deep twilight sky, sometimes racing up the hills, again lighting up the valleys with yellow belt and circle of smoke and fire, but everywhere weird and picturesque beyond the power of words to tell.

I noticed during that drive what I have so often observed out here before—the curious layers of cold air. Sometimes we felt our wraps quite oppressive : generally, this was when we were at the top of a hill, or even climbing up it : then, when we were crossing a valley or a narrow ravine, we seemed to drive into an ice-cold region where we shivered beneath our furs ; and then again in five minutes the air would once more be soft and balmy—crisp and bracing indeed, but many degrees warmer than those narrow arctic belts here and there.

PART X.

I HAVE seen two Kafir weddings lately, and, oddly enough, by the merest chance they took place within a day or two of each other. The two extremes of circumstances, the rudest barbarism and the culminating smartness of civilization, seemed to jostle each other before my very eyes, as things do in a dream. And they went backward, too, to make it more perplexing, for it was the civilized wedding I saw first — the wedding of people whose mothers had been bought for so many cows, and whose marriage-rites had probably been celebrated with a stick, for your Kafir bridegroom does not understand coyness, and speedily ends the romance of courtship by a few timely cuffs.

Well, then, I chanced to be in town one of these fine bright winter mornings (which would be perfect if it were not for the dust), and I saw a crowd round the porch of the principal church. "What is going on?" I asked naturally, and heard, in broken English dashed with Dutch and Kafir, that there was an "umtyado" (excuse phonetic spelling), a "bruitlof," a "vedding." Hardly had I gathered the meaning of all these terms — the English being by far the most difficult to recognize, for they put a click in it — than the bridal party came out of church, formed themselves into an orderly procession and commenced to walk up the exceedingly dusty street two by two. They were escorted by a crowd of well-wishers and a still greater crowd of spectators — more or less derisive, I regret to state. But nothing upset the gravity and decorum of the bride and bridegroom, who walked first with a perfectly happy and self-satisfied expression of face. Uniforms were strictly excluded, and the groom and his male friends prided themselves on having discarded all their miscellaneous red coats for the day, and on being attired in suits of ready-made

tweed, in which they looked queerer than words can say. Boots also had they on their feet, to their huge discomfort, and white felt soft hats stuck more or less rakishly on their elaborately combed and woolly pates. The general effect of the gentlemen, I am sorry to say, was that of the Christy Minstrels, but the ladies made up for everything. I wish you could have seen the perfect ease and grace of the bride as she paced along with her flowing white skirts trailing behind her in the dust and her lace veil thrown over a wreath of orange-flowers and hanging to the ground. It was difficult to believe that probably not long ago she had worn a sack or a fold of coarse salempore as her sole clothing. She managed her draperies, all snowy white and made in the latest fashion, as if she had been used to long gowns all her life, and carried her head as though it had never known red clay or a basket of mealies. I could not see her features, but face and throat and bare arms were all as black as jet, and shone out in strong relief from among her muslin frills, and furbelows. There were many yards of satin ribbon among these same frills, and plenty of artificial flowers, but everything was all white, shoes and all. I am afraid she had "disremembered" her stockings. The principal couple were closely followed by half a dozen other pairs of sable damsels, also "gowned in pure white" and made wonderful with many bows of blue ribbon. Each maiden was escorted by a groomsman, the rear-guard of guests trailing off into colored cottons and patched suits. Everybody looked immensely pleased with him and herself, and I gradually lost sight of them in the unfailing cloud of dust which rises on the slightest provocation at this time of year. I assure you it was a great event, the first smart wedding in Maritzburg among the Kafirs, and I only hope the legal part is all right, and that the bridegroom won't be free to bring another wife home some day to vex the soul of this smart lady. Kafir marriage-laws are in a curious state, and present one of the greatest difficulties in the process of grafting civilized habits on the customs of utter barbarism.

In spite of the imposing appearance of bride and bridegroom, in spite of the good sign all this aping of our ways really is, in spite of a hundred considerations of that nature which ought to have weighed with me, but did not, I fear I took far more interest in a real Kafir marriage, a portion of whose preliminary proceedings I saw two days after this gala procession in white muslin and gray tweed. I was working in the verandah after breakfast — for you must know that it is so cold in-doors that we all spend the middle part of the day basking like lizards in the delicious warmth of sunny air outside — when I heard a distant but loud noise beyond the sod fence between us and a track leading over the hills, in whose hollows many a Kafir kraal nestles snugly. I knew it must be something unusual, for I saw all our Kafirs come running out in a state of great excitement, calling to each other to make haste. G—— too left the funeral obsequies of a cat-murdered pigeon in which he was busily employed, and scampered off to the gate, shouting to me to come and see. So I, who am the idlest mortal in the world, and dearly love an excuse for leaving whatever rational employment I am engaged upon, snatched up the baby, who was supremely happy digging in the dust in the sunshine, called Maria in case there might be anything to explain, and ran off to the gate also. But there was nothing to be seen, not even dust: we only heard a sound of monotonous singing and loud grunting coming nearer and nearer, and by and by a muffled tread of bare hurrying feet shuffling through the powdered earth of the track. My own people had clambered up on the fence, and were gesticulating wildly and laughing and shouting, Tom waving the great wooden spoon

with which he stirs his everlasting "scoff." "What is it, Maria?" I asked. Maria shook her head and looked very solemn, saying "I doan know," but even while she spoke a broad grin broke all over her face, and she showed her exquisite teeth from ear to ear as she said, half contemptuously, "It's only a wild Kafir wedding, lady. There are the warriors: that's what they do when they don't know any better." Evidently, Maria inclined to the long white muslin gown of the civilized bride which I had so minutely described to her, and she turned away in disdain.

Yes, here they come—first, a body of stalwart warriors dressed in skins, with immense plumes of feathers on their heads, their lithe, muscular bodies shining like ebony as they flash past me— not so quickly, however, but that they have time for the *politesse* of tossing up shields and spears with a loud shout of "Inkosi!" which salutation the baby, who takes it entirely to himself, returns with great gravity and unction. These are the vanguard, the flower of Kafir chivalry, who are escorting the daughter of a chieftain to her new home in a kraal on the opposite range of hills. They make it a point of honor to go as quickly as possible, for they are like the stroke oar and give the time to the others. After them come the male relatives of the bride, a motley crew, numerous, but altogether wanting in the style and bearing of the warriors. Their garb, too, is a wretched mixture, and a compromise between clothes and no clothes, and they shuffle breathlessly along, some with sacks over their shoulders, some with old tunics of red or blue and nothing else, and some only with two flaps or aprons. But all wear snuffboxes in their ears—snuffboxes made of every conceivable material—hollow reeds, cowries, tiger-cats' teeth, old cartridge-cases, acorn-shells, empty chrysalises of some large moth — all sorts of miscellaneous rubbish which could by any means be turned to this use. Then comes a more compact and respectable-looking body of men, all with rings on their heads, the Kafir sign and token of well-to-do-ness, with bare legs, but draped in bright-colored rugs or blankets. They too fling up their right arm and cry "Inkosi!" as they race along, but are more intent on urging on their charge, the bride, who is in their midst. Poor girl! she has some five or six miles yet to go, and she looks ready to drop now; but there seems to be no consideration for her fatigue, and I observe that she evidently shrinks from the sticks which her escort flourish about. She is a good-looking, tall girl, with a nice expression in spite of her jaded and hurried air. She wears only a large sheet of coarse brownish cloth draped gracefully and decently around her, leaving, however, her straight, shapely legs bare to run. On her right arm she too bears a pretty little shield made of dun and white ox hide, and her face is smeared over brow and cheeks with red clay, her hair also being tinged with it. She glances wistfully, I fancy, at Maria standing near me in her good clothes and with her fat, comfortable look. Kafir girls dread being married, for it is simply taking a hard place without wages. Love has very rarely anything to do with the union, and yet the only cases of murder of which I have heard have been committed under the influence of either love or jealousy. This has always seemed odd to me, as a Kafir girl does not appear at all prone to one or the other. When I say to Maria, "Perhaps you will want to marry some day, Maria, and leave me?" she shakes her head vehemently, and says, "No, no, I should not like to do that: I should have to work much harder, and no one would be kind to me." Maria too looks compassionately at her savage sister racing along, and murmurs, "Maria would not like to have to run so fast as that." Certainly, she is not in good condition for a hand gallop across these hills, for she is bursting out of all her gowns, although she is growing very tall as well.

There is no other woman in the bridal cavalcade, which is a numerous one, and closes with a perfect mob of youths and boys grunting and shuffling along. Maria says doubtfully, "I think they are only taking that girl to look at her kraal. She won't be married just yet, for they

say the heer is not ready so soon." This information is shouted out as some of the party rush past us, but I cannot catch the exact words amid the loud monotonous song with a sort of chorus or accompaniment of grunts.

Ever since my arrival I have wanted to see a real Kafir kraal, but the difficulty has been to find one of any size and retaining any of the distinctive features of such places. There are numbers of them all about the hills which surround Maritzburg, but they are poor degenerate things, the homes of the lowest class of Kafir, a savage in his most disgusting and dangerous state of transition, when he is neither one thing nor the other, and has picked up only the vices of civilization. Such kraals would be unfavorable specimens of a true Kafir village, and only consist of half a dozen ruinous, filthy hovels whose inhabitants would probably beg of you. For some time past I had been inquiring diligently where a really respectable kraal could be found, and at last I heard of one about eight miles off, whose "induna" or head-man gave it a very good character. Accordingly, we set out on a broiling afternoon, so early in the day that the sun was still beating down on us with all his summer tricks of glowing heat and a fierce fire of brightest rays. The road was steep over hill and dale, and it was only when we had climbed to the top of each successive ridge that a breath of cool breeze greeted us. A strange and characteristic panorama gradually spread itself out before and behind us. After the first steep ascent we lost sight of Maritzburg and its bosky streets. From the next ridge we could well see the regular ring of wooded homesteads which lie in a wide circle outside the primitive little town. Each rising down had a couple or so of these suburban villas hid away in gum trees clinging to its swelling sides. Melancholy-looking sides they were now, and dreary was the immediate country around us, for grass-fires had swept the hills for a hundred miles and more, and far as the eye could reach all was black, sere and arid, the wagon-tracks alone winding about in dusty distinctness. The streams had shrunk away to nothing. and scarcely showed between their high banks. It was a positive relief to horse and rider when we had clambered up the rocky track across the highest saddle we had yet needed to mount. Close on our left rose, some three hundred feet straight up against the brass-bright sky, a big bluff with its basalt sides cut down clean and sharp as though by a giant's knife. In its cold shade a few stunted bushes were feebly struggling to keep their scraggy leaves and branches together, and on the right the ground fell irregularly away down to a valley in which were lovely patches of young forage, making a tender green oasis, precious beyond words in contrast with the black and sun-dried desolation of the hills around. Here too were the inevitable gum trees, not to be despised at this ugly time of year, although they are for all the world like those stiff wooden trees, all of one pattern, peculiar to the model villages in the toys of our youth. With quite as little grace and beauty do these gum trees grow, but yet they are the most valuable things we possess, being excellent natural drainers of marshy soil, kindly absorbers of every stray noxious vapor, and good amateur lightning-conductors into the bargain. Amid these much-abused, not-to-be-done-without trees, then, a gable 'peeped : it was evidently a thriving, comfortable homestead, yet here my friendly guide and companion drew rein and looked around with deep perplexity on his kindly face.

"How beautiful the view is !" I cried in delight, for indeed the distant sweep of ever-rising mountains, the splendid shadows lying broad and deep over the hills and valleys, the great Umgeni, disdaining even this long drought, and shining here and there like a silver ribbon, now widening into a mere, now making almost an island of some vast tract of country, but always journeying "with a gentle ecstasy," were all most beautiful. The burnt-up patches gave only a brown umber depth to the hollows in the island hills, and the rich red soil glowed brightly on the bare downs around us as the westering sun touched and warmed them

into life and color. I was well content to drop the reins on my old horse's neck whilst I gazed with greedy eyes on the fair scene, which I felt would change and darken in a very short while. Perhaps it was also this thought which made my companion say anxiously, "Yes, but look how fast the sun is dropping behind that high hill ; and *where* is the kraal ? It ought to be exactly here, according to Mazimbulu's directions, and yet I don't see a sign of it, do you ?"

If his eyes, accustomed since childhood to every nook and cranny in these hills, could not make out where the kraal hid, little chance was there of mine finding it out. But even he was completely at fault, and looked anxiously around like a deer-hound which has lost the scent. The narrow track before us led straight on into the interior for a couple of hundred miles, and in all the panorama at our feet we could not see trace or sign of living creature, nor could the deadliest silence bring sound of voice or life to our strained ears.

"I dare not take you any farther," Mr. Y—— said : "it is getting much too late already. But how provoking to come all this way and have to go back without finding the kraal !" In vain I tried to comfort him by assurances of how pleasant the ride had been, beguiled by many a hunting-story of days when lions and elephants drank at the stream before us, and when no man's hand ever lost its clasp of his gun, sleeping or waking. We had come to see a kraal, and it was an expedition *manqué* if we could not find it. Still, the sun seemed in a tremendous hurry to reach the shelter of that high hill yonder, and even I was constrained to acknowledge we must not go farther along the rocky track before us. At this moment of despair there came swiftly and silently round the sharp edge of the bluff just ahead of us two Kafir-women, with huge bundles of firewood on their heads, and walking rapidly along, as though in a hurry to get home. To my companion Kafir was as familiar as English, so he was at no loss for pleasant words and still more pleasant smiles with which to ask the way to Mazimbulu's kraal.

"We go there now, O great chieftain!" the women answered with one voice; and, true to the savage code of politeness, they betrayed no surprise as to what *we* could possibly want at their kraal so late. We had scarcely noticed a faint narrow track on the burnt-up ground to our right, but into this the women unhesitatingly struck, and we followed them as best we could. Scarcely three hundred yards away from the main track, round the shoulder of a down, and nestling close in a sort of natural basin scooped out of the hillside, was the kraal, silent enough now, for all except a few old men and babies were absent. The women, like our guides, were out collecting firewood; some of the younger men and bigger children had gone into town to sell poultry and eggs; others were still at work for the farmer whose homestead stood a mile or two away. There must have been at least a hundred goats skipping about beneath the steep hillside down which we had just come—goats who had ventured to the very edge of the shelf along which our bridle-path had lain, and yet who had never by bleat or inquisitive protruded head betrayed their presence to us. In the centre of the excavation stood a large, high, neatly-wattled fence, forming an enclosure for the cattle at night, a remnant of the custom when Kafir herds were ravaged by wild animals and still wilder neighbors. A very small angle of this place was portioned off as a sty for the biggest and mangiest pig it has ever been my lot to behold—a gaunt and hideous beast, yet the show animal of the kraal, and the first object which Mazimbulu pointed out to us. Of course, Mazimbulu was at home: what is the use of being an induna if you have to exert yourself? He came forward at once to receive us, and did the honors of his kraal most thoroughly and with much grace and dignity. Mr. Y—— explained that I was the wife of another inkosi, and that I was consumed by a desire to see with my own eyes a real Kafir kraal. It is needless to say that this was pleasantly conveyed, and a compliment to this particular kraal neatly introduced here.

Mazimbulu—an immensely tall, powerful elderly man, "ringed" of course, and draped in a large gay blanket—looked at me with half-contemptuous surprise, but saluted to carry off his wonder, and said deprecatingly to Mr. Y——: "O chief, the chieftainess is welcome; but what a strange people are these whites! They have all they can desire, all that is good and beautiful of their own, yet they can find pleasure in looking at where we live! Why, chief, you know their horses and dogs have better places to sleep in than we have. It is all most wonderful, but the chieftainess may be sure we are glad to see her, no matter for what reason she comes."

There was not very much to see, after all. About twenty large, substantial, comfortable huts, all of the beehive shape, stood in a crescent, the largest in the middle. This belonged to Mazimbulu, and in front of it knelt his newest wife, resting on her heels and cutting up pumpkins into little bits to make a sort of soup, or what she called "scoff." I think young Mrs. Mazimbulu was one of the handsomest and sulkiest Kafir-women I have yet seen. She was very smart in beads and bangles, her coiffure was elaborate and carefully stained red, her blanket and petticoat were gay and warm and new, and yet she looked the very picture of ill-humor. The vicious way she cut up her pumpkins and pitched the slices into a large pot, the sarcastic glances she cast at Mazimbulu as he invited me to enter his hut, declaring that he was so fortunate in the matter of wives that I should find it the pink of cleanliness! Nothing pleased her, and she refused to talk to me or to "saka bono," or anything. I never saw such a shrew, and wondered whether poor Mazimbulu had not indeed got a handful in this his latest purchase. And yet he looked quite capable of taking care of himself, and his hand had probably lost none of its old cunning in boxing a refractory bride's ears, for the damsel in question seemed rather on the watch as to how far she might venture to show her temper. Such a contrast as her healthy, vigorous form made to that of a slight, sickly girl who crawled out of an adjoining hut to see the wonderful spectacle of an "inkosa-casa"! This poor thing was a martyr to sciatica, and indeed had rheumatism apparently in all her joints. She moved aside her kilt of lynx skins to show me a terribly swollen knee, saying plaintively in Kafir, "I ache all over, for always." Mazimbulu declared in answer to my earnest inquiries that they were all very kind to her, and promised faithfully that a shilling which I put in her hand should remain her own property. "Physic or beads, just as she likes," he vowed, but seemed well content when I gave another coin into his own hand for snuff. There were not many babies —only three or four miserable sickly creatures, all over sores and dirt and ophthalmia. Yet the youth who held our horses whilst we walked about and Mr. Y—— chatted fluently with Mazimbulu might have stood for the model of a bronze Apollo, so straight and tall and symmetrical were his shapely limbs and his lithe, active young body. He too shouted "Inkosa-casa!" in rapturous gratitude for a sixpence which I gave him, and vowed to bring me fowls to buy whenever the young chickens all around should be big enough.

My commissariat is always on my mind, and I never lose an opportunity of replenishing it, but I must confess that I get horribly cheated whenever I try bargaining on my own account. For instance, I sent out a roving commission the other day for honey, which resulted in the offer of a small jar containing perhaps one pound of empty, black and dirty comb and a tablespoonful of honey, which apparently had already been used to catch flies. For this treasure eight shillings were asked. To-day I tried to buy a goat from Mazimbulu, but he honestly said it would be of no use to me, nor could I extract a promise of milk from the cows I saw coming home just then. He declared that there was no milk to be had; and certainly, when one looks at the surrounding pasture, it is not incredible.

Mazimbulu's own hut contained little beyond a stool or two, some skins and mats for a bed, a heap of mealie-husks with which to replenish the fire, his shield and a bundle of assegais and knobkerries. There was another smaller wattled enclosure holding a great store of mealies, and another piled up with splendid pumpkins. At the exact top of Mazimbulu's hut stood a perfect curiosity-shop of lightning-charms — old spear-points, shells, the broken handle of a china jug, and a painted portion of some child's toy: all that is mysterious or unknown to them must perforce be a lightning-charm. They would no more use a conductor than they would fly, declaring triumphantly that our houses, for all their "fire-wires," get more often struck by lightning than their huts. Indeed, Mazimbulu became quite pathetic on the subject of the personal risk I was running on account of my prejudice against his lightning-charms, and hinted that I should come to a bad end some day through it.

By the time we had spent half an hour in the kraal the sun had long since gained the shelter of the western hills and sunk behind them, taking with him apparently every vestige of daylight out of the sky. No one who has not felt it could believe the rapidity of the change in the temperature. So long as there was sunlight it was too hot. In half an hour it was bitingly, bitterly cold. We could not go fast down the rocky tracks, but we cantered over every inch of available space—cantered for the sake of warming ourselves as much as to get home. The young moon gave us light enough to keep on the right track, but I don't think I ever was so cold in my life as when we reached home about half-past six. The wood-fire in the little drawing-room—the only room with a fireplace—seemed indeed delicious, and so did a cup of tea so hot as to be almost scalding. F—— declared that I was of a bright-blue color, and I admit that I came nearer to understanding what being frozen to death meant than I had ever done before. Yet there was not much frost, but one suffered from the reaction after the burning heat of the day and from the impossibility of taking any wraps with one.

Don't think I am going to let you off from my usual monthly grumble about the weather. Not a bit of it! It is worse than ever. At this moment a violent and bitterly cold gale of wind is blowing, and I hear the red tiles flying off the house, which I fully expect will be a regular sieve by the time the rains come. Not one drop of rain have we had these six weeks, and people remark that "the dry season is *beginning.*" Everything smells and tastes of dust—one's clothes, the furniture, everything. If I sit down in an arm-chair, I disturb a cloud of dust; my pillow is, I am convinced, stuffed with it; my writing-table is inches deep in it. All the food is flavored with it, and Don Quixote's enemies could not more persistently "bite the dust" than we do at each meal. Yet when I venture to mention this drawback in answer to the usual question, "Is not this delicious weather?" the answer is always, "Oh, but you can have no dust *here:* you should see what it is in town!" Between us and the town is an ever-flying scud of dust, through which we can but ill discern the wagons. I wonder there are no accidents, for one often *hears* a wagon before and behind one when it is impossible to *see* anything through the choking, suffocating cloud around one. Of a still day, when you carry your own dust quietly along with you, there is nothing for it except to stop at home if you wish to keep your temper. The other day little G—— was about to suffer the extreme penalty of the domestic law for flagrant disobedience, and he remarked dryly to the reluctant executioner, "You had better take care : *I am very dusty.*" It was quite true, for the slipper elicited such clouds of dust from the little blue serge suit that the chastisement had to be curtailed, much to the culprit's satisfaction. As for the baby, he was discovered the other day taking a dust-bath exactly like the chickens, and considered it very hard to be stopped in his amusement. Every now and then we have a dust-storm : there have been two this month already, perfect hurricanes of cold wind driving the dust in solid sheets before them.

Nearer the coast these storms have been followed by welcome rain, but here we are still dry and parched. The only water-supply we (speaking individually) have is brought in buckets from the river, about half a mile off, and one has to wash in it and drink it with closed eyes. But it cannot be unwholesome, thank Heaven! for most of us take nothing else and are very well. I owe it a grudge, however, on account of its extraordinary hardness. Not only does it spoil the flavor of my beloved tea, but it chaps our skins frightfully; and what with the dust in the pores, and the chronic irritation caused by some strange peculiarity in the climate, we are all like nutmeg-graters, and one can understand the common-sense of a Kafir's toilette, into which grease enters largely. Yet in spite of dust and dryness — for everything is ludicrously dry, sugar and salt are so many solid cakes, not to be dealt with by means of a spoon at all—one is very thankful for the cold, bracing weather, and unless there is a necessity for fronting the dust, we contrive to enjoy many of the pleasant sunshiny hours in the verandah; and I rejoice to see the roses blooming again in the children's cheeks. Every evening we have a wood-fire on the open hearth in the drawing-room, and there have been sharp frosts lately. The waving tips of the poor bamboos look sadly yellow, but I have two fine flourishing young camellias out of doors without shelter of any kind, and my supply of roses has never failed from those trees which get regularly watered. The foliage, too, of the geraniums is as luxuriant as ever, though each leaf is white with dust, but the first shower will make them lovely once more.

Quail passed over here a few days ago in dense, solid clouds, leaving many weary stragglers here and there on the veldt to delight the sportsmen. I am told it is a strange and wonderful sight to see these birds sweep—sometimes in the dead silence of a moonlight night, flying low and compactly, beating the air with the monotonous whir of their untiring wings — down one of the wide, empty streets of quiet Maritzburg, so close to the bystander that a stick would knock some over. And to think of the distance they have traveled thus! For hundreds and hundreds of miles, over deserts and lakes at whose existence we can but dimly guess, the little wayfarers have journeyed, from the far interior down to the seaboard of this great continent. Last season a weary pair dropped down among my rose-bushes, but no sportsman knew of their visit, for I found them established there when I came, and jealously guarded their secret for them; but I don't know yet whether any others have claimed my hospitality and protection, in the same way, poor pretty creatures!

I was seized with a sudden wish the other day to see the market here, and accordingly got my household up very early one of these cold mornings, hurried breakfast over, and drove down to the market-square exactly at nine A. M., when the sales commence. Everything is sold by auction, but sold with a rapidity which seemed magical to me. I saw some fine potatoes a dozen yards away from where the market-master was selling with lightning speed wagon-load after wagon-load of fresh green forage. I certainly heard "Two and a halfpenny, two and three farthings — thank you! gone!" coming rather near, and I had gone so far in my own mind as to determine which of my friends—for heaps of people I knew were there—I should ask to manage it for me. But like a wave the bidding swept over my potatoes—I quite looked upon them as mine—and they were gone. So, as I did not want any firewood, and there were only about a dozen huge wagons piled high up with lopped branches and limbs of trees, and as I had begun to perceive that a dozen wagon-loads were nothing to the rapid utterance of the market-master, I went into the market-hall to look at the fruit and vegetables, eggs and butter, with which the tables were fairly well covered. There was very little poultry, and a pair of ducks toward which I felt somewhat attracted went for six shillings sixpence each, directly the bidding began. So I consoled myself by purchasing, still

in a vicarious manner by means of a friend, three turkeys. *Such* a bargain! the only cheap things I have seen in Natal. Only nine shillings ninepence apiece!—beautiful full-grown turkeys— two hens and a cock, just what I wanted. Of course, everybody clustered round me, and began to damp my joy directly by pouring statistics into my ears of the mortality among turkey-chicks and the certain ill-fortune which would attend my efforts to rear them. But it is too early in the season yet for such anxieties, and I am free for the next two months to admire my turkeys as much as I choose without breaking my heart over the untimely fate of their offspring. Yes, these turkeys were the only cheap things : butter sold easily at three shillings ninepence a pound, eggs at three shillings a dozen, and potatoes and other vegetables at pretty nearly Covent Garden prices. It gave one a good idea of the chronic state of famine even so little a town as this lives in to see the clean sweep made of every single thing, live and dead— always excepting my turkeys — in ten minutes after the market-master entered the building. I am sure treble the quantity would have been snapped up quite as quickly. Such odd miscellaneous things!—bacon, cheese, pumpkins, all jumbled together. Then outside for a few moments, to finish up with a few wheelbarrows of green barley, a basket or two of mealies, and some fagots of firewood brought in by the Kafirs; and lo! in something less than an hour it was all over, and hungry Maritzburg had swallowed up all she could get for the day. The market-master was now at liberty — after explaining to a Kafir or two that it was not, strictly speaking, right to sell your wheelbarrow-load twice over, once privately and once publicly— to show me the market-hall, a very creditable building, large and commodious, well roofed and lighted. Knowing as I did the exceeding slowness of building operations in Maritzburg, it struck me as little less than marvelous to hear that it had actually been run up in twenty-one days. No lesser pressure than Prince Alfred's visit about fifteen years ago could have induced such Aladdin-like rapidity; but the loyal Maritzburgers wanted to give their sailor-prince a ball, and there was no room in the whole town capable of holding one-quarter of the people who wanted to see the royal midshipman. So Kafirs and whites and men of all colors fell to with a will, and hammered night and day until all was finished, extempore chandeliers of painted hoops dangling in all directions, flowers and flags hiding the rough-and-ready walls, and the "lion and the unicorn fighting for the crown" in orthodox fashion over the doorway, where they remain to this day. The only thing that puzzles me is whether the floor was at all more even then than now, for at present it is nearly as much up and down as the waves of the Indian Ocean.

Now, too, that there were no more domestic purchases to be made, I could look about and see how quaint and picturesque it all was. In summer the effect must really be charming with the double bordering of acacia trees fresh and green instead of leafless and dusty; the queer little Dutch church, with its hugely disproportionate weathercock shining large and bright in the streaming sunlight; the teams of patient bullocks moving slowly off again through the dust with wagons of forage or firewood to be dragged to their various destinations; and the fast-melting, heterogeneous crowd of Kafirs and coolies, Dutch and English — some with baskets, some with dangling poultry or carefully-carried tins of eggs, but *none* with turkeys. The market-hall and its immediate vicinity became quite deserted, but the crowd seemed reassembling a little lower down, where a weekly auction was being held in a primitive fashion out in the open air beneath the acacia trees. A stalwart Kafir wandered about listlessly ringing a large bell, and the auctioneer, mounted on a table, was effecting what he called a clearance sale, apparently of all the old rubbish in the place. Condemned military stores, such as tents and greatcoats, pianos from which the very ghost of tone had fled years ago, cracked china, broken chairs, crinolines, fiddles, kettles, faded pictures under fly-blown glasses, empty bottles, old baskets, —all were "going, going, gone" whilst we stood there, drifting away to other homes all over the place. I pass every day an ingenious though lowly family mansion made solely and entirely of the sheets of zinc out of boxes, fastened together in some strange fashion : roof, walls, flooring, all are of it. There is neither door nor window facing the road, so I don't know how they are put in, but I can imagine how that hovel must creak in a high wind. What mysterious law of gravitation keeps it down to the ground I have failed to discover, nor do I know how the walls are supported even in their leaning position. Well, I saw the owner of this cot, a Dutchman, buying furniture, and he was very near purchasing the piano under the impression it was a folding-up bedstead. I have always taken such an interest in the zinc dwelling that it was with difficulty I could refrain from giving my opinion about its furniture.

But the sun is getting high, and it is ten o'clock and past—quite time for all housewives to be at home and the men at their business; so the clearance sale ends like a transformation-scene. Kafirs hoist ponderous burdens on their heads and walk off unconcernedly with them, and the odds and ends of what were once household goods disappear round the corner. My early rising makes me feel as dissipated as one does after going to a wedding, and I can't help a reluctance to go back to the daily routine of G——'s lessons and baby's pinafores, it seems so delightful to idle about in the sunshine in spite of the dust. What is there to do or to see? What excuse can any one find at a moment's notice to prevent my going home just yet? It is an anxious thought, for there is nothing to do, and nothing to see beyond wagons and oxen, in the length and breadth of Maritzburg.. Some one fortunately recollects *the* mill—there is only one in the whole place—and avers that wool-scouring is going on there at the present time. At all events, it is a charming drive, and in five minutes we are trotting along, raising a fine cloud of dust on the road which leads to the park. When the river-side has been reached—

poor, shrunken Umsindusi! it is a mere rivulet now, and thoroughly shrunken and depressed—we turn off and follow the windings of the banks for a few hundred yards till we come to where the mill-wheel catches and makes use of a tiny streamlet just as it is entering the river. It is a very picturesque spot, although the immediate country around is flat and uninteresting; but there is such a profusion of willow trees, such beautiful tufts of tall willow-ferns, such clumps of grasses, that the old brick buildings are hidden and shaded by all manner of waving branches. Then in front is the inevitable wagon, the long, straggling span of meagre oxen with their tiny black forelooper and attendant Kafirs. This is indeed beginning at the end of the story, for into the wagon big neat bales all ready for shipment—bales which have been "dumped" and branded—are being lowered by a crane out of a large upper story. Very different do these bales look as they now depart from those in which the wool arrives. With the characteristic untidiness and makeshift fashion of the whole country, the wool is loosely and carelessly stuffed into inferior bales, which become ragged and filthy by the time they reach this, and are a discredit to the place as they pass along the streets. That is the state in which it is brought here and delivered over to the care of the wool-scourers. The first step is to sort it all, sift the coarsest dirt out of it, and then away it goes, first into a bath of soda and water, and afterward into many succeeding tubs of cooler water, until at last it emerges, dripping indeed, but cleansed from burrs and seeds, and white as the driven snow, to be next laid out on a terrace sheltered from dust and wind and dried rapidly under the burning South African sun. Then there is the steam-press, which squeezes it tightly into these neat, trim bales, and a hydraulic machine which gives it that one turn more of the screw which is supposed to constitute the difference between neuralgia and gout, but which here marks the difference between "dumped" and "undumped" bales. The iron bands are riveted with a resounding clang or two, the letters are rapidly brushed in over their iron plate, and the bale is pronounced finished. A very creditable piece of work it is, too—neat and tidy outside and fair and honest inside. I heard none of the usual excuses for dirt and untidiness—no "Oh, one cannot get the Kafirs to do anything." There was a sufficiency of Kafirs at work under the eyes of the masters, but there was no ill-temper or rough language. All was methodical and business-like, every detail seen to and carried thoroughly out from first to last, and the result something to be proud of. The machinery combed and raked and dipped with monotonous patience, and many an ingenious connecting-rod or band saved time and labor. I declare it was the most encouraging and satisfactory thing I have seen since I came, apart from the real pleasure of looking at a bale of wool turned out as it used to be from every wool-shed in New Zealand, instead of the untidy bundles one sees slowly traveling down to Durham, not even well packed in the wagons. Apart from this, it is inspiriting to see the resources of the place made the best of, and everything kept up to the mark of a high standard of excellence. There were no incomplete or makeshift contrivances, and the two bright, active young masters going about and seeing to everything themselves, as colonists ought to do, were each a contrast to the ordinary loafing, pale-faced, unkempt overseer of half a dozen creeping Kafirs that represent the labor-market here.

I feel, however, as if I were rather "loafing" myself, and am certainly very idle, for it is past midday before G—— has half enough examined the establishment and tumbled often enough in and out of the wool-press; so we leave the cool shade of the willows and the mesmeric throb of the mill-wheel, and drive home through the dust once more to our own little house on the hill.

Ever since I began this letter I have been wanting to tell you of an absurd visitor I had the other day, and my poor little story has very nearly been crowded out by other things. A couple of mornings ago I was very busy making a new cotton skirt for "Malia"—for I am her sole dressmaker, and she keeps me at work always, what with growing into a stout grenadier of a girl, and what with rending these skirts upon all occasions. Well, I was getting over the seams at a fine rate on the sewing-machine, which I had moved out into the verandah for light and warmth, when I became aware of a shadow between me and the sun. It was a very little shadow, and the substance of it was the tiniest old Dutchman you ever saw in your life. I assure you my first idea was that I must be looking at a little goblin, he was so precisely like the pictures one sees in the illustrations of a fairy-tale. His long waistcoat of a gay-flowered chintz, his odd, square-tailed coat and square shoes, his wide, short breeches and pointed hat were all in keeping with the goblin theory. But his face! I was too startled to laugh, but it ought to have been sketched on the spot. No apple ever was more rosy, no snake-skin ever more wrinkled. Eyes, blue and keen as steel, gleamed out at me from beneath enormous shaggy brows, and his nose and chin were precisely like Punch's. I wonder what he thought of *me ? My* eyes were as round as marbles, and I do believe my mouth was wide open. He gave a sort of nod, and in a strange dialect said something to which I in my bewilderment answered "Ja," being the one single word of Dutch I know. This misleading reply encouraged my weird visitor to sit down on the steps before me, to take off his hat, mop his thin, long gray locks, and to launch forth with much pantomime into a long story of which I did not understand one word, for the simple reason that it was all literally in High Dutch. Here was a pretty predicament!—alone with a goblin to whom I had just told a flat falsehood, for evidently his first inquiry, of which I only caught the word "Hollands," and which I imagined to refer to gin, must have been a demand as to whether I understood his language! And I had said "Ja!" It was dreadful. In my dismay I remembered having heard

somebody say "Nic," and I even followed it up with a faltering "Stehts nic" ("I don't understand"), which also came to me in my extremity. This contradictory answer puzzled my old gentleman, and he looked at me frowningly; but I had always heard that courage is everything with goblins, so I smiled and said inquiringly "Ja?" again. He shook his head reprovingly, and then by the aid of ticking off each word on his fingers, and stopping at it until he thought I understood, he contrived, by means of German and English and Kafir, only breaking out into Dutch at the very interesting parts, to tell me that he was in search of a little black ox. I must clearly understand that it was "schwartz," and also that the "pfennigs" it had cost were many. The ox seems to have been a regular demon if his story was anything like true. No rest had he had (here a regular pantomime of going to sleep); from over Berg had he come; he had bought this wayward beast from one Herr Schmidt, an inkosi. A great deal of shaking of the head here, which must have meant that this Herr Inkosi had cheated him. Yet I longed to ask how one could get the better of a goblin. I didn't know it was to be done. From the moment the "klein schwartz" ox changed masters my small friend's troubles began. "Früh in de morgen" did that ox get away every day: in vain was it put in kraals at night,.in vain did Kafirs search for it (great acting here of following up a spoor): it was over the berg and far away. He was drie tags mit nodings to eat av mealies. It was a long story, but the *refrain* was always, "Vere hat dat leetel ox, dat schwartzen ox, got to?" If I am to say the exact truth, he once demanded, "Vere das teufels dat leetel ox hat be?" but I looked so shocked that he took off his steeple-crowned hat deprecatingly. "Sprechen Sie Kafir?" I asked in despair, but it was no better. His countenance brightened, and he went through it all again in Kafir, and the "inkomo" was quite as prominent as the ox had been. Of course *I* meant that he should speak to some of my Kafirs about it if he knew their language. I believe we should have been there to this day talking gibberish to each other if little G—— had not appeared suddenly round the corner and taken the matter into his own hands.

"Why, what a queer old man that is, mumsey! Wherever *did* you find him, and what *does* he want?" G—— demanded with true colonial brevity.

"I *think* he is looking for a little black ox," I answered guardedly.

"Ja, wohl, dat is it—ein leetel black ox, my tear" (I trust he meant G——).

"Oh, all right!" G—— shouted, springing up. "Osa (come), old gentleman. There's rather a jolly little black bullock over there: I know, because I've been with Jack there looking for a snake."

The goblin was on his feet in a moment, with every wrinkle on the alert. "Danks, my tear umfan: du air ein gut leetel boy. Früh in de morgen;" and so on with the whole story over again to G——, who understood him much better than I did, and gave me quite a minute account of the "leetel black ox's" adventures. The last thing G—— saw of it it was taking a fence like a springbok, with the goblin and three Kafirs in full chase after it.

PART XI.

THE brief winter season seems already ended and over, so far as the crisp, bracing atmosphere is concerned. For many days past it has been not only very hot in the sun, but a light hot air has brooded over everything. Not strong enough to be called a hot wind, it is yet like the quivering haze out of a furnace-mouth. I pity the poor trees: it is hard upon them. Not a drop of rain has fallen for three months to refresh their dried-up leaves and thirsting roots, and now the sun beats down with a fiercer fire than ever, and draws up the drop of moisture which haply may linger low down in the cool earth. Cool earth, did I say? I fear that is a figure of speech. It almost burns one's feet through the soles of thin boots, and each particle of dust is like a tiny cinder. I think regretfully of the pleasant, sharp, frosty mornings and evenings, even though the days are lengthening, and one may now count by weeks the time before the rain will come, and fruits and vegetables, milk and butter, be once more obtainable with comparative ease. What I most long for, however, is a good pelting shower, a down-pour which will fill the tanks and make water plentiful. I am always rushing out in the sun to see that the horses and the fowls and all the animals have enough water to drink. In spite of all my care, they all seem in a chronic state of thirst, for the Kafirs are too lazy and careless to think that it matters if tubs get empty or if a horse comes home too late to be led down to the river with the rest. The water that I drink myself—and I drink nothing else—would give a sanitary inspector a fit to look at, even after it has passed through two filters. But it goes through many vicissitudes before it reaches this comparatively clean stage. It is brought from the river (which is barely able to move sluggishly over its ironstone bed) through clouds of dust. If the Kafir rests his pails for a moment outside before pouring their contents into the first large filter, the pony, who is always on the lookout for a chance, plunges his muzzle in among the green boughs with snorts of satisfaction; the pigeons fly in circles round the man's head, trying to take advantage of the first favorable moment for a bath; and not only dogs, but even cats, press up for a drop. This is because it is cool, and not so dusty as that in pans outside. There is not a leaf anywhere yet large enough to give shade, and the water outside soon becomes loathsomely hot. Of course it is an exceptionally dry season. All the weather and all the seasons I have ever met with in the course of my life always have been quite out of the ordinary routine. Doubtless, it is kindly meant on the part of the inhabitants, and is probably intended as a consolation to the new-comer. But I am too well used to it to be comforted. Even when one comes back to dear old England after three or four years' absence, and arrives, say, early in May, everybody professes to be amazed that there should be a keen east wind blowing, and apologizes for the black hard buds on the lilac trees and the iron-bound earth and sky with assurances that "There have been *such* east winds this year!" Just as if there are not "such" east winds every year!

After these last few amiable lines it will hardly surprise any one to hear that this is the irritating hot wind which is blowing so lightly. You must know we have hot winds from nearly opposite quarters. There is one from the northeast, which comes down from Delagoa Bay and all the fever-haunted region thereabouts, which is more unhealthy than this. *That* furnace-breath makes you languid and depressed: exertion is almost an impossibility, thought is an effort. But *this* light air represents the healthy hot wind, a nice rasping zephyr —a wind which dries you up like a Normandy pippin, and puts you and keeps you in the most peevish, discontented frame of mind. It has swept over the burning deserts of the interior, and comes from the north-west, and I can only say there is aggravation in every puff of it. The only person toward whom I feel at all kindly disposed when this wind is blowing is Jim. Jim is a new Kafir-lad, Tom's successor, for Tom's battles with Charlie became rather too frequent to be borne in a quiet household. Jim is such a nice boy, and Jim's English is delightful. He began by impressing upon me through Maria that he had "no Inglis," but added immediately, "Jim no sheeky." Certainly he is not cheeky, but, on the contrary, the sweetest-tempered creature you could meet with anywhere. He must be about sixteen years old, but he is over six feet high, and as straight as a willow wand. To see Jim stride along by the side of my little carriage is to be reminded of the illustrations to the *Seven-League-Boots* story. At first, Jim tried to coil and fold and double his long legs into the small perch at the back of the pony-carriage, but he always tumbled out at a rut in the road, and kept me in perpetual terror of his snapping himself in two. Not that there are many ruts now in my road, I would have you know. It is all solid dust, about three feet deep everywhere. A road-party worked at it in their own peculiar way for many weeks this fall, and the old Dutch overseer used to assure me with much pride every time I passed that he "vas making my ladyships a boofler road mit grabels." Of course it was the queen's highway at which he and his Kafirs dug, but it pleased him to regard it as my private path, and this gave him greater courage to throw out "schnapps" as a suggestion worthy of my attention.

Will you believe me when I declare that in spite of all these weary weeks of drought, in spite of this intense blaze of burning sunshine all through the thirsty day, the long stretches of the blackened country are showing tender green shoots round the stumps of the old rank grass

burned away long ago? It seems little short of a miracle when one sees the baked earth, hard as a granite cliff, dry as a last year's bone, and through its parched, pulverized surface little clumps of trefoil are springing everywhere, and young blades of grass. On the mulberry trees, too, the buttons have burst into tufts of dainty leaves, which assert themselves more and more every day, and herald that wealth of freshest greenery in which Natal was clad over hill and dale when first I saw her last November. Then I could not take in that the smiling emerald downs which stretched around me could ever be the arid desolate wasteland they now appear; and now I can scarcely summon up faith enough to believe in the miracle of the spring resurrection close at hand, of which these few lonely leaves and blades are the sign and token.

Yes, Jim's English is very droll—all the more so for his anxiety to practice it, in spite of his protestations to the contrary. Jim is a great meteorologist, unlike the majority of Kafirs, from whom you can extract no opinion whatever. They say the rain-doctor is the proper person to determine whether it is going to be fair or foul weather. I have asked Charlie whether it was going to rain when the heavy clouds have been almost over our heads, just to hear what he would say; and Charlie has answered with Turkish fatalism, "Oh, ma', I doan know: if it like to rain, it will, but if it don't, it won't." Now, Jim does proffer an opinion, expressed by a good deal of pantomime, and Jim is quite as often right as most weather-prophets. Jim studies the skies on account of getting and keeping his wood-heap dry, and prides himself on neat stacks of chopped-up fuel. I gave Jim an orange the other day, and he took it in the graceful Kafir fashion with both hands, and burst forth into all his English at once: "Oh, danks, ma': inkosa-casa vezy kind new face, vezy. Jim no sheeky: oh yaas, all lite!" His meaning can only dimly be guessed at, especially about the new face. I wish with all my heart I *could* get a new face, for this one is much the worse for the South African sun and my inveterate habit of loitering about out of doors whenever I can, and spending most of my waking hours in the verandah.

AUGUST 4.

Since I last wrote there has not been much loitering out of doors, nor has any one who could possibly avoid doing so even put his nose outside. The hot zephyr I alluded to three days ago suddenly changed to a furious hot gale, the worst I have ever seen—hotter than a New Zealand nor'-wester, and as heavy as a hurricane. The clouds of dust baffle description. The direction, too, from whence it came must also have changed, for a sort of epidemic of low fever is hanging about, and the influenza would be ludicrous from the number of its victims if it were not so disagreeable and so dangerous. All the washermen and washerwomen in the whole place are ill, the entire body of Kafir police is on the sick list, all one's servants are laid up —Charlie says pathetically, "Too moch plenty cough inside, ma'"—and everybody looks wretched. The "inkos" which one hears in passing are either a hoarse growl or a wheezy whisper. When you consider how absolutely dry the atmosphere must be, it is difficult to imagine how people catch such constant and severe colds as they do here. I am bound to say, however, that except with this influenza a cold does not last so long as it does in England, but I think you catch cold oftener; and the reason is not far to seek. In these hot winds, or out of the broiling midday sun, some visitor rides up from town, and arrives here or elsewhere very hot indeed. Then he comes into a little drawing-room with its thick stone walls and closed, darkened windows, and exclaims, "How delightfully cool you are here!" but in five minutes he is shivering; and the next thing I hear is that he has cold or fever. Yet what is one to do? I have to keep in-doors all day: I must have a cool room to sit in; and as long as one has not been taking exercise out of doors, it does no harm.

The gale of hot wind seemed to set the whole place on fire. I should not have thought a tussock had been left anywhere, but every night lately has been made bright as day by the glare of blazing hillsides. Then I leave my readers to imagine the state of a house into which all these fine particles of soot filter through ill-fitting doors and windows, driven by a furious hurricane. The other morning poor little G——'s plate of porridge set aside to cool in the dining-room, with every door and window closed, had a layer of black burnt grass on the top in five minutes; and the state of the tablecloth, milk, etc. baffles description. Indeed, one's life is a life of dusting and scrubbing and cleaning generally, if a house is to be kept even tolerably tidy in these parts.

I forget if I have ever told you of the spiders here. They are another sorrow to the careful housewife, spinning webs in every corner, across doorways, filling up spaces beneath tables, flinging their aërial bridges from chair to chair—all in a single night—and regarding glass and china ornaments merely as a nucleus or starting-point for a filmy labyrinth.

AUGUST 10.

Every now and then, when I give way to temper and a hot wind combined, and write crossly about the climate, my conscience reproaches me severely with a want of fairness when the weather changes, as it generally does directly, and we have some exquisite days and nights. For instance, directly after I last wrote our first spring showers fell— very coyly, it is true, and almost as if the clouds had forgotten how to dissolve into rain. Still, the very smell of the moist earth was delicious, and ever since that wet night the whole country has been

> Growing glorious
> Quietly, day by day;

and except in the very last-burnt patches a faint and hesitating tinge of palest green is stealing over all the bleak hillsides. My poor bamboos are still mere shriveled ghosts of the fair green plumes which used to rustle and wave all through the drenching summer weather, but everything else is pushing a leaf here and a shoot there wherever it can, and, and, joy of joys! there has been no dust for a day or two. All looks washed and refreshed: parched-up Nature accepts this shower as the first installment of the deluge which is coming presently. In the mean time, the air is delicious, and even the poor influenza victims are creeping about in the sunshine. The Kafirs have suffered most, and it is really quite sad to see how weak they are, and how grateful for a little nourishing food, which they absolutely require at present.

I took advantage of the first of these new spring days, with their cool air, to make a little expedition I have long had on my mind. From my verandah I can see on the opposite hills, at about my own lofty elevation of fifty feet or so, the white tents beyond the dark walls of Fort Napier. Now, this little spot represents the only shelter and safety in all the country-side in case of a "difficulty" with our swarming dusky neighbors. Here and there in other townships there are "laagers," or loopholed enclosures, within which wagons can be dragged and a stand made against a sudden Kafir raid; but here, at the seat of government, there is a battalion of an English regiment, a thousand strong, and a regular, orthodox fortified place, with some heavy pieces of ordnance. But you know of old how terribly candid I am, so I must confess at once that it was not with the smallest idea of ascertaining for myself the military strength and capability of Fort Napier that I paid it a visit that fine spring morning. No: my object was of the purest domestic character, and indeed was only to see with my own eyes what these new Kafir huts were like, with a view to borrowing the idea for a spare room here. Could anything be more peaceful than such a project? I felt like the old wife in Jean Ingelow's *Brides of Enderby* as I drove slowly up the steep hill, at the brow of which I could already see the pacing sentries and the grim cannon-mouth—

And why should this thing be?
What danger lowers by land or sea?

I might have answered as she did,

For storms be none, and pyrates flee;

for, although there are skirmishes beyond our borders, we ourselves, thank God! dwell in peace and safety within them. Nothing could be more picturesque than the gleaming white points now standing sharply out in snowy vandykes against a cobalt sky, or else toned harmoniously down against a soft gray cloud; now glistening on a background of green hillside, or nestling dimly in a dusty hollow. There is only barrackroom for half the regiment, and the other half, under canvas, takes a good many tents and covers a good deal of ground. Although the soldiers have got through the winter very well, it would not be prudent to trust them to the shelter of a tent during the coming summer months of alternate flood and sunshine. So Kafirs have been busy building nearly a hundred of their huts on an improved plan all this dry weather, and these little dwellings are now just ready for their complement of five men apiece. They are a great step in advance of the original Kafir hut, and it was for this reason I came to see them, lured also by hearing that they only cost four pounds apiece. We are so terribly cramped for room here. I have only ventured on one tiny addition—a dressing-room about as big as the cabin of a ship, which cost nearly eighty pounds to build of stone like the rest of the house. So I have had it on my mind for some time that it would be a very fine thing to build one of these glorified Kafir huts close to the house for a spare room. The real Kafir hut is exactly like a beehive, without door or window, and only a small hole to creep in and out at. These new military huts have circular walls, five feet high and about a dozen feet in diameter, made of closely-woven wattles, and covered within and without with clay. I stood watching the Kafirs working at one for some time. It certainly looked a rude and simple process. Some four or five stalwart Kafirs were squatting on the ground hard by, "snuffing" and conversing with much gesticulation and merriment. They were the off-gang, I imagine. Three or four more were tranquilly and in a leisurely fashion trampling the wet clay and daubing it on with their hands inside and out. They had not the ghost of a tool of any sort, and yet the result was wonderfully good. I wondered why finely-chopped grass was not mixed with the clay, as I have seen the New Zealand shepherds do in preparing the "cob" for their mud walls; but I was told that the Kafir would greatly object to anything so uncomfortable for his bare legs and feet. Of course, the shepherd works up the ugly mass with a spade, whilst here these men slowly trample it to the right consistency. The plastering is really a triumph of (literally) handiwork, though the process is exasperatingly slow. At first the mud comes out all over thumb-marks, and dries so, but in a day or two buckets of water are dashed over it, so as to remoisten it, and then it is once more patiently smoothed all over with the palm of the hand until an absolutely smooth surface is obtained, as flat and flawless as though the best of trowels had been used. A neatly-fitting door and window have meantime been made in the regimental workshop, and hung in the spaces left for them in the wattled walls. More wattles, closely woven together, are put on in the shape of a very irregular dome, and this is thatched nearly a foot deep with long rank grass tied securely down by endless ropes of finely-plaited grass. The result is a spacious, cool, and most comfortable circular room, and those which are finished and fitted up with shelves and camp furniture look as nice as possible. A little tuft of straw at the apex of each dome is at once a lightning-conductor and a finish to the quaint little building. The plastered walls of some huts are whitewashed, but the most popular idea seems to be to tar them and make them still more weather-proof. A crooked stick or two, being merely the rough branch of a tree, stands in the centre and acts as a musket-rack and tent-pole to the little dwelling. The Kafirs get only one pound ten shillings for each hut, and the wooden fittings are calculated to cost about two pounds ten shillings more; but I hear that they grumble a good deal on account of the distance from which they have to bring the grass, all in the neighborhood having been burnt. They also regard it as women's work, for all the kraals are built by women.

On the whole, I am more than ever taken with the idea of a Kafir spare room, and quite hope to carry it out some day, the huts look so cool and healthy and clean. The thatch and mud walls will keep off the sun in the hot weather before us; and as all the huts stand on a gentle slope, there is no fear of their being damp. It is wonderful how well the soldiers have managed hitherto under canvas, and how healthy they have been; but I can quite understand that it is not well to presume upon such good luck during another wet season. As we were up in camp, we looked at all the soldiers' arrangements—the canteen, where mustard and pickles seemed to be the most popular articles of food; the school-house, a wee brick building, in which both the children and the recruits have to learn, and which is also used as a chapel on Sunday. Everything was the pink of neatness and cleanliness, as is always the case where soldiers or sailors live, and I was much struck by the absolute silence and repose of so small an enclosure with a thousand men inside it. I wondered whether a thousand women could have kept so quiet? Of course I peeped into the kitchen, and instantly coveted the beautiful brick oven out of which sundry smoking platters were being drawn. But curry and rice was the chief dish in the bill of fare for that day, and I can only say the smell was excellent and exceedingly appetizing. The view all round, too, was charming. Just at our feet lay the hollow where the men's gardens are. Such potatoes and pumpkins! such cabbages and onions! The men delight in cultivating the willing soil in which all vegetables grow so luxuriantly and easily; and it is so managed that it shall be a profit as well as a pleasure to them. In many ways this encouragement of a taste for gardening is good: there is the first consideration of the advantage to themselves, and it is indirectly a boon to us, for if a thousand men were added to the consumers of the few potatoes and vegetables which daily find their way into the Maritzburg market, I know not what would become of us. Our last stroll was to the brow of another down close by, also crowned with white tents. Beneath it lay the military graveyard, and I have seldom seen anything more poetic and touching than the effect of this lovely garden—for so it looked, a spot of purest green, tenderly cared for—amid the bare winter coloring of all the country-side. The hills folded it softly, as if it were a precious place, the sun lay brightly on it, and the quiet sleeping-ground was made orderly and tranquil by many a sheltering tree and blooming shrub. I promised myself to come in summer and look down on it again when all the wealth of roses and geraniums are out, and when these brown hillsides are green and glorious with their tropic pasture.

You will think I have indeed taken a sudden mania for soldiers and camps when I tell you that a very few days after my visit to Fort Napier I joyfully accepted the offer of a friend to take me to see the annual joint encampment of the Natal Carbineers and D'Urban Mounted Rifles out on Botha's Flat, rather more than halfway between this and D'Urban. Not only was I delighted at the chance of seeing that lovely bit of country more at my leisure than dashing through it in the post-cart, but I have always so much admired the pluck and spirit of this handful of volunteers, who keep up the discipline and prestige of their little corps in the teeth of all sorts of difficulties and discouragements, that I was glad to avail myself of the opportunity of paying them a visit when they were out in camp. For many years past these smart light-horse have struggled on in spite of obstacles to attending drill, want of money, lack of public attention and interest, and a thousand other lets and hinderances. Living as we do in such a chronically precarious position— a position in which five minutes' official ill-temper or ever so trifling an injudicious action might set the whole Kafir population in a blaze of discontent, and even revolt—too much importance cannot, in

my poor judgment, be attached to the volunteer movement; and it seems to me worthy in the highest degree of every encouragement and token of appreciation which it is in our power to give. Of either pence or praise these Natal mounted volunteers (for they would be very little use on foot over such an extent of railway-less country) have hitherto had a very small share, and yet I found the pretty little camp as full of military enthusiasm, as orderly, as severely simple in its internal economy, as though the eyes of all Europe were upon it. Each man there was sacrificing a week of his time was giving up a good deal more than most volunteers give up, and it would make too long a story if I were to enter into particulars of the actual pecuniary loss which in this country attends the lawyer leaving his office, the clerk his desk, the merchant his counting-house, and each providing himself with horses, etc. to come out here twice a year and drill pretty nearly from morning till night. The real difficulty, I fancy, lies in subordinates being able to obtain leave. Every sugar-estate, every office, every warehouse, has so few white men employed in it, exists in such a chronic state of short-handedness, that it is the greatest inconvenience to the masters to let their clerks go out. Both corps are therefore stronger on paper than in the field, but from no lack of willingness to serve on the part of the volunteers themselves.

I don't want to be spiteful or invidious, but I have seen volunteer camps nearer the heart of civilization, where there were flower-gardens round the tents and lovely "fixings" inside, portable couches and chairs, albums, and clocks, besides a French cook and iced champagne flowing like a river. Dismiss from your mind all ideas of that sort if you come with me next year to Botha's Flat. I can promise you scrupulous and exquisite neatness and cleanliness, but in every other respect you might as well be in a real camp on active service. Even the Kafir servants are left behind, the men —some of them very fine gentlemen indeed—cleaning their own horses and accoutrements, pitching their own tents, cooking their own food, and in fact acting precisely as though they had really taken the field in an enemy's country. The actual drill, therefore—though more than half the hours of daylight are spent in the saddle under the instruction of one of the most enthusiastic and competent drill-instructors you could find anywhere—is by no means all that is practiced in these brief, hardly-won camp-days. The men learn to rely solely on their own resources. Their commissariat is arranged by themselves, one single small wagon to each corps conveying tents, forage, stores, firewood—all that is needed for man and horse—for ten days or so. They have no "base of operations" — nothing and nobody to depend upon but themselves. It is literally a "flying camp," and all the more interesting for being so evidently what we shall most need in case of any native difficulty. I don't suppose they ever dream of visitors, for in this languid land few people would journey thirty miles to look at anything, especially in a hot wind. Nor am I sure the volunteers want visitors. It is real, earnest, practical hard work with them, done with their utmost diligence, and without expecting the smallest reward, even in fair words. It strikes me as very remarkable and characteristic of the lack of general interest in public subjects how little one hears of the very men on whom we may at any moment be only too glad to rely. However, I never can attempt to fathom causes : rather let me describe effects for you as best I may.

And a very pretty effect the camp has as we dash round the shoulder of a steep hill with the brake hard down, the leaders plunging wildly along with slack traces, and a general appearance of an impending upset over everything. It has been a lovely drive, though rather hot, but the roads are ever so much better than they were in the summer, and I have never seen the country looking more beautiful, as it seems to grow greener with every mile out of Maritzburg. When the hills open out suddenly and show the great fertile cleft of un-

dulating downs, green ravines with trickling silver threads down them, and purple mountains in the distance stretching away to the coast, which is known as the Inanda Location, one feels as if one were looking at the Happy Valley.

O mortal man, who livest here by toil,
Do not complain of this, thy hard estate,

for neither the imaginary kingdom of Amhara nor any other kingdom in all the fair earth can show a more poetical or suggestive glimpse of scenic beauty. Yet when a few miles more of rushing and galloping through the soft air brings us to the top of the pass of the Inchanga, I make up my mind that *that* is the most beautiful stretch of country my eyes have ever beheld. It is too grand to describe, too complete to break up into fragments by words. Far down among the sylvan slopes of the park-like foreground the Umgeni winds, with the sunshine glinting here and there on its waters : beyond are bold, level mountains with rich deep indigo shadows and lofty crests cut off straight against the dappled sky, according to the South African formation. But we soon climb the lofty saddle, and put the brake hard down again for the worst descent on the road. If good driving and skill and care can save us, we need not be nervous, for we have all these ; but the state of the harness fills me with apprehension, and it is little short of a miracle why it does not all give way at once and tumble off the horses' backs. Luckily, there is very little of it to begin with, and the original leather is largely supplemented by reins or strips of dried bullock hide, so we hold together until the vehicle draws up at the door of a neat little wayside inn, where we get out and begin at once to rub our elbows tenderly, for they are all black and blue. There is the camp, however, on yonder green down, and here are two of the officers from it waiting for us, and wanting to know all about hours and plans and so forth. A little rest and luncheon are first on the programme, and a good deal of soap and water also for us travelers, and then, the afternoon being still young, we mount our horses and canter up the rising ground to where the flagstaff stands. The men are just falling in for their third and last drill, which will last till sundown, so there is time to go round the pretty little spot and admire the precision and neatness, the serviceable, business-like air, of everything. There is the path the sentries tread, already worn perfectly bare, but straight as though it had been ruled: yonder is the bit of sod-fencing thrown up as a shelter to the kettles and frying-pans. The kitchen range consists of half a dozen forked sticks to leeward of this rude shelter, and each troop contributes a volunteer cook and commissariat officer. The picket-ropes for the horses run down the centre of the little camp, and we must look at the neat pile of blankets and nose-bags marked with separate initials. The officers' tents are at one end, and the guard tents at the other, and those for the privates, holding five men each, are between. It is all as sweet and clean and neat as possible, and one can easily understand what is stated almost as a joke—that the first night in camp no one could sleep for his own and his neighbor's cough, and now there is not such a sound to be heard.

We are coming back into camp presently, for I am invited to dine at the officers' mess to-night, so we must make the most of the daylight. It is a gray evening, and the hot wind has died away, allowing the freshness from the hills to steal down to this green spur, which is yet high enough to be out of the cold mists of the valley. The drill is not very amusing for a lady this afternoon, because it is real hard work—patiently doing the same thing over and over again until each little point is perfect — until the horses are steady and the men move with the ease and precision of a machine. But it is just because there is little else to distract one's attention that I can notice what fine stalwart young fellows they all are, and how thoroughly in earnest. Their uniforms and accoutrements are simple, but natty, and clean as a new pin, the horses especially being ever so much better groomed and turned out by their masters' hands than if each had been saddled by his usual Kafir groom. So, after a short while of watching the little squadron patiently wheel and trot and advance by those mysterious "fours," manœuvre across a swamp, charge down a hill, skirmish up that burnt slope over there, and so forth, we leave them hard at work, and canter over some ridges to see what lies beyond. But there is nothing much to reward us, and the only effect of our long evening ride is to make us all ravenously hungry and anxious for six o'clock and dinner. Long before that hour the dusk has crept down, and by the time we have returned, and I have exchanged my riding-habit for a splendid dinner-costume of ticking, it is cold enough and dark enough to make us glad of all the extra wraps we can find, and of the light and shelter of the snug little tent. Here, again, it is real camp fare. I am given *the* great luxury of the encampment—to sit upon a delicious *karosse*, or rug of dressed goat skins. It is snowy white, and soft and flexible as a glove on the wrong side, and on the right it is covered with long, wavy cream-colored hair with black patches at each corner. The ground is strewn with grass, dry and sweet as hay, and carriage candles are tied by wire to a cross stick fastened on a tent-pole: the tablecloth is a piece of canvas, the dishes are billies, but the food is excellent, and, above all, we have tea as the sole beverage for everybody. We are all provided with the best of sauces, and I assure you we very soon find ourselves at our dessert of oranges in a basket-lid. Never have any of us enjoyed a meal more, and certainly everybody except myself has earned it. Then there is a little tinkling and tuning up outside, and the band turns out to play to us. By this time the wind has got up again from another point, and is so bitterly bleak and cold that the musicians cannot possibly stand still, but have to keep marching round and round the little tent, playing away lustily and singing with a good courage. Every now and then a stumble over a tent-peg jerks out a laugh instead of a note, but still there is plenty of "go" and *verve* in the music, and half the camp turns out to join in the chorus of "Sherman's March through Georgia." We all declare loudly that we are going to carry "the flag that makes us free" through all sorts of places, especially from "Atlanta to the sea," and I am quite sure that Sherman's own "dashing Yankee boys" could not possibly have made more noise themselves. This is followed by the softest and sweetest of sentimental songs, given in a beautiful falsetto which would be a treasure to a chorister; but it is really too cold for sentiment, so we have one more song, and then the band sings "Auld Lang Syne" with great spirit, and as the wind is now rising to a hurricane, the musical performances are wound up somewhat hurriedly by "God Save the Queen !" For this the whole camp turns out of their own accord. The cooks leave their fires, the fatigue-party their scrubbing and the lazy ones their pipes. Under the clear starlight, with the Southern Cross sloping up from the edge of yonder dusky hill, with the keen wind sweeping round the camp of this little handful of Englishmen in a strange and distant country, the words of the most beautiful tune in the world come ringing as though straight from each man's heart. Of course we all come out of our tent to stand bareheaded too, and I assure you it is a very impressive and beautiful moment. One feels as one stands here amid the flower of the young colonists, each man holding his cap aloft in his strong right hand, each man putting all the fervor and passion of his loyal love and reverence for his queen into every tone of his voice, that it is well worth coming down for this one moment alone. It is very delightful to see the English people, whether in units or tens of thousands, greet their sovereign face to face, but there is something even more heart-stirring, more inexpressibly pathetic, in such outbursts as this, evoked by none of the glamour and glitter of a royal pageant, but called into being merely by a name, a tune, a sentiment. I often think if I were a queen I should be more really gratified and touched by the ardent and loyal love of such handfuls of my subjects in out-of-the-way corners of my empire, where the sentiment has nothing from outside to fan it, than with the acclamations of a shouting multitude as my splendor is passing them by. At all events, *I* have never seen soldiers or sailors, regulars or volunteers, more enthusiastic over our own anthem. It is followed by cheer upon cheer, blessing upon blessing on the beloved and royal name, until everybody is perfectly hoarse from shouting in such a high wind, and we all retreat into the tiny tents for a cup of coffee and—what do you think? Stories. I am worse than any child in my love of stories, and we have one or two really good *raconteurs* in the little knot of hosts.

Of course one of the first inquiries I make is whether any snakes have been found in the tents, and I hear, much to my disappointment—because the bare fact will not at all lend itself to a story for G—— when I get home—that only one little one had crept beneath a folded great-coat (which is the camp pillow, it seems), and been found in the morning curled up, torpidly dozing in the woolen warmth. No, it is not a story G—— will ever care about, for the poor little snake had not even been killed: it was too small and too insignificant, they say, and it merely got kicked out of its comfortable bed. To console me for this bald and incomplete adventure, I am told some more snake-stories, which, at all events, *ought* to have been true, so good are they. Here are two for you, one of which especially delights me.

Hard by this very camp a keen sportsman was lately pursuing a buck. He had no dogs except a pet Skye terrier to help him in the chase—nothing but his rifle and a trusty Kafir. Yet the hard-pressed buck had to dash into a small, solitary patch of thorny scrub for shelter and a moment's rest. In an instant the hunter was off his pony, and had sent the Kafir into the bush to drive out the buck, that he might have a shot at it the moment it emerged from the cover. Instead of the expected buck, however—I must tell you the story never states what became of *him*—came loud cries in Kafir from the scrub of, "Oh, my mother ! oh, my friends and relations ! I die ! I die!" The master, much astonished, peeped as well as he could into the little patch of tangled briers and bushes, and there he saw his crouching Kafir stooping, motionless, beneath a low branch round which was coiled a large and venomous snake. The creature had struck at the man's head as he crept beneath, and its forked tongue had got firmly imbedded in the Kafir's woolly pate. The wretched beater dared not stir an inch: he dared not even put up his hands to free himself; but there he remained motionless and despairing, uttering these loud shrieks. His master bade him stay perfectly still, and taking close aim at the snake's body, fired and blew it in two. He then with a dexterous jerk disentangled the barbed tongue, and flung the quivering head and neck outside the bushes. Here comes the only marvelous part of the story. "How did he know it was a poisonous snake?" I ask. "Oh, well: the little dog ran up to play with the head, and the snake—or rather the half snake—struck out at it and bit it in the paw, and it died in ten minutes."

But the following is *my* favorite Munchausen: There was once a certain valiant man of many adventures whose Kafir title was "the prince of—fibs," and he used to relate the following experience: One day—so long ago that breech-loading guns were unknown, and the process of reloading was a five-minute affair—he came upon a large and deadly snake making as fast as it could for its hole hard by. Of course, such a thing as escape could not be permitted, and as there was no other weapon at hand, the huntsman determined to shoot the huge reptile. But first the gun must be loaded, and whilst this was being done, lo! the snake's head had already disappeared in the hole: in another instant the whole body would have followed. A sudden grasp at the tail, a rapid, bold jerk, flung the creature a yard or two off. Did it attempt to show fight? Oh no: it glided swiftly as ever toward the same shelter from which it had been so rudely plucked. The ramrod was rapidly plied, the charge driven home, but there was yet the percussion-cap to be adjusted.

Once more the tail was grasped, the snake pulled out and flung still farther away. Again did the wily creature approach the hole. In another instant the cap would be on and the gun cocked, but everything depended on that instant. The sportsman kept his eye fixed on his artful foe even whilst his fingers deftly found and fixed the percussion-cap. What, then, was his horror and dismay to find that he had, for once, met his match, and that the snake, recognizing the desperate nature of the position, and keeping a wary eye on the hunter's movements, instead of going into his hole for the third time in the usual method, had turned round and was backing in *tail first!* Is it not delightful?

As soon as we had finished laughing at this and similar stories it was high time to break up the little party, although it was only about the hour at which one sits down to dinner in London. Still, there were early parades and drills and Goodness knows what, and I was very tired and sleepy with my jolting journey and afternoon on horseback. So we all went the "grand rounds," lantern in hand, and with a deep feeling of admiration and pity for the poor sentries pacing up and down on the bleak hillside, walked down to the little inn, where a tiny room, exactly like a wooden box, had been secured for me, the rest of the party climbing heroically up the hill again to sleep on the ground with their saddles for a pillow. This was playing at soldiers with a vengeance, was it not? However, they all looked as smart and well as possible next morning, when they came to fetch me up to breakfast in the camp. Then more drill —very pretty this time—a sham attack and defence, and then another delightful long ride over a different range of hills. It was a perfect morning for exploring, gray and cool and cloudy — so different from the hot wind and scorching sun of yesterday. We could not go fast, not only from the steep up-and-down hill, but from the way the ground was turned up by the ant-bears. Every few yards was a deep burrow, often only a few hours' old; and unless you had seen it with your own eyes I can never make you believe or understand the extraordinarily vivid color of this newly-turned earth. During yesterday's journey I had noticed that the only wild-flower yet out was a curious lily growing on a fat bulb more than half out of the ground, and sometimes of a deep-orange or of a brilliant-scarlet color. With the recollection of these blossoms fresh in my mind, I noticed a patch of bright scarlet on the face of an opposite down, and thought it must, of course, be made by lilies. As I was very anxious to get some bulbs for my garden, I proposed that we should ride across the ravine and dig some up. "We can come if you like," said the kindest and pleasantest of guides, "but I assure you it is only a freshly-dug ant-bear's hole." Never did I find belief so difficult, and, like all incredulous people, I was on the point of backing up my hasty opinion by half a dozen pairs of gloves when the same friendly guide laughingly pointed to a hole close by, bidding me look well at it before risking my gloves. There was nothing more to be said. The freshly scratched-out earth was exactly like vermilion, moist and brilliant in color—"a ferruginous soil," some learned person said; but, however that may be, I had never before seen earth of such a bright color, for it was quite different from the red-clay soil one has seen here and in other places.

The line of country we followed that morning was extraordinarily pretty and characteristic. The distant purple hills rolled down to the gently-undulating ground over which we rode. Here and there—would that it had been oftener!—a pretty homestead with its sheltering trees and surrounding patches of pale-green forage clung to the steep hillside before us. Then, as we rode on, one of the ravines fell away at our feet to a deep gully, through which ran a stream-

let among clustering scrub and bushes. In one spot the naked rock stood out straight and bare and bold for fifty yards or so, as though it were the walls of a citadel, with a wealth of creeping greenery at its foot, and over its face a tiny waterfall, racing from the hill behind, leapt down to join the brook in the gully. We saw plenty of game, too—partridges, buck, two varieties of the bald-headed ibis, secretary-birds, and, most esteemed of all, a couple of paauw (I wonder *how* it is spelt?), a fine kind of bustard, which is quite as good eating as a turkey, but daily becoming more and more scarce. There were lots of plover, too, busy among the feathery ashes on the newly-burned ground, and smaller birds chirruped sweetly every now and then. It was all exceedingly delightful, and I enjoyed it all the more for the absence of the blazing sunshine, which, however it may light up and glorify the landscape, beats too fiercely on one's head to be pleasant. If only we women could bring ourselves to wear pith helmets, it would not be so bad; but with the present fashion of hats, which are neither shade nor shelter, a ride in the sun is pretty nearly certain to end in a bad headache. At all events, *this* ride had no worse consequence than making us very hungry for our last camp-meal, a solid luncheon, and then there was just time to rush down the hill and clamber into the post-cart for four hours of galloping and jolting through the cold spring evening air. My last look was at the white tents of the pretty camp, the smoke of its fires and the smart lines of carbineers and mounted rifles assembling to the bugle-call for another long afternoon of steady drill down in the valley, or "flat," as it is called—a picturesque and pretty glimpse, recalling the memory of some very pleasant hours, the prettiest imaginable welcome, and a great deal of hearty and genuine hospitality.

PART XII.

I HAVE had many pleasant cups of tea in my life, indoors and out of doors, but never a pleasanter cup than the one I had the other day in a wagon, or, to speak more exactly, by the side of a wagon—a wagon, too, upon which one looked with the deepest respect, for it had just come down from a long journey up the country, where it had been trekking these four months past—trekking night and day right up to the territory of the Ama-Swazies, through the Thorn country, over hundreds of miles of these endless billowy hills, rolling in wearying monotony day after day; but—and this "but" made up for every other shortcoming—amid hunting-grounds happier than often fall to the lot of even the South African explorer. And there were the spoils of the little campaign spread out before us. The first result, however, which struck me was the splendid health of the travelers. Sunburned indeed they were, especially the fair young English girl-face which had smiled good-bye to me from the depths of a sun-bonnet last April. But who would not risk a few shades of tan to have gone through such a novel and delightful journey? I never saw two people look so well in all my life as this adventurous couple, and it was with one voice they declared they had enjoyed every moment of the time. And what a pleasant time it must have been, rewarded as they were—and deserved to be—by splendid sport! On the fore part of the wagon lay a goodly pile of skins and quantities of magnificent horns, from the ponderous pair on the shaggy buffalo-skulls down to taper points which might have belonged to a fairy buck, so slender, so polished, so inexpressibly graceful, were they. But the trophy of trophies was the skin of a lion, which had been shot in the earliest morning light some twenty yards from the hunter's tent. It was a splendid skin, and the curved claws are to be made into a necklace and earrings for the sportsman's wife, who indeed deserves them for bearing her share of the dangers and discomforts of the expedition so cheerfully and bravely. It was very difficult to elicit the least hint of what the discomforts were, or might have been, until at last my eager questions raked out an admission that a week of wet weather (the only one, by the way, in all the four months) was tedious when cooped up under the tilt of the wagon, or that some of the places up and down which the lumbering, unwieldy conveyance had crept were fearful to look at and dangerous to travel, necessitating a lashing together of the wheels by iron chains, as well as the use of the ordinary heavy brake. Yet there had been no upset, no casualty, no serious trouble of any sort; and I think what these English travelers were more impressed with than anything else was the honesty of the Kafirs. The wagon with its stores of food and wine, of comforts and conveniences of all sorts, had been left absolutely alone by the side of a track crossed and recrossed every hour by Kafirs, and twenty miles short of the place whither the tent had been carried for greater facilities of getting at the big game. The oxen were twenty miles off in another direction, under no one's care in particular; the wagon stood absolutely alone; and yet when the moment of reassembling came every bullock was forthcoming, and nothing whatever of any description was missing from the unguarded wagon. The great attraction to the Kafirs along the line of travel had been the empty tins of preserved milk or jam: with tops and bottoms knocked out they made the most resplendent bangles, and became a violent fashion up among the Thorns.

Nor was that grand lion's skin the only one. There were quagga skins, wolf skins, buck skins of half a dozen different species, eland skins, buffalo skins, lynx and wild-cat skins enough to start a furrier's shop, and all in excellent preservation, having been tightly pegged out and thoroughly dried. The horns—or rather the skulls—were still a little high, and needed to be heaped well to leeward before we settled down to tea, camping on kegs and boxes and whatever we could find. I was made proud and happy by being accommodated with a seat on the lion skin; and exactly opposite to me, tranquilly grazing on the young grass, was the identical donkey which had attracted the king of animals to the spot where his fate awaited him. Although camped in the very heart of the lion country, the hunter had neither seen nor heard anything of his big game until this donkey chanced to be added to the stud, and then the lions came roaring round, half a dozen at a time. A huge fire had to be kept up night and day, and close to this the unhappy ass was tethered, for his life would not have been worth much otherwise; and he seems to have been thoroughly alive to the perils of his situation. Lions can resist anything except ass-flesh, it appears; but it is so entirely their favorite delicacy that they forget their cunning, and become absolutely reckless in pursuit of it. When at the last extremity of terror, the poor donkey used to lift up his discordant voice, and so keep the prowling foe at bay for a while, though it invariably had the double effect of attracting all the lions within earshot. And so it was that in the early dawn the hunter, hearing the lion's growls coming nearer and nearer, and the poor donkey's brays more and more frequent, stole out, rifle in hand, just in time to get a steady shot at the splendid brute only fifteen yards away, who was hungrily eyeing the miserable ass on the other side of the blazing fire. In spite of all legends to the contrary, a lion never attacks a man first, and this lion turned and moved away directly he saw the sportsman's leveled rifle. Only one shot was fired, for the dull thud of the bullet told that it had struck the lion, and nothing upon earth is so dangerous as a wounded lion. The huge beast walked slowly away, and

when the full daylight had come the sportsman and a few Kafirs followed up the blood-flecked trail for a quarter of a mile, or less, to find the lion lying down as if asleep, with his head resting on his folded fore paw, quite dead. I don't think I ever understood the *weight* of a lion until I was told that it took two strong Kafirs to lift one of its ponderous fore feet a few inches even from the ground, and it was almost more than ten men could manage to drag it along the ground by ropes back to the tent. Twenty men could scarcely have carried it, the size and weight of the muscle are so enormous. The Kafirs prize the fat of the lion very highly, and the headman of the expedition had claimed this as his perquisite, melting it down into gourds and selling it in infinitesimal portions as an unguent. I don't know what the market-price up country was, but whilst we were laughing and chatting over our tea I saw the crafty Kafir scooping out the tiniest bits of lion's fat in return for a shilling. One of my Kafirs asked leave to go down and buy some. "What for, Jack?" I asked. "Not for me, ma' —*for my brudder:* make him brave, ma'—able for plenty fight, ma'." I am certain, however, that this was a ruse, and that Jack felt his own need of the courage-giving ointment.

Talking of Jack, reminds me of a visit I had the other day from a detachment of his friends and relatives. They did not come to see Jack: they came to see me, and very amusing visitors they were. First of all, there was a bride, who brought me a young hen as a present. She was attended by two or three scraggy girls of about fifteen, draped only in short mantles of coarse cloth. The bride herself was exceedingly smart, and had one of the prettiest faces imaginable. Her regular features, oval outline, dazzling teeth and charming expression were not a bit disfigured by her jet-black skin. Her hair was drawn straight up from her head like a tiara, stained red and ornamented with a profusion of bones and skewers, feathers, etc., stuck coquettishly over one ear, and a band of bead embroidery, studded with brass-headed nails, being worn like a fillet where the hair grew low on the forehead. She had a kilt—or series of aprons, rather—of lynx skins, a sort of bodice of calf skin, and over her shoulders, arranged with ineffable grace, a gay table - cover. Then there were strings of beads on her pretty, shapely throat and arms, and a bright scarlet ribbon tied tight round each ankle. All the rest of the party seemed immensely proud of this young person, and were very anxious to put her forward in every way. Indeed, all the others, mostly hard-working, hard-featured matrons, prematurely aged, took no more active part than the chorus of a Greek play, always excepting the old induna or headman of the village, who came as escort and in charge of the whole party. He was a most garrulous and amusing individual, full of reminiscences and anecdotes of his fighting days. He was rather more frank than most warriors who

Shoulder their crutch and show how fields are won,

for the usual end of his battle-stories was the naïve confession, "And then I thought I should be killed, and so I ran away." He and I used up a great many interpreters in the course of the visit, for he wearied every one out, and nothing made him so angry as any attempt to condense his conversation in translating it to me. But he was great fun—polite, as became an old soldier, full of compliments and assurances that "now, the happiest day of his life having come, he desired to live no longer, but was ready for death." The visit took place on the shady side of the verandah, and thither I brought my large musical-box and set it down on the ground to play. Never was there such a success. In a moment they were all down on their knees before it, listening with rapt delight, the old man telling them the music was caused by very little people inside the box, who were obliged to do exactly as I bade them. They were all in a perfect ecstasy of delight for ever so long, retreating rapidly, however, to a distance whenever I wound it up. The old induna took snuff copiously all the time, and made me affectionate speeches, which resulted in the gift of an old great-coat, which he assured me he never should live to wear out, because he was quite in a hurry to die and go to the white man's land, now that he had seen me. We hunted up all manner of queer odds and ends for presents, and made everybody happy in turn. As a final ceremony, I took them through the house: tiny as it is, it filled them with amazement and delight. My long looking-glass was at once a terror and a pleasure to them, for they rather feared bewitchment; but I held up the baby to see himself in it, and then they were pacified, saying, "The chieftainess never would go and bewitch that nice little chieftain." As usual, the pictures were what they most thoroughly enjoyed. Landseer's prints of wild cattle elicited low cries of recognition and surprise: "Zipi in korno!" ("Behold the cows!") My own favorite print of the three little foxes was much admired, but pronounced to be "lill catties." The bride was anxious to know why I kept the beds of the establishment on the floor and allowed people to walk over them. She did not consider that a good arrangement evidently; nor could she understand how matting could be of any use except to sleep on. At last it became time for "scoff," and they all retired to partake of that dainty, the old induna having begged leave to kiss my hands, which he did very gallantly, assuring me he had never been so happy before in all his life, and that he could quite believe now what I had told him about the great white queen over the sea being just as careful for and fond of her black children as of her white ones. I made a great point of this in my conversations with him, and showed them all Her Majesty's picture, to which they cried "Moochlie!" ("Nice!"), and gave the royal salute. I must say I delight in these little glimpses of Kafir character; I find in those whom I come across, like my visitors of last week, so much simple dignity with shrewd common sense. Their minds, too, seem peculiarly adapted to receive and profit by anything like culture and civilization, and there certainly is a better foundation on which to build up both these things than in any other black race with which I am acquainted.

Such an expedition as we have just made! It reminded me exactly of the dear old New Zealand days, only that I should have been sure to have had a better horse to ride in New Zealand than here. I have a very poor opinion of most of the animals here : anything like a tolerable horse is rare and expensive, and the ordinary run of steeds is ugly to look at, ill-groomed and ill-favored, besides not being up to much work. Upon this occasion I was mounted on a coarsely-put-together chestnut, who was broken in to carry a lady a few evenings ago whilst I was getting ready for my ride. However, beyond being a little fidgety and difficult to mount, owing to lurking distrust of my habit, he has no objection to carry me. But he is as rough as a cart-horse in his paces, and the way he stops short in his canter or trot, flinging all his legs about anywhere, is enough to jolt one's spine out of the crown of one's head. As for his mouth, it might as well be a stone wall, and he requires to be ridden tightly on the curb to keep him from tripping. When you add to these peculiarities a tendency to shy at every tuft of grass, and a habit of hanging the entire weight of his head on your bridle-hand as soon as he gets the least bit jaded, it must be admitted that it would be easy to find a pleasanter horse for a long, hurried journey. Still, on the principle of all's well that ends well, I ought not to be so severe on my steed, for the expedition ended well, and was really rather a severe tax on man and beast. This is the way we came to take it :

Ever since I arrived, now nearly a year ago, I have been hearing of a certain "bush" or forest some forty-five or fifty miles away, which is always named when I break into lamentations over the utter treelessness of Natal. Latterly, I have had even a stronger craving than usual to see something more than a small plantation of blue gums, infantine oaks and baby firs, making a dot here and there amid the eternal undulation of the

low hills around. "Seven-Mile Bush" has daily grown more attractive to my thoughts, and at last we accepted one of many kind and hospitable invitations thither, and I induced F—— to promise that he would forego the dear delight of riding down to his barn-like office for a couple of days, and come with Mr. C—— and me to the "bush." This was a great concession on his part; and I may state here that he never ceased pining for his papers and his arm-chair from the moment we started until we came back.

It was necessary to make a very early start indeed, and the stars were still shining when we set off, though the first sunbeams were creeping brightly and swiftly over the high eastern hills. It was a fresh morning, in spite of the occasional puff of dust-laden air, which seemed to warn us every now and then that there was such a thing as a hot wind to be considered, and also that there had not been a drop of rain for these last five months. The whole country seems ground to powder, and the almost daily hot winds keep this powder incessantly moving about; so it is not exactly pleasant for traveling. We picked up our Kafir guide as we rode through the town, and made the best of our way at once across the flats between this and Edendale, which we left on our right, climbing slowly and tediously up a high hill above it; then down again and up again, constantly crossing clear, cold, bright rivulets—a welcome moment to horse and rider, for already our lips are feeling swollen and baked; across stony reefs and ridges cropping out from bare hillsides; past many a snug Kafir kraal clinging like the beehives of a giant to the side of a steep pitch, with the long red wagon-track stretching out as though for ever and ever before us. The sun is hot, very hot, but we have left it behind us in the valleys below, and we sweep along wherever there is a foothold for the horses, with a light and pleasant air blowing in our faces. Still, it is with feelings of profound content that at the end of a twenty-mile stage we see "Taylor's," a roadside shanty, looking like a child's toy set down on the vast flat around, but uncommonly comfortable and snug inside, with mealie-gardens and forage-patches around, and more accommodation than one would have believed possible beneath its low, thatched eaves from the first bird's-eye glance. The horses are made luxuriously comfortable directly in a roomy, cool shed, and we sit down to an impromptu breakfast in the cleanest of all inn-parlors. I have no doubt it would have been a very comprehensive and well-arranged meal, but the worst of it was it never had a chance of being taken as a whole. Whatever edible the nice, tidy landlady put down on her snowy cloth vanished like a conjuring trick before she had time to bring the proper thing to go with it. We ate our breakfast backward and forward, and all sorts of ways, beginning with jam, sardines, and mustard, varied by eggs, and ending with rashers of bacon. As for the tea, we had drunk up all the milk and eaten the sugar by the time the pot arrived. The only thing which at all daunted us was some freshly-made boers' bread, of the color of a sponge, the consistency of clay and the weight of pig iron. We were quite respectful to that bread, and only ventured to break off little crusts here and there and eat it guardedly, for it was a fearful condiment. Still, we managed to eat an enormous breakfast in spite of it, and so did the horses; and we all started in highest condition and spirits a little before two o'clock, having had more than a couple of hours' rest. After riding hard for some time, galloping over every yard of anything approaching to broken ground, we ventured to begin to question our guide—who kept up with us in an amazing manner, considering the prominence of his little rough pony's ribs—as to the remaining distance between us and "Seven-Mile Bush." Imagine our horror when he crooked his hand at right angles to his wrist, and made slowly and distinctly five separate dips with it, pointing to the horizon as he did so! Now, the alarming part was, that there were five distinct and ever-rising ranges of hills before us, the range which made a hard ridge against the dazzling sky being of

a deep and misty purple, so distant was it. We had been assured at Taylor's that only twenty-five miles more lay between us and the "bush," and those mountains must be *now* at least thirty miles off. But the guide only grins and nods his head, and kicks with his bare heels against his pony's pronounced ribs, and we hasten on once more. On our right hand, but some distance off, rises the dark crest of the Swartzkopf Mountain, and beneath its shadow, extending over many thousand acres of splendid pasture-ground, is what is known as the Swartzkopf Location, a vast tract of country reserved—or rather appropriated—to the use of a large tribe of Kafirs. They dwell here in peace and plenty, and, until the other day, in prosperity too. But a couple of years ago lung-sickness broke out and decimated their herds, reducing the tribe to the very verge of starvation and misery. However, they battled manfully with the scourge, but it gave them a distrust of cattle, and they took every opportunity of exchanging oxen for horses, of which they now own a great number. What we should have called in New Zealand "mobs" of them were to be seen peacefully pasturing themselves on the slopes around us, and in almost every nook and hollow nestled a Kafir kraal. Here and there were large irregular patches of brown on the fast greening hillsides, and these straggling patches, rarely if ever fenced, were the mealie-gardens belonging to the kraals.

By four of the clock we have made such good way that we can afford immediately after crossing Eland's River, a beautiful stream, to "off saddle" and sit down and rest by its cool banks for a quarter of an hour. Then, tightening up our girths, we push off once more. It has been up hill the whole way, just excepting the sudden sharp descent into a deep valley on the farther side of each range; but the increasing freshness—nay, sharpness—of the air proved to us how steadily we had been climbing up to a high level ever since we had passed through Edendale. From this point of the journey the whole scenic character of the country became widely different from anything I have hitherto seen in Natal. For the first time I began to understand what a wealth of beauty lies hidden away among her hills and valleys, and that the whole country is not made up of undulating downs, fertile flats and distant purple hills. At the top of the very first ridge up which we climbed after crossing Eland's River a perfectly new and enchanting landscape opened out before us, and it gained in majesty and beauty with every succeeding mile of our journey. Ah! how can I make you see it in all its grandeur of form and glory of color? The ground is broken up abruptly into magnificent masses — cliffs, terraces and rocky crags. The hills expand into abrupt mountain-ranges, serrated in bold relief against the loveliest sky blazing with coming sunset splendors. Every cleft—or *kloof*, as it is called here — is filled with fragments of the giant forest which until quite lately must have clothed these rugged mountain-sides. Distant hill-slopes, still bare with wintry leanness, catch some slanting sun-rays on their scanty covering of queer, reddish grass, and straightway glow like sheets of amethyst and topaz, and behind them lie transparent deep-blue shadows of which no pigment ever spread on mortal palette could give the exquisite delicacy and depth. Under our horses' feet the turf might be off the Sussex downs, so close and firm and delicious is it—the very thing for sheep, of which we only see a score here and there. "Why are there not more sheep?" I ask indignantly, with my old squatter instincts coming back in full force upon me. Mr. C—— translates my question to the Kafir guide, who grins and kicks his pony's ribs and says, "No can keep ship here. Plenty Kafir dog: eat up all ships two, tree day." "Yes, that is exactly the reason," Mr. C—— says, "but I wanted you to hear it from himself." And ever after this, I, remembering the dearness and scarcity of mutton in Maritzburg, and seeing all this splendid feed growing for nothing, look with an eye of extreme disfavor and animosity on all the gaunt, lean curs I see prowling about the kraals. Almost every Kafir

we meet has half a dozen of these poaching-looking brutes at his heels, and it exasperates me to hear that there *is* a dog law or ordinance, or something of that sort, "only it has not come into operation yet." I wish it would come into operation to-morrow, and so does every farmer in the country, I should think. Yes, in spite of this fairest of fair scenes —and in all my gypsy life I have never seen anything much more beautiful—I feel quite cross and put out to think of imaginary fat sheep being harried by these useless, hideous dogs.

But the horses are beginning to go a little wearily, and gladly pause to wet their muzzles and cool their hoofs in every brook we cross. I am free to confess that I am getting very tired, for nothing is so wearying as a sudden, hurried journey like this, and I am also excessively hungry and thirsty. The sun dips down quite suddenly behind a splendid confusion of clouds and mountain-tops, lights up the whole sky for a short while with translucent masses of crimson and amber, which fade swiftly away into strangest, tenderest tints of primrose and pale green, and then a flood of clear cold moonlight breaks over all and bathes everything in a differing but equally beautiful radiance. Three ridges have now been climbed, and the pertinacious guide only dips his hand twice more in answer to my peevish questions about the distance. Nay, he promises in wonderful Dutch and Kafir phraseology to show me the "baas's" house (whither we are bound) from the very next ridge. But what a climb it is! and what a panorama do we look down upon from the topmost crag before commencing the steep descent, this time through a bit of dense forest! It is all as distinct as day, and yet there is that soft, ineffable veil of mystery and silence which moonlight wraps up everything in. We look over immense tree-tops, over plains which seem endless beneath the film of evening mist creeping over them, to where the broad Umkomanzi rushes and roars amid great boulders and rocks, leaping every here and there over a crag down to a lower level of its wide and rocky bed. In places the fine river widens out into a mere, and then it sleeps tranquilly enough in the moonlight, making great patches of shimmering silver amid the profound shadows cast by hill and forest. Beyond, again, are mountains, always mountains, and one more day's journey like this would take us into Adam Kop's Land. As we look at it all now, it does indeed seem "a sleepy world of dreams;" but in another moment the panorama is shut out, for we are amid the intense darkness of the forest-path, stepping carefully down what resembles a stone ladder placed at an angle of 45°. Of course I am frightened, and of course my fright shows itself in crossness and in incoherent reproaches. I feel as if I were slipping down on my horse's neck; and so I am, I believe. But nobody will "take me off," which is what I earnestly entreat. Both my gentlemen retain unruffled good-humor, and adjure me "not to think about it," coupled with assurances of perfect safety. I hear, however, a great deal of slipping and sliding and rolling of displaced rocks even after these consoling announcements of safety, and orders are given to each weary steed to "hold up;" which orders are not at all reassuring. Somebody told me somewhere—it seems months ago, but it must have been early in the afternoon—that this particular and dreadful hill was only three-quarters of a mile from the "baas's;" so you may imagine my mingled rage and disappointment at hearing that it was still rather more than three miles off. And three miles at this stage of the journey is equal to thirteen at an earlier date. It is wonderful how well the horses hold out. This last bit of the road is almost flat, winding round the gentlest undulation possible, and it is as much as I can do to hold the chestnut, who has caught sight evidently of twinkling lights there under the lee of that great wooded cliff. No sound can ever be so delightful to a wearied and belated traveler as the bark of half a dozen dogs, and no greeting more grateful than their rough caresses, half menace and half play. But there is a much warmer and more cordial welcome

waiting for us behind the *sako bono* of the dogs, and I find myself staggering about as if the water I have been drinking so freely all day had been something much stronger. On my feet at last in such a pretty sitting-room! Pictures, books, papers, all sorts of comforts and conveniences, and, sight of joy! a tea-table all ready, even to the tea-pot, which had been brought in when the dogs announced us. If I had even sixpence for every cup of tea I drank that evening, I should be a rich woman to the end of my days. As for the milk, deliciously fresh from the cow, it was only to be equaled by the cream; and you must have lived all these months in Natal before you can appreciate as we did the butter, which looked and tasted like butter, instead of the pale, salt, vapid compound, as much lard as anything else, for which we pay three shillings and sixpence a pound in Maritzburg, and which has been costing six shillings in Port Elizabeth all this winter.

It is always a marvel to me, arriving at night at these out-of-the-way places, which seem the very Ultima Thule of the habitable globe, *how* the furniture, the glass and china, the pictures and ornaments and books, get there. How has anybody energy to think of transporting all these perishable articles over that road? Think of their jolting in a bullock-wagon down that hill! One fancies if one lived here it must needs be a Robinson-Crusoe existence; instead of which it is as comfortable as possible; and if one did not remember the distance and the road and the country, one might be in England, except for the Kafir boys, barefooted and white-garmented, something like choristers, who are gliding about with incessant relays of food for us famished ones. The sweet little golden-haired children, rosy and fresh as the bough of apple-blossoms they are playing with, the pretty châtelaine in her fresh toilette, — all might have been taken up in a beneficent fairy's thumb and transported, a moment ago, from the heart of civilization to this its farthest extremity. As for sleep, you must slumber in just such a bed if you want to know what a good night's rest is, and then wake up as we did, with all memories of the long, wearying day's journey clean blotted out of one's mind, and nothing in it but eagerness not to lose a moment of the lovely fresh and cool day before us. Even the sailing clouds are beautiful, and the shadows they cast over the steep mountains, the broad rivers and the long dark belt of forest are more beautiful still. Of course, the "bush" is the great novelty to us who have not seen a tree larger than a dozen years' growth could make it since we landed; and it is especially beautiful just now, for although, like all native forests, it is almost entirely evergreen (there is a more scientific word than that, isn't there?), still, there are patches and tufts of fresh green coming out in delicate spring tints, which show vividly against the sombre mass of foliage. But oh, I wish they had not such names! Handed down to us from our Dutch predecessors, they must surely have got changed in some incomprehensible fashion, for what rhyme or reason, what sense or satire, is there in such a name as "cannibal stink-wood"?—applied, too, to a graceful, handsome tree, whose bark gives out an aromatic though pungent perfume. Is it not a libel? For a tree with a particularly beautifully-veined wood, of a deep amber color, they could think of no more poetical or suggestive name than simply "yellow-wood:" a tree whose wood is of a rich veined brown, which goes, too, beautifully with the yellow-wood in furniture, is merely called "iron-wood," because it chances to be hard; and so forth.

Before going to the "bush," however, we consider ourselves bound to go and look at the great saw-mill down by the Umkomanzi, where all these trees are divided and subdivided, cut into lengths of twenty feet, sawn into planks, half a dozen at a time, and otherwise changed from forest kings to plain, humdrum piles and slabs and posts for bridges, rooftrees, walls, and what not. There is the machinery at work, with just one ripple, as it were, of the rushing river turned aside by a little sluice, to drive the great wheel round and set all the mysterious pistons and levers moving up and down in their calm, monotonous strength, doing all sorts of miraculous things in the most methodical, commonplace manner. I was much struck by the physiognomy of the only two white men employed about this mill. There were some assistant Kafirs of course, but these two in their widely-different ways were at once repellent and interesting. One of them was, I think, the biggest man I ever saw. To say that he looked like a tall tree himself among his fellows is to give you, after all, the best idea of his enormous height and powerful build. He moved huge logs about with scarcely an effort, and it was entirely for his enormous physical strength that our host kept him in his place. I did not need to be told he was one of the most persistent and consistent bad characters imaginable, for a single glance at his evil countenance was enough to suggest that he could hardly be a very satisfactory member of society. He had only one eye, and about as hangdog, sullen, lowering a countenance as one would see out of the hulks. His "mate" was a civil, tidy, wizen-looking, elderly man, who might have appeared almost respectable by the side of the bigger villain if his shaking hand and bleared, restless eyes had not told *his* story plainly enough. Still, if he could only be kept out of temptation the old man might be trusted; but our host confessed that he did not half like retaining the services of the other, and yet did not know where to find any one who would or could do his work so easily and admirably. It is almost impossible to get any men to come and live up here, so far away from their fellow-creatures and from everything except their work; so one has to put up with a thousand drawbacks in the service one is able to procure. I was glad when we turned our backs upon that villainous-looking giant and strolled beneath a perfect sun and sky and balmy air toward the lowest kloof or cleft where the great "bush" ran down between two steep spurs. The grass of the downs over which we walked had all the elasticity of tread of turf to our feet, but they ended abruptly in a sort of terrace, under which ran a noisy, chattering brooklet in a vast hurry to reach the Umkomanzi over yonder. It is easy to scramble down among the tangle of ferns and reeds and across the boulders which this long dry winter has left bare, and so strike one of the Bushmen's paths without difficulty, and get into the heart of the forest before we allow ourselves to sit down and look around us. How wonderfully poetical and beautiful it all is!—the tall, stately trees around us, with their smooth magnificent boles shooting up straight as a willow wand for sixty feet and more before putting forth their crown of lofty branches, the more diminutive undergrowth of gracefulest shrubs and plumy tufts of fern and lovely wild flowers— violets, clematis, wood-anemones and hepaticas—showing here and there a modest gleam of color. But indeed the very mosses and lichens at our feet are a week's study, and so are the details of the delicate green tracery creeping close to the ground. The trees, the actual great forest trees, are our delight, however, and we never weary of calling to each other to "come and look at this one," extemporizing measuring-lines from the endless green withies which hang in loops and festoons from the higher branches. Thirty feet round five feet from the ground is not an uncommon measurement, and it is half sad, half amusing to see how in an hour or so we too begin to look upon everything as timber, to call the most splendid trees "blocks" (the woodman's word), and to speculate and give opinions as to the best way of "falling" the beautiful stems. Up above our heads the foliage seems all interlaced and woven together by a perfect network of these monkey ropes —a stout and sturdy species of *liane*, really—such as I have seen swinging from West India forest trees. Here they are actually used as a sort of trapeze by the troops of baboons which live in these great woods, coming down in small armies when the mealies are ripe, and carrying off literally armsful of cobs. The Kafirs dread the baboons

more than anything else, and there is a regular organized system of warfare between them, in which the baboons by no means get the worst. I heard a sickening story of how only last season the Kafirs of a kraal close by, infuriated by their losses, managed to catch an old baboon, leader of his troop, and skinned him and let him go again into the woods. It is too horrible to think of such cruelty, and it seemed a blot upon the lovely idyllic scene around us. All the wild animals with which the bush was teeming until a very few years ago are gradually being driven farther and farther back into the highest part, which has not yet been touched by axe or hatchet. There are still many kinds of buck, however—we saw three splendid specimens grazing just outside—besides other game. It must—not so long ago, either—have been the quiet forest home of many a wild creature, for there are pits now to be seen, one of which we came across with sharp stakes at the bottom, dug to trap elephants, whose bones lie there to this day. Tigers also have been seen, and panthers and leopards, but they grow scarcer every year. The aboriginal inhabitants of the border country beyond, the little Bushmen—the lowest type of human creatures—used to come down and hunt in great numbers here in this very spot where we are sitting, and traces of their ingenious methods of snaring their prey are to be seen in many places.

As I sat there, with the tinkle of the water in my ears, sole break in the "charmèd silence" around, I could not make up my mind which was the most enchanting, to look up or down—up to where the tenderest tint of cobalt blue showed through the flicker of green leaves nearly a hundred feet above us, and where a sudden terror among the birds drove them in bright-plumaged flight from bough to bough; or down on the ground among the delicious brown leaves and wonderful minutiæ of diminutive tendril and flower. Here and there were fallen crimson and yellow leaves, riveting the eye for a moment by their vivid glow, or the young fronds of a rare fern over yonder are pushing up their curled horns of pale green. A month hence it will be all carpeted with wild flowers, and the heaths will be spires of tiny bells. There is also a coarse but sweet grass, growing luxuriantly, on which the cattle love to feed when all the herbage outside is parched and burned to the very root.

As I read over what I have written, I am filled with a deep disgust to perceive how impossible it has been for me to catch even the faintest reflection of the charm of that forest-glade—how its subtle beauty is not, by any poor words of mine, to be transferred to paper—how its stillness and its life, its grandeur and its delicate prettinesses, the aroma of the freshly-cut logs, the chirrup of the cicalas, the twitter of the birds, all, all escape me. Yet I shall have failed indeed if I have not been able to convey to you that it was a delicious hour, and that I enjoyed every moment of it. I am only a woman, so I was content to sit there plaiting a crown of ferns, and thinking how I should tell you all about it some day, perhaps. My companions conversed together, and their talk was entirely about killing something—"sport" they called it—how best they could get a shot at those graceful bucks over yonder; what a pity the close season had begun; what partridges there were; when the wild-ducks would come down to that large mere shining in the distance; whether there were any wild-pigeons; how far into the unexplored bush one must penetrate to get a shot at a panther; and so forth. It seemed a desecration to talk of taking life on such a heavenly morning, and I was glad when it all ended in a project of a fishing-excursion after a late luncheon.

As we found we should be obliged to start early to-morrow morning, I decided to stay at home and rest this afternoon; and I did not regret my resolution, for it was very pleasant by the fire, and our beautiful morning turned into a raw, cold drizzle. But, as the people about here say, it has really forgotten how to rain, and it is more like a Scotch mist than anything else. Whatever it may be call-

ed, it blots out mountain and forest and river, and causes the fishing-excursion to turn into the dismalest failure. Next morning, too, when we start after breakfast, we are all glad of our waterproofs (what *should* I do without my ulster?), and the ground is as slippery as though it had been soaped. Our farewells are made, and we declare that we have no need of our Kafir guide again, though I confess to misgivings as to how we are to find our road through so thick a mist. It has also been decided, for the sake of the horses, to take them only as far as Taylor's to-night, and so break the journey. But the question is, Shall we ever find Taylor's? for it is a little off the track, and we cannot see five yards to our right hand or our left. We are obliged to go very slowly, and there are places, steep up and down hill, where in spite of precaution and picking out grass or stones to go over, our horses' feet fly from under them, and we each in our turn come down on the damp red clay in an awkward sprawl. However, we do not disgrace ourselves by tumbling off, and my poor habit fares the worst, for the chestnut always seems to pick himself up, in some odd way, by its help; and the process is not beneficial to it. Eland's River is crossed early in the afternoon, and then, slippery or not, we are forced to push on, for it seems as though it intended to be pitchy dark by four o'clock, and the mist turns into a thick, fine rain. At last, about half-past four, we hear on our left the joyful sound of barking dogs and crowing cocks, and the horses of their own accord show a simultaneous desire to turn off the track, to which, with its guiding wagon-wheels, we have so persistently clung. If it be *not* Taylor's—if it turns out that these sounds come only from a Kafir kraal— then indeed I don't know what we shall do, for we can never find the track again. It is an anxious moment, and Taylor's is so small and so low that we are as likely as not to ride right over it; but no, there is a wagon, and behind the wagon, and not much higher, is a thatched roof, and under that thatched roof are warmth and food and shelter and a warm, cordial welcome: all of which good things we are enjoying in five minutes' time. As for the horses, they are rubbed down and put to stand in a warm shed, with bedding up to their knees and a perfect orgie of mealies and green forage before them in boxes. Let us hope they enjoyed the contrast between indoors and out of doors as much as we did. At all events, they were freshness itself next morning, when we made another start —not quite so early, for only the lesser half of our long journey lay before us, and the flood of sunshine made it worth while to wait a little and let the soapy clay tracks have a chance to get dry.

It was exquisitely fresh and balmy about nine o'clock, when, after a capital breakfast, we did start at last, and the well-washed hills had actually put on quite a spring-green tint since we passed them a couple of days ago from yesterday's long looked-for, much-wanted rain. I went through many anxieties, however, on that return journey, because my two companions, who were in the most tearing, school-boy spirits, insisted on leaving the road with its guiding marks of wagon-wheels, as well as every landmark to which I fondly clung, and taking me across country, over hill and dale, through swampy hollows and over rocky goat-paths, until I was quite bewildered and thoroughly incredulous as to where we should emerge. It is true that the dark crest of Swartzkopf lay steadily to our left, just where it should be, but I invariably protested we were all wrong when I had any leisure or breath to do anything but "hold on with my eyelids" up and down hill. At last we climbed our last hill-face, and there, below us, literally smiling in the sunshine, lay the pretty little mission settlement of Edendale. We were exactly where we wanted, topographically speaking, to be, but between us and Edendale the mountain dropped sheer down, as it seemed to me, and naught but a goat-path was there. "Of course we are going to get off and lead our horses down," I fondly hope. No such thing! I can't very well get off by myself, for the precipice is so sheer that I should certainly drop down a hun-

dred feet or so. F—— steadily declines to "take me off,' and begins to slip and slither down the track on horseback. I feel my saddle getting into all sorts of odd positions, and I believe I am seated on my horse's ears, although I lean back until I can nearly touch his tail. It is really horrible. I get more and more cross every moment, and scold F—— and reproach Mr. C—— furiously all the way down, without eliciting the smallest sign of remorse from either. But it is very difficult to remain cross when once we have reached the foot of that cruel descent, for it is all inexpressibly lovely and calm and prosperous that beautiful spring morning. Everybody seems busy, and yet good-humored. The little black children grinned and saluted on their way to school; the elders cried "Sako bono, inkosa!" as they looked up from their basket-plaiting or their wagon-making; the mill-wheel turned merrily with a busy clatter inexpressibly cool and charming; the numerous fowls and ducks cackled and quacked as they scuttled from under our horses' feet. We rode down the main street, with its neat row of unburnt brick houses on either hand, across a little river, and so, under avenues of syringas whose heavy perfume filled the delicious air, out into the open country once more. It is nearly a dead level between this and Maritzburg, and the road is in good order after the long winter drought; so we make the best of our way, and hardly draw rein until we are under the lee of the hill on which Fort Napier stands. Here is a villainous bit of road, a perfect study of ingenuity as to cross-drains, holes and pitfalls generally; so the horses take breath once more for an easy canter down the quiet straight streets of the sleepy little Dutch town. Our cottage lies beyond it and across the river, but it is still early, hardly noon in fact, when we pull up at our own stable-door, and the horses seem every whit as fresh and in as good condition as when we started, yet they have gone close upon one hundred miles from first to last,

> Over hill, over dale,
> Through brush, through brier.

SEPTEMBER 25.

I declare I have not said anything about the weather for a long time. I cannot finish more appropriately than by one of my little meteorological reports. The skies are trying to remember how to rain; we have every now and then a cold, gray day—a day which is my particular delight, it is so like an English one; then rain more or less heavy, and an attempt at a thunderstorm. The intervening days are brightly glaring and exceedingly hot. Everything is bursting hurriedly and luxuriantly into bloom; my scraggy rose-bushes are thickly covered with buds, which blow into splendid roses after every shower; the young oaks are a mass of tender, luxuriant green, and even the unpoetical blue gums try hard to assume a fresh spring tint; the fruit trees look like large bouquets of pink blossom, and the laquot trees afford good sport for G—— in climbing and stone-throwing. On the veldt the lilies are pushing up their green sheaths and brilliant cups through the still hard ground, the black hill-slopes are turning a vivid green, and the weeds are springing up in millions all over my field-like flower-beds. Spring is always lovely everywhere, but nowhere lovelier than in "fair Natal."